Mastering Augmented Reality Development with Unity

Create immersive and engaging AR experiences with Unity

Indika Wijesooriya

www.bpbonline.com

Copyright © 2024 BPB Online

All rights reserved. No part of this book may be reproduced, stored in a retrieval system, or transmitted in any form or by any means, without the prior written permission of the publisher, except in the case of brief quotations embedded in critical articles or reviews.

Every effort has been made in the preparation of this book to ensure the accuracy of the information presented. However, the information contained in this book is sold without warranty, either express or implied. Neither the author, nor BPB Online or its dealers and distributors, will be held liable for any damages caused or alleged to have been caused directly or indirectly by this book.

BPB Online has endeavored to provide trademark information about all of the companies and products mentioned in this book by the appropriate use of capitals. However, BPB Online cannot guarantee the accuracy of this information.

First published: 2024

Published by BPB Online
WeWork
119 Marylebone Road
London NW1 5PU

UK | UAE | INDIA | SINGAPORE

ISBN 978-93-55518-330

www.bpbonline.com

Dedicated to

My beloved wife, **Thilini**

&

My mother, **Swarna**

About the Author

Indika Wijesooriya has over 8 years of extensive experience working with Unity, coupled with a profound involvement in crafting AR applications since 2014. In 2017, he successfully attained a degree in Engineering intertwined with Computer Science, further solidifying his expertise in the field.

Notably, Indika held the distinguished position of Chief of Innovation at Arimac, a prominent end-to-end digital solutions provider renowned for its active engagement in the development of AR and VR applications on a global scale. His instrumental contributions to the advancement of immersive and emergent technologies have garnered both local and international accolades.

Indika's passion is towards 3D real-time development, AR VR, and research and sharing his knowledge with enthusiasts around the world.

About the Reviewer

Sumaya is a visionary Unity XR developer with a passion for exploring the realms of the Metaverse and Gen AI concepts. With a profound love for merging technology and creativity, Sumaya has become a trailblazer in the world of virtual reality (VR) and augmented reality (AR) development. Having spent years honing her skills in Unity, Sumaya's expertise lies in crafting captivating XR experiences that blur the lines between the physical and digital worlds. Her fascination with the potential of the Metaverse and Gen AI has driven her to delve deeper into cutting-edge XR technologies, constantly seeking new ways to shape the future of immersive digital experiences. With an ever-curious mind and openness to new ideas, Sumaya continues to push the boundaries of XR development, inspiring others to join her in shaping the world of tomorrow.

Acknowledgement

I would like to express my deepest gratitude to my wife, Thilini, whose unwavering encouragement and unconditional support have been instrumental in bringing this book to fruition. Her belief in me and constant motivation were an invaluable source of inspiration throughout this journey. I extend my heartfelt thanks to Chamira Jayasinghe, CEO of Arimac, for opening my eyes to the vast world of immersive technology. His guidance and mentorship have played a pivotal role in shaping my career and fueling my passion for AR development.

I would like to extend my appreciation to Lou, Mike, and Jerry from Circuit Stream. Their support and guidance have helped me discover my passion for teaching and sharing knowledge with others. Their expertise and collaboration have been instrumental in shaping the content of this book. I would also like to acknowledge Dejan, my dear friend, for his unwavering motivation and continuous support. His belief in my abilities has been a driving force throughout this writing process. I am grateful to Mana Saei and Leena Prasad for their insightful reviews and valuable comments on the manuscript. Their expertise and constructive feedback have immensely contributed to the quality of this book.

Special thanks to the team at BPB Publications for their unwavering dedication and support in making this book a reality. Their expertise in the publishing process and their commitment to delivering top-notch content have been instrumental in bringing this book to readers worldwide.

Finally, I would like to express my sincere appreciation to all the readers and supporters of this book. Your interest and enthusiasm for augmented reality development have been the driving force behind my commitment to sharing knowledge and empowering others in this exciting field. Thank you for joining me on this journey.

Preface

Augmented Reality has been a key component of immersive technologies in the past decade. With the entrance of web3 and related technologies, Augmented reality has become a key player in providing extended user experiences for the people around the world. Whether its education, training, manufacturing, healthcare or military, Augmented reality can help people augment and enhance the core components of them. One of the major challenges for an enthusiast to start building AR applications is the knowledge of the tools as there are many available in the current context.

This book will introduce Augmented reality, their use cases, and the history to better understand about it. The second section will focus mainly on the available tools and technologies to develop AR applications. Later on, the book will introduce the Unity 3D engine, fundamentals of C# programming with Unity, vector mathematics and implementing AR applications with Unity followed by the best practices in building AR applications.

By the end of the book, readers will have a comprehensive knowledge on bringing an idea into an augmented reality application and use C# and Unity 3D engine to design and develop a prototype, or maybe a finished application.

Chapter 1: Getting Started with Augmented Reality- In this chapter, we are going to learn about the key concept of Augmented Reality. The technology behind AR applications and the principles of content recognition. The idea is to get some knowledge about the underlying technology to better understand the behaviour. Also, it provides a brief history of Augmented Reality and the existing and future use cases of the technology.

Chapter 2: Visualizing AR Environment and Components- In this chapter, we will be discussing about the placement of objects in a virtual world and how these are mapped to generate the illusion of Augmented Reality. Realizing how different Augmented Reality setups work is provided and to better understand these principles, an introduction to basic mathematical theories is discussed.

Chapter 3: Exploring Tools and Development Platforms- This chapter provides an in-depth introduction to currently available tools and technologies to build AR applications and experiences, and their running platforms. We also compare the pros and cons of each available tool and discuss about multiple use cases to better understand what platform and tools suits the best for the fulfilment of that use case.

Chapter 4: Up and Running with Unity 3D- In this chapter, we use Unity3D engine as the core development tool for the rest of the book and we go through the steps of installing the necessary tools and setup the computer for development. Also, we will be building a 3D scene in Unity 3D. This will be useful to know about the Unity engine, the tools, and an introduction to 3D concepts that helps us build AR application in future chapters. Additionally, we dive deep into the key components of Unity. We learn the structure of GameObject and the components, and the main components in Unity will be discussed.

Chapter 5: Creating Your First Custom Component- In this chapter, we get an introduction to C# with Unity creating our first custom component. We go through the steps of creating a base script, understand the basic components of a C# script and how the execution of a C# script works. Finally, we will be creating a simple Clock using the concepts we learnt throughout the chapter.

Chapter 6: Refreshing C# Concepts with Unity- In this chapter, we will be exploring the C# programming to build functionality. Throughout this chapter, we will be building an endless top-down shooting game that are targeted towards mobile. We will be learning C# concepts with Unity, using the key unity components that are relevant in building interactive applications.

Chapter 7: Trying Out First 3D Mobile App Development- During this chapter, we continue the development of the top-down shooter game and install the application on the mobile device. We go through two different mobile platforms, Android and iOS understanding each device requirement, and how you set up the project settings accordingly. Alternatively, we check different debugging methods while your app is running in your device.

Chapter 8: Building Marker-based AR Apps with Vuforia- In this chapter, we will be building an Augmented Reality treasure hunt game using the Vuforia AR SDK. This section covers the introduction to marker-based tracking with Vuforia SDK, its key capabilities and use of Marker based tracking. We go through the steps of creating a Vuforia account, registering the application, and using the Vuforia portal to configure the project trackers. We also download the SDK, install it in Unity and test with the PC web camera.

Chapter 9: Developing Marker-based Dynamic AR Apps- In this chapter, we go beyond the default use cases of marker-based AR to dynamic application design. We will be building two AR applications. One is a sample AR machine inspection tool, and the other is a dynamic AR billboard that changes the experience without app updates. In the sample AR inspection tool, we will be using a marker system to uniquely identify different objects without making significant changes to the marker graphic. In the dynamic billboard, we go beyond Unity to host files in the cloud to build a dynamic AR app that can change the content and markers without updating the app.

Chapter 10: Marker-less AR Apps with AR Kit and AR Core- In this chapter, we will be building multiple mini projects that covers most AR detection modes provided by ARKit and ARCore that works with iPhones/iPads and Androids subsequently. We will learn the similarities in both and use AR Foundation as a cross-platform method to build the AR apps.

Chapter 11: World Scale AR App with Niantic Lightship- In this chapter, we will be developing mini projects that uses the Niantic lightship SDK. The objective of this is to get started with building world scale AR applications that reacts to the environment obstacles including collision and occlusion. During the first project development, we understand the environment capturing by the SDK to build a simple throwing experience in AR. The second project will learn the process of scanning an environment to build custom (private/public) area-based AR applications.

Chapter 12: Best Practices in Augmented Reality Application Design- In this chapter, we talk about different best practices in AR application design and development. This can be categorised as design-based practices, development practices and Sample project snippet for all the best practices mentioned below.

Chapter 13: AR App Performance Optimization- In this chapter, we will be learning key performance metrics that can be considered in building AR applications and optimization techniques to optimize our AR apps to reduce the resource requirements needed. We will identify key necessary actions to mitigate the performance related challenges in your app.

Code Bundle and Coloured Images

Please follow the link to download the
Code Bundle and the *Coloured Images* of the book:

https://rebrand.ly/z6y0enl

The code bundle for the book is also hosted on GitHub at **https://github.com/bpbpublications/Mastering-Augmented-Reality-Development-with-Unity**. In case there's an update to the code, it will be updated on the existing GitHub repository.

We have code bundles from our rich catalogue of books and videos available at **https://github.com/bpbpublications**. Check them out!

Errata

We take immense pride in our work at BPB Publications and follow best practices to ensure the accuracy of our content to provide with an indulging reading experience to our subscribers. Our readers are our mirrors, and we use their inputs to reflect and improve upon human errors, if any, that may have occurred during the publishing processes involved. To let us maintain the quality and help us reach out to any readers who might be having difficulties due to any unforeseen errors, please write to us at :

errata@bpbonline.com

Your support, suggestions and feedbacks are highly appreciated by the BPB Publications' Family.

> Did you know that BPB offers eBook versions of every book published, with PDF and ePub files available? You can upgrade to the eBook version at www.bpbonline.com and as a print book customer, you are entitled to a discount on the eBook copy. Get in touch with us at :
>
> **business@bpbonline.com** for more details.
>
> At **www.bpbonline.com**, you can also read a collection of free technical articles, sign up for a range of free newsletters, and receive exclusive discounts and offers on BPB books and eBooks.

Piracy

If you come across any illegal copies of our works in any form on the internet, we would be grateful if you would provide us with the location address or website name. Please contact us at **business@bpbonline.com** with a link to the material.

If you are interested in becoming an author

If there is a topic that you have expertise in, and you are interested in either writing or contributing to a book, please visit **www.bpbonline.com**. We have worked with thousands of developers and tech professionals, just like you, to help them share their insights with the global tech community. You can make a general application, apply for a specific hot topic that we are recruiting an author for, or submit your own idea.

Reviews

Please leave a review. Once you have read and used this book, why not leave a review on the site that you purchased it from? Potential readers can then see and use your unbiased opinion to make purchase decisions. We at BPB can understand what you think about our products, and our authors can see your feedback on their book. Thank you!

For more information about BPB, please visit **www.bpbonline.com**.

Join our book's Discord space

Join the book's Discord Workspace for Latest updates, Offers, Tech happenings around the world, New Release and Sessions with the Authors:

https://discord.bpbonline.com

Table of Contents

1. Getting Started with Augmented Reality 1
    Introduction 1
    Structure 2
    Objectives 2
    Augmented reality implementation and application 2
    History of augmented reality 4
        1968 – The Sword of Damocles 4
        1975 – Videoplace by Myron Krueger 5
        1999 – AR Toolkit 6
        Augmented reality over the years 7
    Augmented reality across the world 8
        Augmented reality in entertainment 8
        AR in manufacturing and logistics 10
        Real estate 11
        Health 11
        Education 11
        Marketing and retail 12
    Augmented reality enabling technologies 13
        Image recognition and tracking 13
        Simultaneous localization and mapping 15
    Machine learning and artificial intelligence 17
    Conclusion 18
    Key points 18
    Multiple choice questions 19
        Answers 19

2. Visualizing AR Environment and Components 21
    Introduction 21
    Structure 21

Objectives 22
Basics of mathematics for 3D visualization 22
Understanding the 3D environment 24
Vector mathematics 28
Basic trigonometry 31
Understanding different spaces 33
Context recognition concepts 34
Placement of virtual objects on physical worlds 35
Converting physical input to virtual interactions 36
Conclusion 37
Key points 38
Multiple choice questions 38
      Answers 39

3. Exploring Tools and Development Platforms 41
Introduction 41
Structure 41
Objectives 42
AR platforms 43
      Smartphones Android, iOS 43
      Magic Leap 46
      Snapchat spectacles 47
      Other wearables 48
      WebXR AR 50
      Social AR 50
AR development tools 51
      Native 51
      Social AR- Spark AR, Snapchat Lens Studio, TikTok 52
      Apple Reality Composer 53
      8th Wall 54
      Unity 3D 54
      AR software development kits 55

  Microsoft mixed reality toolkit 55

  ARToolkit 55

  Wikitude 56

  Easy AR 56

  Vuforia 56

  ARCore 57

  ARKit 57

  AR Foundation 57

  Niantic Lightship 58

 Conclusion 59

 Key points 59

 Questions 60

  Answers 60

4. Up and Running with Unity 3D 61

 Introduction 61

 Structure 61

 Objectives 62

 Installing Unity 3D 62

  Installing Android SDK, Java SDK 64

 Installing Xcode in MacOS 65

 Installing Visual Studio / Visual Studio Code 66

 Creating a project and setting up the target platform 68

 Unity Engine user interface 69

 Using the tools to create and manipulate primitive objects 71

 Understanding lights 74

 Creating materials 77

 Manipulating the virtual camera 79

 Using the Unity package manager 81

 Importing content into Unity 82

 Importing assets from the Unity asset store 83

 The structure of the GameObject 84

  Components of Unity 84
    Transform 85
    Mesh Renderer 85
    Colliders 85
    Rigid body 86
  Creating prefabs 87
  Conclusion 88
  Key points 89
  Multiple choice questions 89
    Answers 90

5. Creating Your First Custom Component 91
  Introduction 91
  Structure 91
  Objectives 92
  Introduction to C# in Unity 92
  Exploring the MonoBehaviour 93
  Serialized variables 94
  Debug class of Unity 95
  Time in Unity 96
  GetComponent 97
  Building a simple 3D clock 99
  Conclusion 102
  Key points 102
  Multiple choice questions 103
    Answers 104

6. Refreshing C# Concepts with Unity 105
  Introduction 105
  Structure 105
  Objectives 106
  Setting up the scene 106
  Movement of the player 107

Creating a bullet for the player to shoot 109
Shooting bullets 113
Setting up the enemy 115
Setting up the player 121
Spawning and destroying enemies 123
Game UI 125
    Game manager *126*
Adding audio and polishing 129
    Adding the main menu *131*
    Switching scenes *133*
    The next steps *134*
Conclusion 135
Key points 135
Multiple choice questions 136
    Answers *137*

7. Trying Out First 3D Mobile App Development 139
Introduction 139
Structure 139
Objectives 140
Unity Build settings 140
    Android build settings *140*
    Icon *141*
    Resolution and presentation *141*
    Splash image *142*
    Other settings *142*
    Publishing settings *143*
    iOS build settings *144*
        Identification | Bundle Identifier *144*
        Identification | Provisioning profile and Signing team ID *144*
        Configuration | Target Device, SDK and minimum iOS version *145*
        Configuration | Camera Usage Description *145*

　　　　　Configuration | Requires AR Kit support...145
　　Building Unity apps 145
　　　　Building for Android 145
　　　　　　Building for Android without ADB..146
　　　　Building for iOS..148
　　Unity script debugging with Visual studio 150
　　Debugging the app for both platforms...152
　　　　Using the ADB console for Android...152
　　　　Using the XCode Console for iOS 153
　　Conclusion..153
　　Key points...153
　　Questions..154
　　　　Answers...154

8. **Building Marker-based AR Apps with Vuforia**..155
　　Introduction..155
　　Structure...155
　　Objectives...156
　　Introduction to Vuforia..156
　　　　Create a Vuforia developer account and login.................................156
　　　　Downloading and installing the SDK..157
　　　　Setting up a basic AR scene..158
　　Using Image Targets...159
　　　　Choosing the best markers/targets..163
　　　　Additional features of Image Targets...165
　　Using cylinder targets..166
　　Using Multi targets..170
　　Development of an AR treasure hunt game..174
　　Conclusion..182
　　Key points...182
　　Question...182

9. Developing Marker-based Dynamic AR Apps 183

Introduction 183

Structure 183

Objectives 184

Machine inspection tool 184

    Unity serialization and deserialization 186

    Creating a simple mock API 192

    Using UnityWebRequest to request data based on input 193

    Vuforia VuMark introduction 195

    Designing a VuMark using Adobe Illustrator 195

        Design step 1 197

        Design step 2 198

        Design step 3 198

        Design step 4 199

        Design step 5 200

    Connecting the marker recognition with networking to request dynamic data and displaying them in AR 202

        Downloading VuMark targets 202

        Decoding VuMark data 203

        Using decoded values to retrieve data from the remote server through API 206

Dynamic AR billboard 214

    Setting up the AR poster project 214

    Implementing Vuforia Cloud targets 216

    Creating asset bundles in Unity 221

        Installing asset bundle browser 221

    Uploading the asset bundles in the cloud 223

    Updating the meta files to update AR experience 223

    Downloading content and displaying in AR 224

Conclusion 227

Key points 227

Questions 227

10. Marker-less AR Apps with AR Kit and AR Core 229

Introduction 229

Structure 229

Objectives 230

Setting up AR Foundation 230

Setting up a marker-less tracking scene 232

Simulating the scene in the editor 234

Plane detection and tracking: building an AR object viewer 235

Placing the object on a scanned plane 235

Move object on touch if the object is placed already 237

Scaling the object with two touches 238

Rotating the object with a single touch and drag 240

Face tracking – Creating an AR face filter with AR Foundation ... 243

Default face tracking setup 243

Adding custom objects around a face 244

Adding face interactions 246

Device tracking: building an AR shooter 249

Setting up the enemy 250

Setting up the Game Manager 251

Additional components of AR Foundation 256

AR human body manager 256

Point clouds 256

Anchors 256

Image tracking 256

Conclusion 256

Key points 257

Question 257

11. World Scale AR App with Niantic Lightship 259

Introduction 259

Structure 259

Objectives 260

Setting up Niantic Lightship with Unity	260
Downloading required tools and assets	261
Adding a new license key and authenticating an application	261
Setting up a simple plane tracking scene	262
Setting up the camera	263
Object placement in AR	265
Object occlusion	268
Environment meshing	269
Setting up the scene to mesh the environment boundaries	269
Creating a simple physics simulation in AR	270
Creating an object to throw	270
Throwing the ball at runtime	271
Introduction to Niantic lightship VPS	273
Scanning an environment for VPS	274
The flow of VPS scan recognition	276
Importing the scanned location	277
Adding anchors using the VPS authoring tool	278
Updating the prefab with proper visual elements	280
Using Niantic API to restore anchor data	281
Using Niantic VPS for scalable AR applications	285
Conclusion	286
Key points	286
Question	286

12. Best Practices in Augmented Reality Application Design 287

Introduction	287
Structure	287
Objectives	288
Safety is key	288
Showing warnings at the beginning	288
Showing warnings while using the AR app	290
Guide the user with the interactions	291

- Be mindful of the scale 293
- Use audio and visual cues 294
  - *Indicating objects that are out of camera view* 294
  - *Adding visual markers on interactable objects* 295
  - *Using 3D audio cues* 296
  - *Showing physical properties in visual cues* 297
- Free flow restrictions 300
- AR interactions 301
  - *Using a reticle to interact with smaller objects* 301
  - *Interacting with objects further from camera* 302
- UI considerations 303
- Conclusion 304
- Key points 304
- Question 305

13. AR App Performance Optimization 307
- Introduction 307
- Structure 307
- Objectives 308
- Performance metrics 308
  - *Frames per second* 308
  - *Tris and verts* 310
  - *Draw calls* 310
- Optimization of a 3D app 311
  - *GPU instancing* 311
  - *Static and dynamic batching* 312
  - *Occlusion culling and frustum culling* 313
  - *Textures and UV maps* 314
  - *Light baking* 317
  - *UI optimizations* 318
- Optimization considerations in coding 319
- Conclusion 321

Key points	321
Questions	321
Answers	*322*
Index	**323-330**

CHAPTER 1
Getting Started with Augmented Reality

Introduction

Before building **Augmented Reality** (**AR**) applications, we must understand what AR is and how hardware and software technology is combined to present an AR application to the end user. The second decade of the 21st century can be seen as a pivotal period for Immersive technology, mainly AR and virtual reality. One of the main reasons for the exponential growth in the AR field can be the escalated CPU power of mobile smartphones. The processing power required to perform real-time image processing calculations while estimating virtual element poses was unavailable in mobile devices. Therefore, technology did not have a better reach towards the masses.

A practical definition for AR can be: It is a view of the real physical world in which some elements are computer generated and graphically enhanced, allowing extended capabilities in terms of input and output.

The definition seems unrealistic, but the motivation for AR has been there since decades ago through science fiction stories. Almost a century ago, the golden age of comics introduced many superheroes and characters with superhuman and *augmented* abilities, who were placed in scenarios where these characters used AR technologies as in science fiction. **Holograms** have been one of the key elements to demonstrate advanced technologies within the stories. These holograms and augmented elements in the physical world had many things in common, such as interactivity with hands or voice, feedback from the elements with animations, showing information with text or sound effects, and the flexibility to spawn them anywhere, regardless of the context. Even though humans are not advanced as they predicted to be in the movies, we can see rapid development in research and development to invent such concepts.

Structure

In this chapter, we will cover the following topics:

- Augmented reality implementation and application.
- History of augmented reality.
- Augmented reality across the world.
- Augmented reality enabling technologies.
- Machine learning and artificial intelligence.

Objectives

By the end of this chapter, you will know that AR was not invented during the last decade but is a topic with a history of many decades. You will also learn the fundamental technologies used to create AR applications and the use cases of AR in different industries.

Augmented reality implementation and application

Let us consider a holographic AR implementation that may be implemented in the future. The technology behind the implementation must first capture and identify the context. There may be a hardware component with built-in sensors to recognize the people, objects, planes, and the world around them.

And once the context has been captured, the collected data must be converted into a virtual environment so that a virtual object can be placed on top of it. This conversion may be done using computer algorithms placed within the holographic device. This process can also be identified as the transformation layer.

The final steps of the implementation may include a presentation layer, which consists of all the audio and visual feedback, interactions, logic, etc. The users of the holographic device may use this presentation layer to generate AR content. The final layer would be the output layer which generates the accumulated set of components so that the user can see the final implementation. In a hologram, this is the final holographic output. In 2023, we still have a long way to go and years of research and development to implement a non-blocking output layer for a real hologram. *Figure 1.1* represents the conceptual representation of a Holographic AR implementation:

Figure 1.1: *Conceptual representation of a hologram*
(**Source**: *https://pixabay.com/photos/science-hologram-artificial-fiction-4642115/*)

Currently, existing AR systems are very advanced but are not yet able to visualize the AR content without another screen or a wearable in between the actual and virtual worlds. Consider a wearable AR device as an example. Such a device contains a camera and other sensors at the front to capture the world around it and uses software to recognize the context. Like the hologram example above, objects can be placed in the virtual environment generated within the presentation layer. Finally, the generated 3D content will render on the wearable screen, mapping to the physical world that can be seen through the glass.

A smartphone-based AR application would be the same, except that the final output layer would be through the mobile screen, having the camera input as the background. In these AR applications, the camera input must be captured and rendered inside the 3D space behind the 3D models, giving an illusion of how the 3D models are placed in the real-world context. *Figure 1.2* illustrates the structure of an AR application:

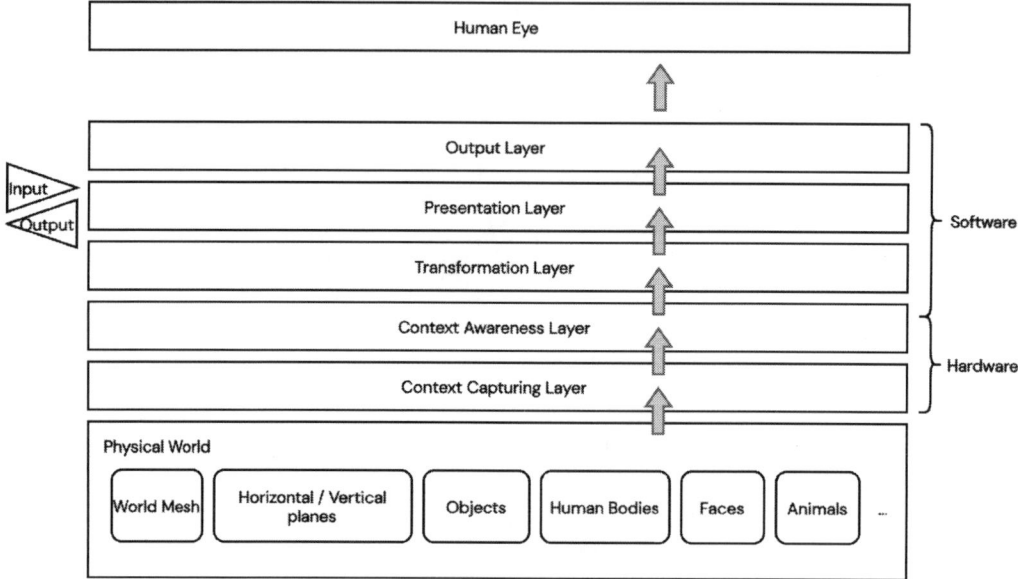

Figure 1.2: Structure of an AR application

History of augmented reality

In order to understand where we stand with widespread AR development, it is better to know the brief history of AR and where everything started.

1968 – The Sword of Damocles

The first implementation of AR that can be found in the history books is not through a computer screen but a prototype head-mounted display. *Prof. Ivan Sutherland*, an American computer scientist and a widely known computer graphics expert, created the first head-mounted display in 1968, known as **The Sword of Damocles**. The fundamental of that device is to create an illusion on the transparent display depending on a concept known as the *kinetic depth effect*.

The display is fixed to the ceiling of a room and can be worn by the user. The linkage in the ceiling measures the pose of the head and transfers that data to the computer program. A miniature cathode ray tube attached to the side of the display projects the image onto the eyeglass display optics, changing the orientation of the image based on the movement of the head. The research paper on this implementation can be obtained within chapter *A head-mounted three-dimensional display* of the Fall Joint Computer Conference journal in 1968. *Figure 1.3* features the above-mentioned display:

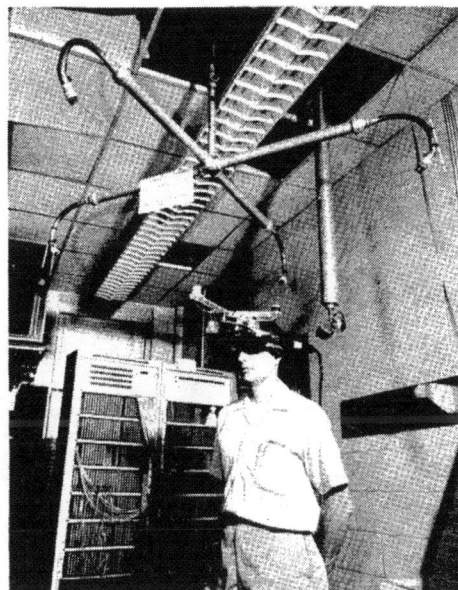

Figure 1.3: The first head-mounted display and how a 3D object can be seen through it.
(**Ref**: *Fall Joint Computer Conference Journal, 1968*)

1975 – Videoplace by Myron Krueger

Another implementation of artificial reality, even though it is not directly an augmented reality, can be seen through one of the first augmented interactive applications, which was known as **Videoplace**. The idea behind the application is to use external sensors and capture the context and interactivity without the use of goggles, buttons, gloves, or anything attached to the user.

The application used a camera to capture the user in front of a projector screen in front of the person. The captured video is transmitted to a computer, which performs image processing to generate a silhouette of the person with an additional interactive element as a separate layer. The layers are generated in different flat colors to differentiate each. The processed final image is then projected to the same projection screen using a back projector. This does not completely fulfill the requirement of AR, but it can be recognized as a step towards artificial reality and contained image recognition algorithms. *Figure 1.4* is an illustration of the videoplace system:

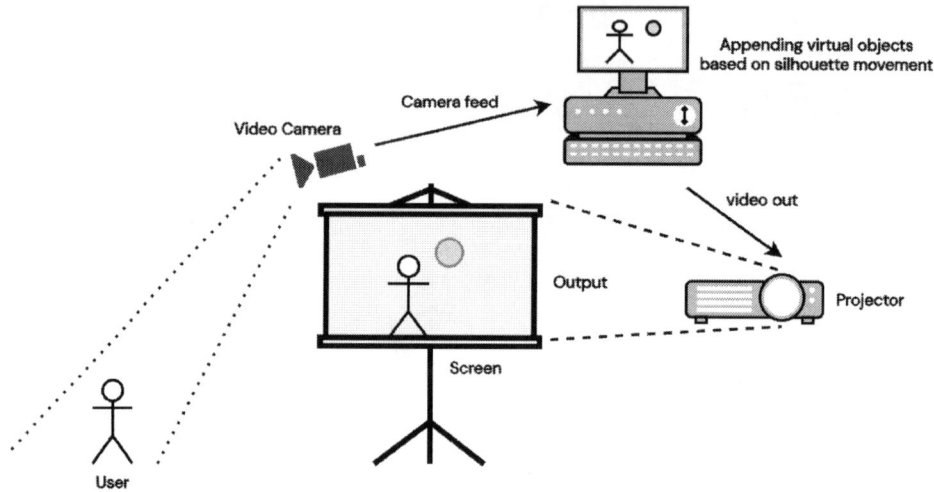

Figure 1.4: Structure of the videoplace system

1999 – AR Toolkit

Ever since the first AR implementations, technology has improved to move away from hardware-only solutions to programmable software solutions. One of the major implementations of such solutions is the AR Toolkit, which is a library that was developed in 1999 by *Dr. Hirokazu Kato* of Nara Institute of Science and Technology.

AR Toolkit was known as the world's first Mobile Augmented Reality Software Development Toolkit was incorporated after it, and a version was released to the public. The library was used in early OS-based smartphone devices such as Symbian around 2005, all the way to iOS and Android during the 2010 era.

Early versions of the AR Toolkit focused on predefined physical AR trackers (also known as **Fiducial markers**) to recognize the planes and visualize virtual 3D objects following the orientation of the trackers. Later versions of the AR Toolkit introduced *Natural Feature Tracking*, which allowed developers to train natural features of colorful images rather than using predefined AR trackers.

Figure 1.5 illustrates an AR Toolkit fiducial tracker, which is an example of an AR target:

Figure 1.5: Example of an AR target (AR Toolkit fiducial tracker)

More information on AR Toolkit can be found at:

http://www.hitl.washington.edu/artoolkit.html

Augmented reality over the years

Ever since the development of the AR Toolkit, many developers and organizations have stepped into the field of research and development of AR software development kits and supportive hardware. This was followed by the development of smartphone devices and their easy accessibility, which encouraged engineers and developers to focus more on handheld devices. Early software-based AR applications leveraged the power of desktop computers and attached web cameras to generate 3D models using magazine covers as image targets. A magazine advertisement done for MINI in 2008 is an example of one of the first AR implementations as a commercial use case. It can be found at:

https://www.youtube.com/watch?v=HTYeuo6pIjY

Esquire magazine worked with Hollywood actor *Robert Downey Jr.* to color their magazine with AR, and it can be found at:

https://www.youtube.com/watch?v=wp2z36kKn0s

The introduction of Google Glass in 2014 has become one of the key events in the history of AR. It was the first AR-inspired wearable device targeted at consumers. From 2010 to 2015, many software-based development kits and libraries were developed, targeting mainly mobile operating systems. Qualcomm Vuforia, AR Toolkit open source, MetaIO (acquired by Apple to develop its current AR SDK, ARKit), Wikitude, and ARMedia are some of the early adaptors of AR in the domain of smart handheld devices.

In 2016, Microsoft joined the AR market by introducing the *HoloLens*, which is the world's first wearable augmented reality tracking and meshing device, as can be seen in *Figure 1.6*:

Figure 1.6: Microsoft HoloLens. Kai Kowalewski, CC BY-SA 4.0
(*Source*: https://creativecommons.org/licenses/by-sa/4.0, via Wikimedia Commons)

Apple released its native AR SDK, known as AR kit, and Google started working on a hardware-software implementation known as Google Tango. The project was discontinued and later announced again as a complete software-based implementation known as ARCore. Google also invested in a wearable AR device, Magic Leap, an alternative to Microsoft HoloLens.

In the later chapters of this book, we will dive into some of the most popular AR development tools currently available to develop AR applications in cross-platform devices.

Augmented reality across the world

In order to build AR applications, it is better to research and understand the use cases of AR in various disciplines. Emerging technologies during the last couple of decades have been used in various applications outside the field of computer science. This section explores some of the use cases of AR currently in the world.

Augmented reality in entertainment

Many use cases of AR that are consumer-based circle around entertainment. In 2016, *Niantic* released its widely popular location-based game Pokémon Go. Niantic has been working with location-based games before stepping into AR, such as Ingress.

Pokémon Go innovatively implemented *catching a Pokémon using a pokéball* interaction using an AR interface within the game. This was a major boost for AR technology as more people could experience AR for the first time.

With the release of Pokémon go and smartphones having native AR capabilities, many games were developed that used AR as the backbone. Minecraft World, Harry Potter Wizards Unite, and Jurassic World Alive are some of the popular games that have been released since then. Stepping out of the mass outreach of AR games, the technology has also been used in various physical activations and live events. Video-based AR technologies such as Vizrt and Wtvision have taken over the world, offering real-time AR over broadcast. We have seen how various augmented content appear on television news, sports events, and other live shows to make the shows more interesting through television. Vizrt technologies have been used over thousands of TV events around the world. Mainly covering sports events and news, some of their customer stories include Eurovision, ausbiz, Mediacorp in Singapore, CNN-NEWS18, Al-Jazeera documentaries, and many more.

Figure 1.7 features the use of AR in a museum:

Figure 1.7: Augmented reality at Museu de Mataró linking to Catalan
(**Source**: Kippelboy, CC BY-SA 3.0,
https://creativecommons.org/licenses/by-sa/3.0>, via Wikimedia Commons)

AR has been used in art galleries and museums around the world. In 2021 the *Muséum National d'Histoire Naturelle* in Paris launched an AR experience. The experience was called REVIRE and allowed visitors to hire a Microsoft HoloLens and interact with digital animals throughout the museum. The National Museum of Singapore has an AR installation called **Story of the Forest**. An AR installation known as ReBlink is available at the Art Gallery of Ontario, Toronto enhancing the art experience of the artwork within the gallery. Google has a virtual museum with AR capabilities, allowing users to visit an AR gallery virtually. It can be found at:

https://artsandculture.google.com/project/ar

These are just a fraction of the thousands of AR installations all around the world.

We explored some of the existing AR-related use cases in the world. Thinking of the future, AR can replace many entertainment channels such as television, billboards, and live events. Think of an AR wearable device that can turn your living room into a stadium with live matches running on your coffee table. Imagine how a wall in your room can be converted to a large cinema screen where you can watch the latest movies without stepping out of your room. The possibilities of AR in the entertainment world are endless, provided the correct tools and technologies.

AR in manufacturing and logistics

Google Glass had many challenges in reaching the consumer market even though it is the first ever widely announced wearable display device. The device has a camera mounted to the front of it, and there is no indication to the outside world whether the user is capturing the surrounding and streaming a video to a third party. This caused many conflicts with regard to security and privacy. Ultimately, Google discontinued the product to the public as a consumer device and revived it to be used in enterprise applications, mainly focusing on manufacturing, logistics, and anything that requires hands-free work but with access to additional information. Currently, Google Glass provides real-time collaboration, access to training visualizations, and voice input, enhancing the capabilities of factory workers. Even though this is not a completely AR-enabled device, this has been used by many larger organizations across the world, including DHL, Schenker, Samsung, and Volkswagen.

Mainly, AR has been used in factories for maintenance assistance, machine operation training, and data visualization in real-time for machinery data retrieval and preventive maintenance. Dynamic arrangement of manufacturing facilities leverages AR for navigation within the factories. Imagine a logistics facility that rearranges the inside of the facility rapidly based on its dynamic adaptations. This may be an overhead for the facility to change the navigation system along with its rearrangements. This can be easily overcome by setting up navigation in AR that can instantly replace the data points. Imagine a wearable within a factory that allows machine supervisors to just look at the machine and visualize its sensory and machinery data in real-time next to the machine itself. This reduces the overhead time the teams spend searching through data logs through a separate interface matching the data to the machines. Imagine a 3D machine or vehicle construction that can be previewed through AR in a collaborative environment. This allows the designers and engineers working together to visualize the elements on a real-life scale and thus reduces the time required to make foam models of the machine. There are limitless possibilities where AR can be beneficial in the manufacturing industry.

Real estate

In 2020, Unity, a leading 3D development engine, teamed up with Autodesk Revit, a **Building Information Modelling (BIM)**, to create a tool known as Unity Reflect. This allowed creators to link BIM model data to a 3D environment in real-time. Unity, known for AR, used the same links to visualize 3D models of buildings and architecture in real time in an AR environment. A great use case of this turned out to be the client's ability to visualize their building design exactly on the building site as a 1:1 scale on-site in AR while the architects change the model data in real time according to the client's needs.

Similarly, many real estate agencies use AR to enhance the customer experience in buying real estate by providing AR virtual tours. Imagine an application allowing people to go to real estate locations and visualize the price charts and how different buildings appear without spending for concept creators. Imagine, as a real-estate agency, your customers being able to freely walk around within any available houses with the AR app providing additional information to their needs. Using AR technologies, the realtors get a competitive advantage in providing more unique personalized experiences to their customers.

Health

Imagine visualizing a 3D reconstruction of the bone structure of a patient while walking around it instead of taking multiple X-ray images. AR can allow that to happen, provided the hardware and software required to obtain scan data of a patient are available. AR is a great alternative to the current healthcare imaging solutions. Many of the imaging output channels can be replaced by a simple AR wearable that can use its surroundings to import as many 3D visualizations to the environment as possible. Imagine a surgeon performing surgery and being able to visualize patients' vital data on top of the patient's body parts. The surgery can be done faster, reducing the time required for the professionals to look away from the patient. Also, such use cases reduce the surgeons making errors due to misreading information.

AR can also be used in medical training. Instead of using custom-made physical dummies for health-related simulations, AR glasses can be used to quickly change training scenarios for the trainees to perform interactions and get trained more efficiently.

Education

As mentioned in the previous sub-section, training can be offered in any competency. It can be the health industry, manufacturing, logistics, and also a common school classroom. Schools invest heavily in chemical and physics laboratories, not only by building new labs but also by maintaining them. Imagine an enhanced school physics laboratory where the students can create AR-based tabletop physical simulations while changing the parameters of the objects dynamically. This allows the students to learn the activities by trying out limitless scenarios without changing any physical object in the lab. Imagine a wearable AR headset that can convert your living room to a classroom with your friends. Microsoft HoloLens provides shared experiences with the help of *spatial anchors* allowing people to connect, share, and learn the same experience. Science books make use of marker-based AR to allow the experiments to be viewed out of the book by using a mobile application. The ability to move around freely to observe 3D constructions enabled the engagement of the students to learn by doing rather than learn by memorizing.

Marketing and retail

One of the widely used AR applications can be found within marketing and retail use cases of AR. IKEA Place is a great initiative done by the company to allow people to add furniture to their own space to visualize whether the piece of furniture fits properly. Dulux has built an AR app to scan any wall and immediately change the color to any available color by them. There are many marketing enabler AR apps currently in the market, such as Blippar, 8th wall (acquired by Niantic), Zappar, and Augment, which allow companies to use their platforms as authoring tools to build content for their marketing campaigns. Children's cereal producers use AR apps to extend their cereal boxes for children to collect and play custom-made games for rewards. E-commerce sites make use of AR product viewers to spawn the 3D models of products into a user's space to visualize them on a real-life scale. Companies like Nike and Adidas use the power of AI and AR and have built apps such as Wannakicks and Wyking AR to visualize shoes directly attached to your feet. Product visualization, product configurators, and marketing engagement activities have become the key entry points of AR in retail. Unlike decades ago, the spectrum of possibilities has expanded with the introduction of AR. It does not only provide the *wow factor* to the customers but also creates unforgettable memories in their minds about the products and services that have been marketed with AR. Many businesses have been leveraging the use of AR, providing marketing and retail solutions around AR to bigger companies around the world. Leading service-oriented companies, such as Accenture and Volume Global, have already filled their portfolios with AR case studies around the world, and there is more to come.

Any of the readers of this book hopes to provide services with AR solutions, think of the problems that are faced in different disciplines across the world, and evaluate how those problems can be solved using AR. There are many AR use cases that create problems than offering solutions. Therefore, it is vital to understand the requirement and measure the importance of AR, which can replace the existing workflows. Considering the costs, maintainability, and usefulness of AR technology, any industry can leverage it for higher savings, higher profits, and higher engagement.

Augmented reality enabling technologies

AR heavily relies on computer vision. The use of additional data, such as depth sensing for meshing, catalyzes the accuracy of the trackers. Ever since the use of machine learning and AI, the accuracy of target detection and tracking and the extended capabilities of AR have expanded. The following section explores some of the computer vision techniques that enable AR.

Image recognition and tracking

In order to enable AR in a predefined target image (for example, a poster, magazine cover, photo, QR code, and so on), the features of the image must be matched and recognized. This process is known as feature detection and matching. Once the image has been detected, the data can be used to track the image with its movement with respect to the position of the camera. These algorithms are used not only for AR but in many applications. Robot navigation systems, image retrieval, object tracking, motion detection, and segmentation are some of the other applications of feature detection and matching. A feature of an image can be recognized as a piece of information in the image that can be used by the computer program to recognize the image. As an example, the points and edges of an image can be used as features of the image. The challenge of image detection is to detect and capture the features, collect information about the appearance around the feature point, and match similar features with a known feature distribution set. These feature points are identified by various algorithms based on either the brightness of the image or the boundary/edge details of the image.

A feature recognition algorithm gets an image as an input and outputs a series of vectors. The output of an image would be a series of encoded data in a machine-understandable format. This is known as a feature descriptor. The information that is generated from an image is supposed to be independent of the orientation and the transformation of the image. Therefore, the output data remains the same regardless of the movement of the image. This provides one of the fundamental abilities of AR, which is the ability to track a detected image based on the image features by recognizing and tracking the image detected. *Figure 1.8* illustrates a colored poster and how its transformed feature points are aligned together:

Figure 1.8: *Features of an image (features are marked with x)*

The neighborhood around a feature point is known as a local descriptor, which resembles the appearance of an area around its feature point. The basic flow of feature detection and matching can be listed as follows:

- Use image processing methods to detect certain points. They can be based on the contrast of the image, edge detection, etc.
- Capture the information around the detected feature point.
- Generate a local descriptor, an encoded vector that describes the region around the feature point.
- Match the local descriptors based on another factor, such as the time, predefined descriptor, etc.

Following are the image processing algorithms that support feature detection and tracking:

- Harris Corner Detector
- **Scale Invariant Feature Transform (SIFT)**

- **Speeded Up Robust Feature (SURF)**
- **Binary Robust Independent Elementary Features (BRIEF)**
- **Features from Accelerated Segment Test (FAST)**
- **Oriented FAST and Rotated BRIEF (ORB)**
- **Binary Robust Invariant Scalable Key points (BRISK)**

Open CV is a library of computer vision algorithms that is under Apache open-source license. In-depth details of all the above algorithms can be read via OpenCV documentation:

https://docs.opencv.org/

Simultaneous localization and mapping

Simultaneous Localization and Mapping (SLAM) has been an integral part of not only AR but of many research areas in the engineering field, such as robotics. The basic idea of SLAM is to use the cameras and other sensors of the computational device to generate a virtual map of the surroundings. Once the map has been generated, the information is then fed into its own movement system, where it can localize itself within the virtual map.

SLAM can be achieved in many ways depending on the device. For robots, it uses cameras, LiDAR sensors, motion, and other sensors to map the virtual world. Some systems use beacons placed around the world to help the device map the environment more accurately. However, for mobile AR, it is only the camera, the gyroscope, the accelerometer, and other movement-based sensors that can be used to map the environment.

For example, let us consider a mobile AR solution that works on top of a SLAM integration. The ultimate goal is to capture the world around us and convert it into a map. The flow of the process can be listed as follows.

- Use the camera of the device to capture the image, the gyroscope, and the accelerometer to capture the pose and the movement vectors of the device.
- Extracting the features based on the input data. As described in the image processing section, a feature descriptor is used to convert the image data to vector data, such as key points and neighborhood data.
- Association of data is done to neglect the features that have been captured before. This is a repetitive process. Therefore, the features that were captured in one frame (in one iteration) should be passed to the other frame. Instead of duplication, similar data points must be recognized. This is also known as a loop closure.

- The data that was captured is used to determine the movement of all the feature points and transferred to map construction. Based on the algorithm, the generated map will be a point cloud or a sparse reconstruction based on the distribution of the feature points. *Figure 1.9* illustrates how feature detection and tracking is done:

Figure 1.9: Feature detection and tracking

- The mapped data is used again with the pose of the capturing device to map its position with respect to the generated virtual space. This is known as a SLAM estimate, as can be seen in *Figure 1.10*:

*Figure 1.10: Example of a SLAM estimate. Martin Holzkothen, Michael Korn, CC BY 3.0 (**Source**: https://creativecommons.org/licenses/by/3.0, via Wikimedia Commons)*

In AR, SLAM is mainly used for environment detection where there are no predefined trackers, such as in images, posters, or QR codes to enable tracking. The first frames captured through the camera are used to generate the feature vectors in real time, and the same are used over time to convert the mapped point data to planes and obstacles.

Recent AR frameworks not only capture still images or an unknown environment but also faces, body parts, barcode data, textual data on billboards, and many more. Based on the processing power required just for SLAM and feature descriptors, heading for more traditional image processing may result in unnecessary processing overhead. Therefore, machine learning and artificial intelligence are used to enhance the capabilities of AR.

Machine learning and artificial intelligence

Machine learning has become one of the key factors in the growth of artificial intelligence throughout recent years. Machine learning algorithms have been used in many use cases, such as object recognition, natural language processing, predictive analytics, and automated processing of many tasks that span across multiple disciplines.

AR, too has seen an uprising with the integration of machine learning. The concept of machine learning for computer vision is as follows:

- Collection of data samples.
- Training data using the collected samples.
- Generate the machine learning model.
- Test the generated model.
- Use it in implementation.

Consider an AR solution that tracks human hair to change color while showing a 3D sunglass over the eyes. Machine learning models can be used to detect the face and the pose of the face, generating a face feature model to be modified in a 3D environment. At the same time, another machine learning algorithm will be extracting the image features to detect only the hair portion changing color.

There are multiple machine learning algorithms that are available within Open CV. An in-depth analysis of these algorithms can be learned through the following link:

https://docs.opencv.org/4.x/dc/dd6/ml_intro.html

Deep learning is a type of machine learning which works by mimicking a human brain solving problems. Unlike standard machine learning algorithms, deep learning uses artificial neural networks for representation learning and predictive modeling.

Deep learning algorithms in computer vision can be used not just for recognition but for image generation as well. **Generative Adversarial Networks (GANs)** are widely used in generating images based on training data and a generator. There are AR applications that can capture a human face to directly convert to an animated character in real time. These algorithms use modified versions of GANs to generate a new image based on the trainset and a generator and replace the content from the original camera.

Currently, most of the AR development kit providers make use of the technologies discussed in this chapter. Image descriptors are used for marker training for later recognition, which can be used directly in AR applications that can track predefined targets. SLAM, or at least modified or enhanced versions, has been used by many marker-less AR SDK developers such as Apple, Android as well as Microsoft. The use of machine learning and AI works as a catalyst to provide unique and enhanced AR experiences to the user.

In the next chapter of this book, the difference between marker-based and marker-less AR is discussed.

Conclusion

Now we know how people looked at AR from a technical point of view and the research done around the technologies related to AR, such as image processing and machine learning-related recognition technologies. Even after decades, technology is still in its early stages but growing exponentially due to the growth of supporting technologies. We also looked at the history of AR, use cases, and potential use cases of AR in different industries that sums up the objectives of AR.

From the next chapter onwards, we aim to dive deeper into the principles behind AR applications, the tools available for building AR apps, and the steps of building and deploying AR apps with different interaction methods.

Key points

- AR technologies are built on top of image recognition.
- Image recognition uses different mathematical algorithms to extract images to data that computers can process, which are known as descriptors.
- Real-time area recognition technologies use cameras and other sensors to capture and determine the position with respect to the environment. This is known as SLAM.
- Machine learning technologies are used to extend tracking accuracy and implement additional features.

Multiple choice questions

1. **What was The Sword of Damocles in the context of AR?**
   a. A famous sword used in an AR-based video game.
   b. The first-ever AR headset prototype developed by Ivan Sutherland.
   c. A mythical weapon depicted in an AR-themed movie.
   d. An AR app used to teach sword-fighting techniques.

2. **Who developed the AR Toolkit, a popular open-source software library for creating AR applications?**
   a. Dr. Richard Feynman
   b. Dr. Hirokazu Kato
   c. Dr. Alan Turing
   d. Dr. Grace Hopper

3. **What does SLAM stand for in the context of AR and robotics?**
   a. Simultaneous Location and Mapping
   b. Sensory Light and Motion
   c. Spatial Localization and Measurement
   d. Systematic Learning and Management

4. **Which of the following is an example of how AI is used in AR applications?**
   a. Creating 3D models from physical objects in real-time.
   b. Enabling seamless integration of AR content on mobile devices.
   c. Providing AR glasses with extended battery life.
   d. Generating holographic displays without the need for any hardware.

Answers
1. b
2. b
3. a
4. a

Join our book's Discord space

Join the book's Discord Workspace for Latest updates, Offers, Tech happenings around the world, New Release and Sessions with the Authors:

https://discord.bpbonline.com

CHAPTER 2
Visualizing AR Environment and Components

Introduction

In the previous chapter, we learned what makes **Augmented Reality (AR)** a reality and how AR is being used in different industries. In this chapter, we will be stepping a bit further into the concepts of 3D and learning the basics of mathematics that are required for building applications that make use of 3D virtual spaces. This chapter can be considered the basic building block of any computer graphics application. Our intention is to better understand how a virtual world is generated, how virtual objects are placed in such a world, and how real input is converted into a virtual interaction.

In order to understand some of the concepts we discuss during this chapter, let us take a step back and go through the basics of mathematics, as the related terminology will be helpful in the long run.

Structure

In this chapter, we will cover the following topics:

- Basics of mathematics for 3D visualization
- Understanding the 3D environment

- Vector mathematics
- Basic trigonometry
- Understanding different spaces
- Context recognition concepts
- Placement of virtual objects on physical worlds
- Converting physical input to virtual interactions

Objectives

After completing this chapter, you will have a basic knowledge of mathematics relevant to 3D application development, a sound understanding of 2D and 3D spaces, and how the augmented reality components are placed in a virtual environment mapping a real physical space.

Basics of mathematics for 3D visualization

Ever since the 1st grade, we learn about numbers. When we grow older, we learn different types of numbers. Even if this book assumes your basic mathematical skills, understanding the underlying concepts will be beneficial for 3D interaction development.

We can start with the number Zero (0). Anything that is not a zero can be either positive or negative. We use the minus sign (-) in front of the number to denote a negative number. Check out these examples:

Zero: 0

Positives: 1, 6, 89, 1.98, 2.37384723, 98.1823

Negatives: -1, -5, -0.1212, -0.6, -10.1829, -124.123632

Any number, regardless of being positive or negative, can also be a whole number without a fractional component. These whole numbers are known as **integers**. Between two integers, there exists an infinite number of non-integers. These numbers contain a fractional component or a part of an integer component to represent a fraction of the proceeding integer with respect to the ending integer. In computing, these fraction numerals are known as **floating-point arithmetic**. Any number that is not an integer is represented as a **float**, and it is written with a decimal point dividing the whole number and the fractional component. These floating points can either be rational or irrational. A simple fraction can express rational numbers, while irrational numbers cannot be expressed easily. Here are a few examples:

Integers: -2, -23, -1, 3, 6, 34, 1234346.

Floats: -43.234, -1.234234, -0.55, 21.001, 45.23507, 23.56.

Rational: 2.5 or 5/2, -4.5 or -9/2, 2.34 or 117/50.

Irrational: $\sqrt{8}$, $\sqrt{11}$, $\sqrt{50}$ These numbers cannot be expressed as a fraction.

Computers use numbers for mathematical processing. Even though the underlying process uses binary calculations, computers can perform various mathematical calculations on numbers. In computer languages such as C#, the following symbols are used to denote mathematical calculations:

- **Addition**: Plus, sign (+)

    1+2 = 3

- **Subtraction**: Minus sign (-)

    10-2 = 8

- **Multiplication**: Star sign (*)

    23 * 3 = 69

- **Division**: Back slash (/)

    10/2 = 5

- **Modulus (Remainder after division)**: Percentage sign (%)

    10 % 3 = 1

When building 3D applications, one of the many areas in mathematics that we cannot leave out is Algebra. It is a branch of mathematics that represents problems in mathematical expressions. This is where the term variable comes into play. In programming, there are different types of variables. When it comes to mathematical calculations, we can consider numbers as integers and floats. Variables can be defined based on the type, and mathematical expressions can be written using combined numbers, variables, and mathematical operations:

$$Area = diameter * \pi$$

Here, the **Area** is a variable that represents the final value. The **diameter** is a variable that can hold any value. π is just a constant that represents a floating-point value of approximately **3.14**. In programming, we combine the use of all in order to calculate the properties of objects. Imagine a scenario of an AR experience that captures the diameter of a circular object and provides the area of that object. As a developer, we can use a similar calculation to simply represent the area to the user.

Now that we have understood the basic steps of mathematics, it is time to step into the 3D world. However, before jumping into 3D, we need two more steps to check-in. We can start by understanding the Cartesian coordinate system with 1D and 2D mathematics.

Understanding the 3D environment

Draw a line on a sheet and divide the line into ten similar sections. Now, number the section breaks from 0 to 10. The result would look like *Figure 2.1*:

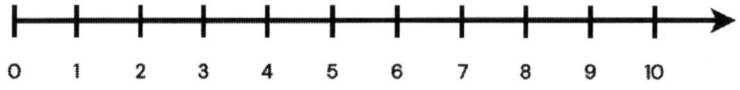

Figure 2.1: Number Line

Now, we can represent a number on this line by adding a dot. The dot can be moved based on various mathematical calculations. As an example, check the *Figure 2.2 (for, $9 - 5 + 3 - 4$)*:

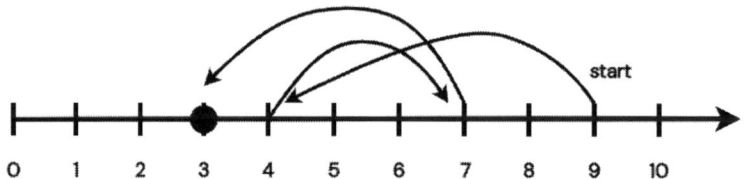

Figure 2.2: Representing a calculation in a number line

In mathematics, this can be considered as a one-dimensional space. Any variable or number can be represented as a point on the line. In a situation where a floating number has to be presented on the line, it can be represented within two integer sections as a proportion. *Figure 2.3* represents the real number π on a one-dimensional line:

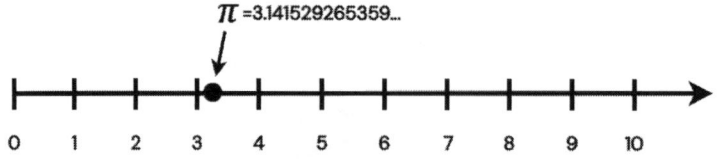

Figure 2.3: Representing a number in a number line

Now, let us go a bit further. With a line, we could represent a position of just one number. If we combine two lines, we can represent two numbers. But if we keep the lines perpendicular to each other, we can use the two numbers to represent a position on a plane. This can now be identified as a two-dimensional Cartesian plane. A checkerboard is a great example for this, as can be seen in *Figure 2.4*:

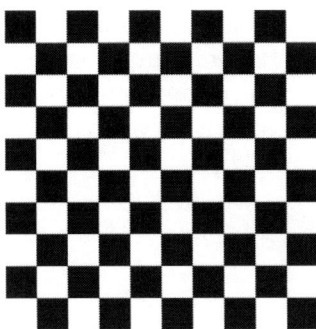

Figure 2.4: A Checkerboard

A checkerboard uses numbers to represent square shapes. Numbering the horizontal and the vertical plane, any square in the checkerboard can be represented using two numbers. In Chess, one line is numbered, and the other line is represented using the alphabet. Similarly, we can represent a position on a plane using two lines. We call the combination of the two lines the **coordinate system.** We represent these lines as **axes**. As a practice, a horizontal axis is labeled as the *x-axis* and the vertical line as the *y-axis*. A mathematical representation of a point on a plane will be given as (x,y). If you consider where the two lines should be merged perpendicularly, there can be many depending on the use case. In general, two lines representing negative to positive merges on 0 respectively. The point is the center of the coordinate system and is known as the **origin.**

For example, (5,3) represents a point in the 2D space where the x value is 5 and the y value is 3. This can be used to specify many mathematical representations. As an example, a position of a given plane that can be visually represented is shown in *Figure 2.5*:

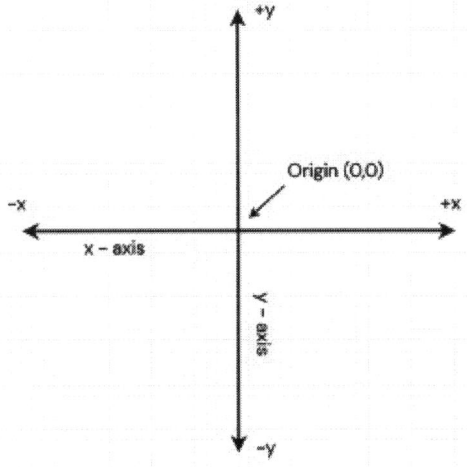

Figure 2.5: 2D Cartesian plane

Similar to the 1D line positioning, integers and any positive and negative number can be represented using the 2D coordinate system. Imagine a 2D Cartesian plane placed on a table, and you keep a pencil vertically, right on top of the origin. You may visualize a three-dimensional view of it, as illustrated in *Figure 2.6*:

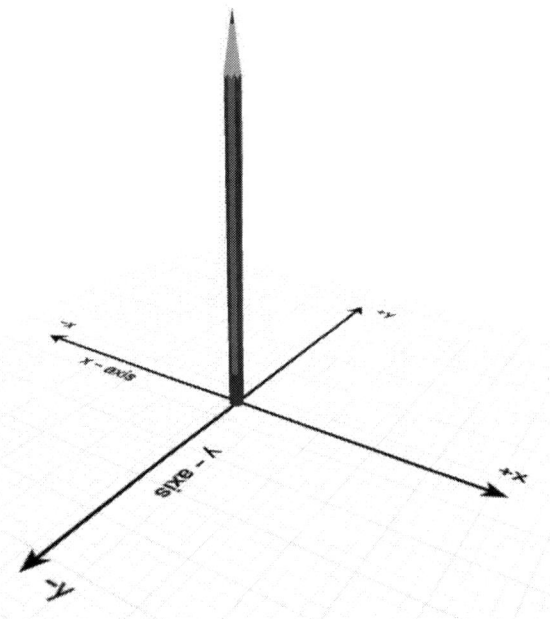

Figure 2.6: Placing a pencil on a 2D Cartesian plane

Source: "Pencil" (https://skfb.ly/6TAAV) by Akshat, licensed under
Creative Commons Attribution (http://creativecommons.org/licenses/by/4.0/)

Visualizing the three-dimensional space is a bit difficult to describe. However, imagining a real-world example helps us understand how the three dimensions are placed with respect to each axis.

Now, we convert the pencil to another virtual line, giving it the label *z*. Imagine a point placed on the plane of *x-y*. If we lift it directly parallel to the pencil, or the z-axis, now we will get a floating dot in the air. The position of the point can now be represented with respect to the origin point of the plane by using x, y, and z numbers. The orientation of the x, y, and z axis may change, but three values can now give the position of any point. A visual representation of a position in the 3D space and a 3D Cartesian space is shown in *Figure 2.7*:

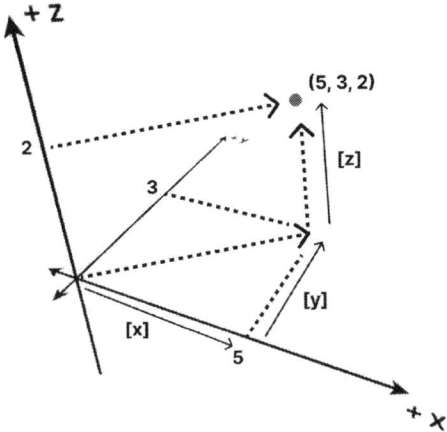

Figure 2.7: A point in a 3D Cartesian space

Now that we know how a 3D space is represented imagine flipping one of the axes. As an example, change the z-axis's minus to plus and plus to minus. Now you may realize that both coordinate systems can never be aligned on top of each other. This is because all the 3D coordinate spaces are not equal. There are two different 3D coordinate spaces regardless of the change of axis direction. We call them the left-handed coordinate space and the right-handed coordinate space. Any similar-handed coordinate system can be rotated and aligned on each other, while the opposite is impossible.

Try to align both hands, as shown in *Figure 2.8*, and see whether you can align them together in any way. You may realize that any two fingers can be aligned, while the other can never be:

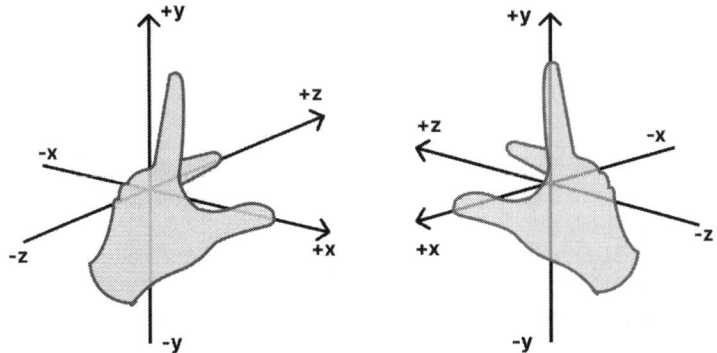

Figure 2.8: Left and Right handedness of 3D coordinate space

In 3D application development, we will manipulate objects using transform values, mainly on position, rotation, and scale. The transformations use the coordinate spaces of the 3D system to perform these calculations. Considering the rotation of any point with respect to the origin, it can be defined by the handedness of the coordinate space.

A positive rotation can be clockwise or counterclockwise based on the coordinate space. This is known as the left-hand rule or the right-hand rule. If you rotate anything around a given axis, consider making a fist of either of your hands. Point your thumb up towards the positive direction of the axis. Now the rest of the fingers will be curved and rotated towards the positive direction of the rotation. This is illustrated in *Figure 2.9*:

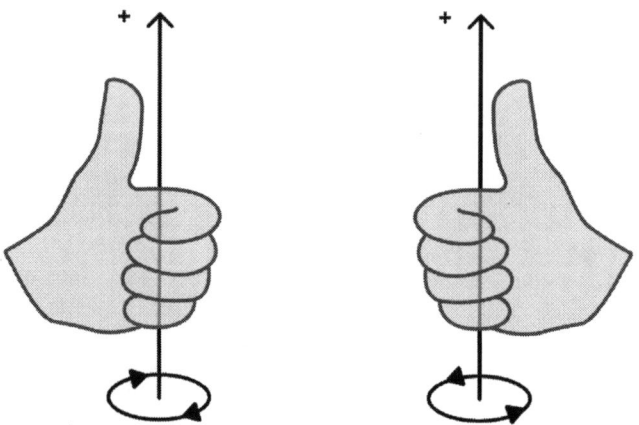

Figure 2.9: *Left-hand and right-hand rule for positive rotation*

In this book, we will be using the Left-hand rule and the left-hand-based coordinate system mainly because Unity 3D engine uses the left as its three-dimensional space. Simply put, any rotation that we perform with a positive amount will result in a clockwise rotation.

Vector mathematics

In mathematics, a vector is a collection of numbers. It can be just one number or a list of numbers within a single entity. The number of elements in a vector can define the number of dimensions of the vector. As an example, check the following set of vectors:

- **Vector1:** (34.45), (-12.4), (0.0)
- **Vector2:** (12.3, 3.45), (1,5), (-1, -4)
- **Vector3:** (45.6, 22.2, 6.2), (-1, -4, 6), (0, 0, 0)

In physics, a vector is known as an entity with a magnitude and a direction. Usually, this applies to 2D and 3D modes since a single number cannot define a direction, and more than three values cause complexity in defining directions. Imagine placing a ring at the center of a board and pulling it towards a given direction using a thread. The pull that you apply can be known as the force. The force and direction are variables, and each can change, keeping the other constant. This allows the force to be applied in various different ways in this 2D plane. Hence it has the characteristics to be defined mathematically. The same force can be applied using two forces that are perpendicular to each other, as shown in *Figure 2.10*:

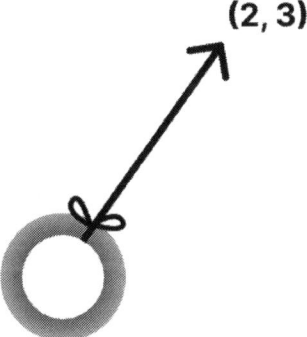

Figure 2.10: Pulling a ring with a string with (2,3) force

Instead of pulling the ring with just one thread, you can get the same movement with two threads that pull the ring horizontally and vertically. The resultant will be the ring moving diagonally based on the forces by the two threads. The two forces can now be determined with just two numbers, or we can say: a 2D vector. This can be seen in *Figure 2.11*:

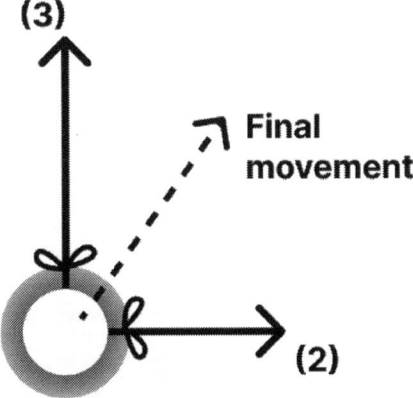

Figure 2.11: Pulling a ring with two perpendicular strings

The representation of a 2D vector can be done on a Cartesian plane, as shown in *Figure 2.12*:

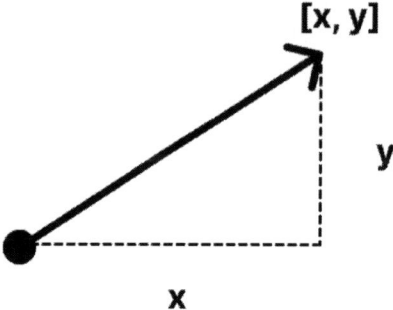

Figure 2.12: Representation of a vector in 3D space

Similarly, a 3D vector can be represented on a 3D Cartesian plane. Imagine the ring is being pulled out by another force upwards; the resultant can be a movement in the 3D space. This can be seen in *Figure 2.13*:

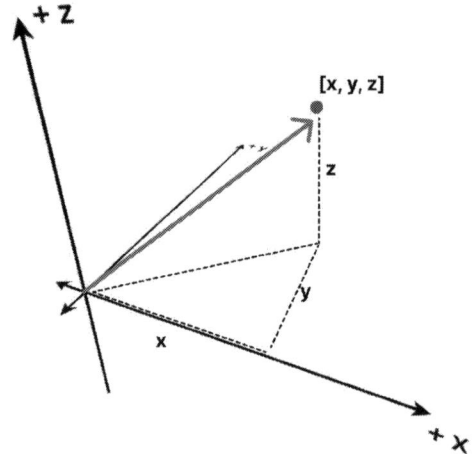

Figure 2.13: Representation of a vector in 3D space

Terminology of vectors

- **Magnitude**: This is the size or length of the vector. The magnitude is always positive.

  For example, the magnitude of [3,4] vector is 5.

- **Direction**: This is the direction that the vector is pointing towards.

  For example, the direction of the [4,4] vector is 45^0 clockwise from north.

- **Negating a vector**: Changing the direction of the vector to the opposite direction. This way, all the numbers representing the vector will be multiplied by -1.

  For example, the negation of [4, -6] is [-4, 6].

- **Unit vector:** The vector with the same direction but a magnitude of 1.

  For example, the unit vector of [3,3], [5,5], [6,6], etc., is [1,1].

- **Dot product:** Given two vectors, the dot product is the multiplication of both magnitudes and the cosine of the angle between the two vectors. Generally, this determines if another vector is perpendicular to a given vector.

- **Cross product**: Given two vectors, this gives another vector perpendicular to both. The direction of the resultant vector depends on the angle between the given two vectors.

However, the vectors represent both scalar and directional components, and they are used in physics-based calculations to represent transform values, forces, and velocities in 3D development tools.

Basic trigonometry

The vectors generate virtual triangles in 3D and 2D spaces, which involves transformations, rotations, angles, etc. Therefore, having a basic knowledge of the fundamentals of Trigonometry helps build 3D applications. Consider a circle divided into 360 pieces. One of these pieces is known as 1 degree (1^0). The total circle is 360^0, and half of it is 180^0. This is illustrated in *Figure 2.14*:

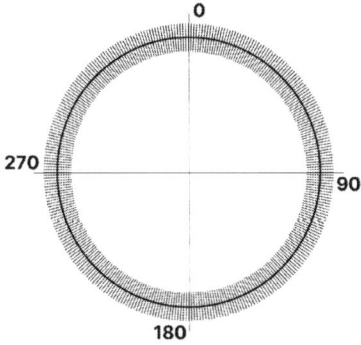

Figure 2.14: A circle has 360 divisions, each called a degree

Consider a circle of radius R. Place a dot on the circumference of the circle and move it on the circle such that the distance traveled is exactly R. Given that, the total rotation covered by the dot with respect to the center of the circle is known as a **Radian,** as shown in *Figure 2.15*:

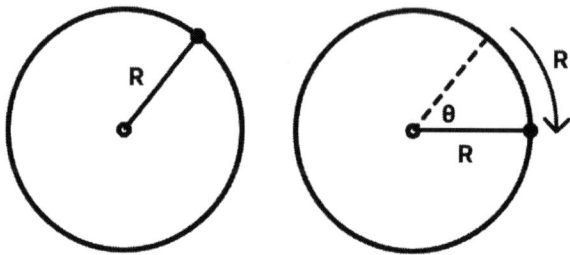

Figure 2.15: Defining a radian angle

The dot should travel roughly 6.2831.. radians to complete a full circle. This amount is an **irrational** number, and half of it is generally known as the constant π. 2π radians are equal to 360⁰ degrees. Any angle can be represented using either degrees or radians. If you take a right triangle with one angle being θ, the edges of the triangle can be used to determine the trigonometric functions, as shown in *Figure 2.16*:

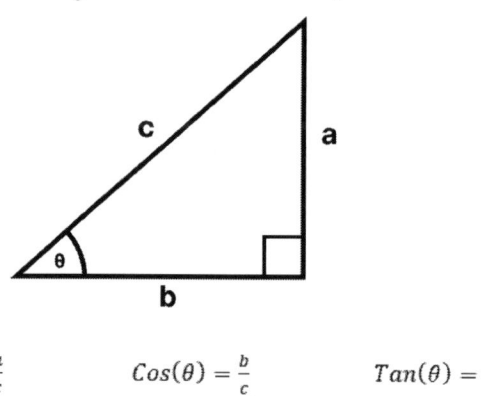

$$Sin(\theta) = \frac{a}{c} \qquad Cos(\theta) = \frac{b}{c} \qquad Tan(\theta) = \frac{a}{b}$$

Figure 2.16: A right triangle

Representing rotations in 3D space can be tricky. You can use vectors and angles to present the orientation of the x, y, and z components of a vector, or you can use the number of degrees with respect to each axis which is known as **Euler angles**. However, this can be harder than it seems when you want to rotate something around a given axis.

Imagine you are looking at something above and immediately turning your back to look at something below. This whole rotation path should be calculated and presented in a 3D environment. A straightforward way is to use a 3D vector representing the degrees. However, the rotation needs to be done in a sequence. Rotate x, then y, and then z by changing the values separately. This flow of the change of values ends when it meets the loss of the degree of freedom, known as the **Gimbal Lock.**

Therefore, instead of using vectors, or Euler angles for rotations, we use **Quaternions** to determine rotations in the 3D space.

Quaternions are based on complex numbers. Many 3D programs, like Unity, use quaternions for rotation-based calculations, and they can be converted to Euler angles and vice versa. Therefore, as developers, we are not required to provide quaternion inputs directly for rotation-based interpolations.

Understanding different spaces

Imagine the world as a three-dimensional cubic space. If you assume your house's front door to be the origin point of that 3D Cartesian space, you may visualize your position with respect to that origin. If you stand on the door, your position will be exactly (0, 0, 0). If you move away to your house next door, your position has changed towards the horizontal plane. If you climb a tree, now your position has a third-dimensional value. When you consider a 3D world a Cartesian plane, you can define everything in the world with respect to a given origin point. This is known as the **world space**.

Now imagine you have a large wooden box in your hand with another wooden ball fixed inside that box. Because the ball is fixed inside the box, there is no movement inside. Now, consider the position of the ball with respect to the center of the wooden box. Does it change if you move the wooden box around the neighborhood? The answer is no because the ball's position is fixed with respect to the center of the box. Now consider the position of the ball with respect to your front door. When you move around with the box, the position of the ball changes only with respect to the origin. If you release the ball inside the box, now the ball can be freely moved within the box; hence the position with respect to the center of the box is changed. The box can be identified as a **local space**, and this is illustrated in *Figure 2.17*:

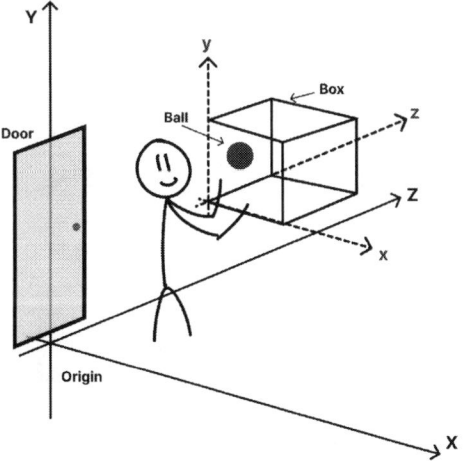

Figure 2.17: World space and Local space

If you consider the ball having its own virtual space, this is also a local space. Sometimes it can be considered as **object space** as well. In 3D spatial applications, space is important to determine the poses of objects with respect to either the world or a given local space. Using different coordinate spaces is more convenient and thus easy to manipulate in different situations.

Context recognition concepts

We mainly discuss two types of AR. If you consider the workflow of AR recognition, identifying the space to generate 3D content is the first step. This identification can either be based on a pre-defined environment or an environment that is created in real-time. Under this, the two types of AR can be:

- Marker-based
- Marker-less

As discussed in *Chapter 1, Getting Started with Augmented Reality* marker-based recognition requires a pre-defined context. This is known as a tracker that has been converted to a mathematical model, in which a comparison is made to build the virtual world. Now let us consider a scenario where a marker has been recognized in the 3D world. Once such a pre-defined target is detected, a virtual space is created in the 3D world with respect to the marker. The marker can then be in any position of the 3D world space, but any object that is placed on the marker will be considered the marker as its space. Therefore, the marker's local space is considered the space of the AR content. In multi-target tracking, there can be multiple image targets placed around the world. Any 3D content that tracks these image targets is placed in the world space, but the positioning will take place according to the orientation and the position of the target image. Refer to *Figure 2.18* for an illustration of the same:

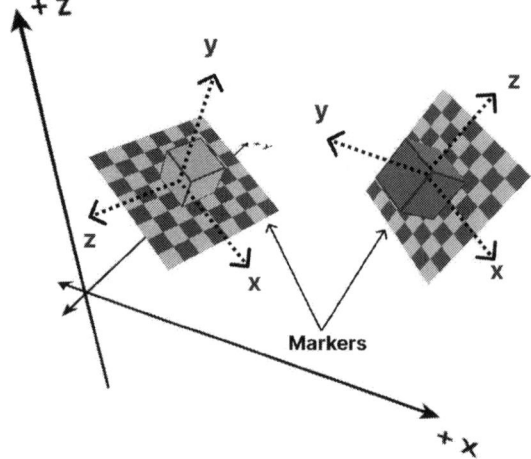

Figure 2.18: AR markers use their own local space within the world space

In a marker-less environment, the starting point of the experience can be considered as the world origin. Scanning the world around will keep generating virtual planes inside the 3D world, which are placed with respect to world space. These virtual planes cannot be moved once tracked. If moved, the scan has to be restarted to recalculate the planes/ targets. Similar to marker-based tracking, objects that are placed on the planes will be with respect to those planes. Depending on the tracking algorithm, the targets can be moved or placed constantly. In marker-less tracking environments, we use a concept known as **device tracking**, that is, based on the movement of the capturing device, the pose of the virtual camera within the virtual world also moves at a 1:1 proportion.

Placement of virtual objects on physical worlds

In AR, virtual objects are placed on physical objects, and that illusion is presented to the user. In a virtual 3D space, a virtual camera can capture 3D objects. The movement of this virtual camera maps to the movement of the capturing device. Both the movements are aligned, and both virtual and physical environments are aligned to provide the final output to the user. Consider a mobile augmented reality use case, as shown in *Figure 2.19*:

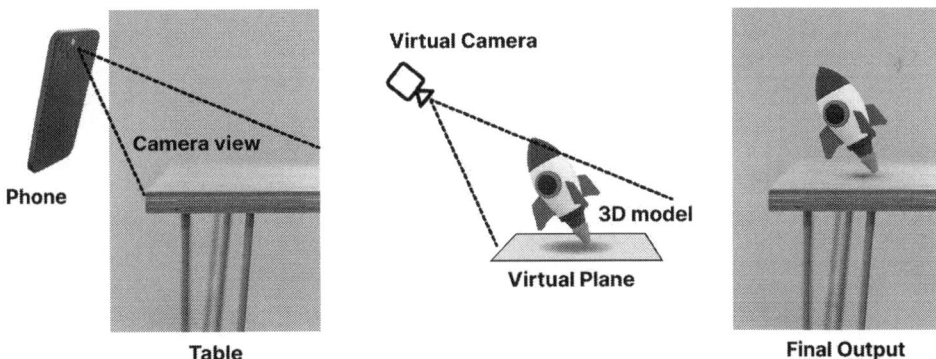

Figure 2.19: Alignment of 3D objects in a marker-less AR application

In *Figure 2.19*, the user is scanning a tabletop. Based on the scans, a virtual plane is generated in the 3D space, and the movement of the device is mapped with the virtual camera in the 3D space. The final output is the combination of the 3D space and the physical camera input. The placement of the objects can be presented as seen in *Figure 2.20*:

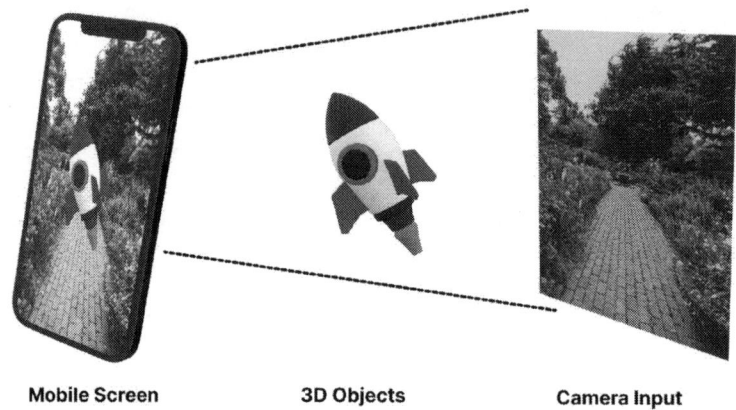

Mobile Screen **3D Objects** **Camera Input**

Figure 2.20: How the final output is aligned on the phone screen

The algorithms are used to track and place the 3D objects, determine the pose of 3D models, mapping the physical object properties with the virtual planes.

Converting physical input to virtual interactions

In AR applications, input is one major component to consider, regardless of the channel. It can be a wearable, a mobile AR app, or a fixed AR display; input must be captured and transferred to the application, and feedback must be provided based on the input.

Let us start with a mobile AR application. Imagine that, as a user, you can see a 3D object placed on your table. You are supposed to tap on the object and manipulate it based on your touch input. It can be just a button press or a swipe to rotate, pinch to scale, or touch and hold to move. Even if the world you are interacting with is 3D, the touch input is captured through a 2D screen, which is your mobile screen. Therefore, the 2D screen tap details must be converted into 3D. One of the methods of identifying such interaction is known as **Ray casting**. Imagine this as a laser that is sent from the mobile screen to the 3D world. A visual representation is shown in *Figure 2.21*:

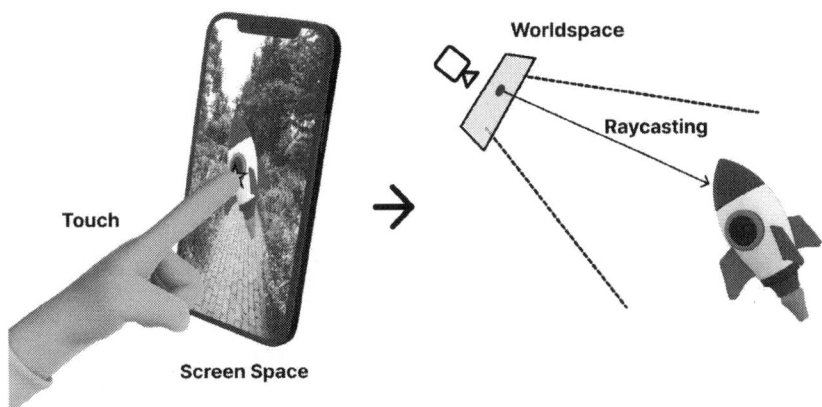

Figure 2.21: Converting a touch input to a ray cast input in 3D space

In ray casting, the screen point details are converted to the world space coordinates to determine a world space origin point for the interaction. Then, a virtual ray (more like a laser) is sent parallel to the camera direction. If the ray hits a 3D object, the result will be returned to the application logic. Any interaction can then be continued based on the 2D positional differences of the touch input. An in-depth look into such input will be discussed in *Chapter 5, Creating Your First Custom Component*.

In wearable devices, handheld controllers use the same methods to interact with objects. In these use cases, the controller or hand-tracking algorithms generate a virtual representation of the controller within the 3D world. There will be a 3D model with the other 3D models which tracked the controllers to perform interactions in the 3D environment. Devices like **HoloLens** and **Magic Leap** have hand tracking, which provides native support to integrate a 3D model that tracks hands. Using collision-based triggers and ray casts are generally used to interact with virtual content.

Conclusion

During this chapter, we covered the fundamental mathematical concepts to understand the 3D environment and how objects can be placed in a 3D environment when building AR applications. The placement and implementation methods on different platforms will differ, but the fundamental structure remains the same.

In the next chapter, we will explore some popular development tools and frameworks available to build and distribute AR applications.

Key points

- Numbers can be represented in single-dimension number lines.
- 2D cartesian planes are used to represent 2D positions, and 3D spaces are used to represent positions in 3D.
- Vectors are used to represent positions, rotations, and other physical properties of objects in 3D spaces.
- A 3D space can be global or local to an object with respect to its orientation.
- AR applications match real-world poses with virtual world poses and provide a combination of both to the end user.

Multiple choice questions

1. Which of the following is a negative floating point irrational number?
   a. 1.23
   b. -2.44542324562364323….
   c. -2.56
   d. -5

2. In Unity 3D engine, the right is the x-axis, the up is the y-axis, and the forward is the z-axis. What is the handness of the 3D space?
   a. Up
   b. Right
   c. Left
   d. Down

3. A Museum is requesting to build an AR app that allows you to scan paintings and show animating views in 3D. What method is the most suitable?
   a. Marker-based AR
   b. Marker-less AR
   c. Location-based AR
   d. Device tracking

4. An AR app is being built to scan the ceiling and place virtual chandeliers. What will be the most suitable method from the following?

   a. Marker-based AR

   b. Marker-less AR

   c. Location-based AR

   d. Device tracking

5. An AR application uses two different images to spawn 3D characters on top of them. When one gets closer to the other, both characters start to fight. Which of the following is true regarding this application?

   a. Both characters and the markers are in the world space

   b. One character is in world space, and the other is in the marker's local space.

   c. Both the markers are in local space, and the character is in world space on top of the markers.

   d. Both the markers move in world space, while the characters use the local space of the markers individually.

Answers

1. b
2. c
3. a
4. b
5. d

Join our book's Discord space

Join the book's Discord Workspace for Latest updates, Offers, Tech happenings around the world, New Release and Sessions with the Authors:

https://discord.bpbonline.com

CHAPTER 3
Exploring Tools and Development Platforms

Introduction

Now that we understand the AR principles and the underlying concepts behind AR applications let us use this chapter to have a look at available AR platforms and tools to build AR applications. You can also go beyond the scope of the book and use the image recognition algorithms and 3D tools to create your own AR framework. However, there has been an exponential growth in available tools to build AR apps that we can evaluate and choose based on the use case, the target audience, the target platform, and the complexity of the application.

Currently, there are two main ways you can build AR applications. It can be for an AR-based wearable such as Microsoft **HoloLens, Magic leap** or **Epson Moverio**. You can also build mobile app-based AR experiences which merely use your mobile phones as the platform. This chapter provides an overview of all the platforms, understands their pros and cons based on the use case, and evaluates the available technologies for each platform development.

Structure

In this chapter, we will cover the following topics:

- AR platforms

- Smartphones (Android, iOS)
- Microsoft HoloLens
- Magic Leap
- Snapchat spectacles
- Other wearables
- WebXR (AR)
- Social AR

- AR development tools
    - Native
    - Social AR – Spark AR, Snapchat Lens Studio, TikTok
    - Unity 3D
    - Apple Reality Composer
    - 8th Wall

- AR SDKs
    - Microsoft Mixed Reality Toolkit (MRTK)
    - Wikitude
    - Easy AR
    - Vuforia
    - ARCore
    - ARKit
    - AR Toolkit
    - AR Foundation
    - Niantic lightship

Objectives

After completing this chapter, you will be able to understand a requirement, evaluate all the available platforms, and choose the platform that meets the requirement. You will also evaluate available AR frameworks and SDKs for the selected platform and choose one to start the development.

AR platforms

If you are an end user of any AR application, you will use an AR-enabled platform to get your experience. Currently, handheld devices and wearable devices are used to provide AR experiences. This section covers the most popular AR platforms available in the world to build and run AR experiences.

Smartphones Android, iOS

Smartphones are the earliest adaptors of AR applications in the consumer space. Of course, AR experiences have been made for desktop computers with webcams, early camera phones, and smartphones such as Nokia Symbian devices throughout the decade. However, with developer-friendly operating systems such as iOS (Apple) and Android, software development has grown exponentially, focusing on image processing and augmented reality. This resulted in smartphones being the most used platform to experience AR applications today.

Based on the previous chapters, we learned that just camera input may not be enough to recognize context. However, smartphones already came up with sensors that can help any AR-based algorithms work. Sensors like the accelerometer to measure the movement and the gyroscope to measure the alignment of the device with respect to the world have been a catalyst for AR algorithms. Early smartphone AR applications were limited to what third-party developers could offer. ARToolkit, the first-ever AR software development kit, was initially ported to Symbian operating system devices and then into Android devices. However, it was able to track fiducial markers and black and white pre-defined planes to view AR content. SDKs such as **Wikitude** and **Vuforia** enabled natural feature tracking, which allowed the developers to use any image target for marker-based AR. With the introduction of the AR kit by Apple and AR Core by Android, the AR development field developed exponentially, allowing the developers to build marker less and marker-based AR without third-party tool involvement.

Apple iPhones use an operating system known as iOS, built by Apple Inc. However, the Android operating system is open source and can be used by any hardware manufacturer, given it has the licenses to use it. Therefore, we cannot limit Android devices to one electronics manufacturer, as any company can make them. Leading Android device manufacturers include Samsung, Sony, Huawei, and Xiaomi. The features of all of these devices, including the AR capabilities depend on the hardware capabilities and the performance of the device. *Figure 3.1* features an Apple iPhone running iOS:

Figure 3.1: Apple iPhone running iOS

The following figure illustrates a Google Pixel device running Android OS HoloLens:

Figure 3.2: Google Pixel device running Android OS Microsoft HoloLens

Developed in 2016, Microsoft HoloLens is the first ever consumer-targeted AR wearable device in the world. Even though it was available in the market, their target audience used to be professionals and corporations to participate in the pre-production of the device. The HoloLens device still does not target the everyday consumer and relies mainly on corporate implementations such that the cost of one device goes over 3000 US dollars in 2022.

Microsoft HoloLens is a head-mounted wearable device that consists of a front tinted visor, a pair of transparent combiner lenses, and an array of sensors at the top of the device that is mounted to a cushioned head strap. The array of sensors includes an accelerometer, gyroscope, and magnetometer to capture the device's orientation and position, an energy-efficient depth camera, a 2.4-megapixel photographic video camera, a four-microphone array, and an ambient light sensor. The sensor technology is said to be a successor of Microsoft's depth sensor technology, **Kinect,** which used to be an add-on camera for Xbox 360. HoloLens runs a modified spatial version of the Windows 10 operating system.

The operating system runs on a custom-made holographic processing unit designed and developed by Microsoft, especially for the device. Using the cameras and the sensors, it has the capability for spatial mapping, hand gesture recognition, and voice and speech recognition. The device works by projecting augmented content onto the inner pair of sensors that aligns with the physical objects around it. The core system does not provide recognition technologies such as image tracking and anchoring. Still, spatial mapping can be extended, and additional tracking tools can be used to augment its capabilities. *Figure 3.3* shows a Microsoft HoloLens 2 device:

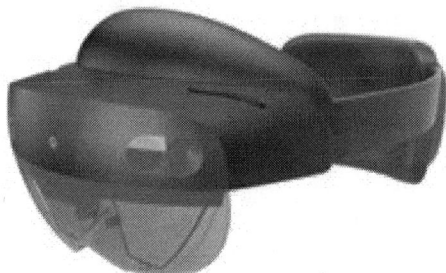

Figure 3.3: Microsoft HoloLens 2

Microsoft has released two versions of HoloLens so far. The second version HoloLens 2 has a longer battery life, increased field of view, higher processing power, and additional features such as improved voice and gesture recognition and eye tracking. Developing applications on HoloLens requires a Windows software developer kit and only supports Microsoft Windows development environments. Unity 3D engine can also be used to develop 3D applications that can run on HoloLens, and Microsoft has released official Unity developer kits to get started easily. Their operating system can be downloaded separately as an emulator, so the developers can develop and test applications without having a HoloLens. *Figure 3.4* shows a HoloLens emulator:

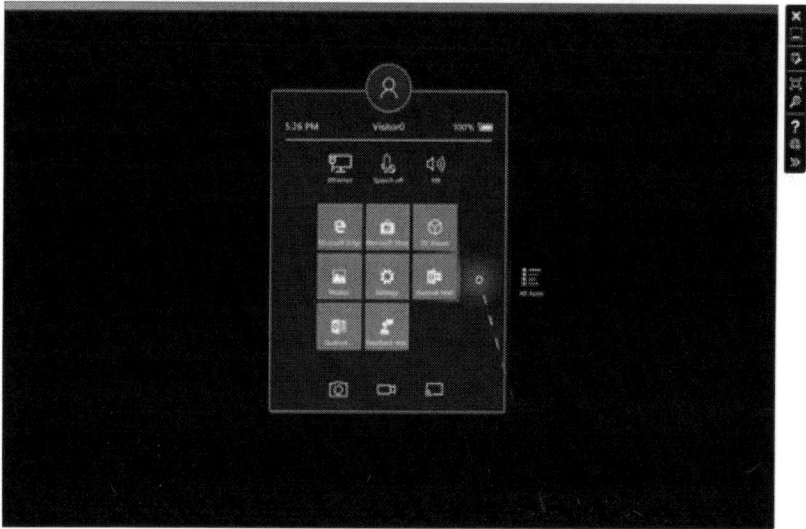

Figure 3.4: HoloLens Emulator

More information on Microsoft HoloLens and available developer tools can be found at: **https://www.microsoft.com/en-us/hololens/developers**

Magic Leap

The Magic Leap is a wearable AR headset designed and developed by Magic Leap Inc. The company was founded in 2010 and has focused mainly on AR and computer vision research until 2015. Between 2010 and 2015, magic leap raised over 2 billion US dollars from investors, including Google and Alibaba. Based on their investor portfolio, industry enthusiasts have had a higher interest in their technology.

After eight years of research and development, they released their first version of the magic leap device in July 2018. At the time of writing this chapter, the Magic Leap 2 has been revealed but is not available in the market until the end of 2022. The Magic Leap device is a wearable compact headset that rests on the nose, wrapping around the face and distributing the weight of it similar to a spectacle. The latest version of the device has a depth camera, 12.6-megapixel color camera, ambient light sensor, 4x eye tracking cameras, positional sensors (gyro, magnetometer, accelerometer), and an altimeter. The device has 16GB of massive RAM for a standalone device with a storage capacity of 256 GB. The device can have over 3 hours of continuous use with a 7-hour sleep mode with battery life. Unlike the HoloLens device, the Magic Leap package has a controller for precise input and a separate compute pack, which moves the processing components out of the wearable. The release version of the

Magic Leap 2 costs 3299 USD and the enterprise version is valued at 5000 USD. *Figure 3.5* shows a Magic Leap 2 device:

Figure 3.5: *Magic Leap 2*

The device used its operating system known as Lumin OS. However, the second version of the device runs an **Android Open-Source Project (AOSP)** based operating system, which supports WebXR and OpenXR, allowing developers to create applications targeting multiple platforms without the hassle of platform dependencies.

Snapchat spectacles

Snap Inc. is one of the leading AR-based companies in the world offering AR face filters through their mobile social media app, Snapchat. Their initial spectacles implementation was a simple wearable spectacle with a camera attached to it for quick photo and video capturing in order to support people to create more content easily. Ever since their research has focused more on AR. Snap Inc released its AR filter authoring tool, Snapchat lens studio. Lens studio allowed developers to create and integrate augmented reality applications within the Snapchat application. Along with the research and development effort put into the Snapchat lenses and lens studio, the company released a developer version of the spectacles, which leverages the power of Snapchat lenses to run AR applications. *Figure 3.6* features a Snapchat spectacle AR:

Figure 3.6: *Snapchat Spectacles AR*

This does not have a consumer version and is only available for aspiring creators, AR development companies, and individuals heavily involved in AR development. However, their consumer version with just a front camera is available for purchase, which does not provide an AR view through the lenses. Developing AR apps on this device cannot be done directly. Since it uses the same AR effect backend, the developers must design and build AR filters using their authoring tool, Lens Studio.

Other wearables

While the Holo Lens and the Magic Leap are the most expensive but the most precise AR headsets available in the market, other players are developing their hardware, mainly for enterprise use cases. Vuzix is one of the oldest Virtual Reality hardware companies in the world. They currently design and produce their AR wearable known as Vuzix Blade. This device primarily focuses on being a heads-up display, but marker-based AR applications can be developed and run using additional software. *Figure 3.7* features a Vuzix Blade device:

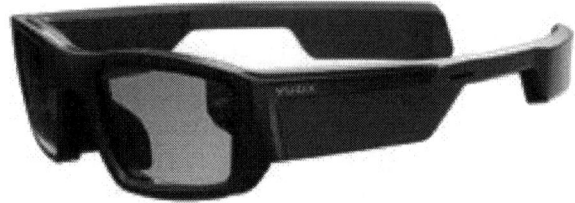

Figure 3.7: Vuzix Blade

Nreal is another company that specializes in building AR smart glasses. They have multiple AR wearable devices. Their implementation uses a standard Android smartphone as the processing device, while the wearable becomes a display while using the real world as the background. This has a 6-degree-of-freedom space recognition capability, hand tracking, and plane detection capabilities. Therefore, we can develop apps that use such capabilities allowing the users to use the existing space as an AR world. *Figure 3.8* shows a Nreal Air device:

Figure 3.8: Nreal Air

Epson Moverio is a similar device developed by Seiko Epson Corp and uses Android as its operating system. Their device capability is similar to Nreal devices. Their development kits provide direct access to the pose tracking sensors for custom AR application development which leverages plane tracking, device tracking, object, and image tracking, and so on. *Figure 3.9* features the Epson Moverio device:

Figure 3.9: Epson Moverio

Apple Vision Pro: Revealed in mid-2023, Apples Vision Pro has been a device that was discussed by many spatial computing enthusiasts over the world. It is not an augmented reality device which has a transparent front surface but consists of 12 cameras that capture the world and projects into the eye through stereo lenses. Additionally, it has cameras within the device that captures your face and projects to outside. The concept of using a camera to work as a channel between the human eye and the world is known as passthrough. This is the first device to use both ways so that observers outside can see the users eye movement. At the time of writing this book, it is not released to the public as a consumer device, but the first device is priced at US$ 3499, which is one of the expensive devices for wearable immersive technology devices. Refer to *Figure 3.10*:

Figure 3.10: Apple Vision Pro with external battery

WebXR AR

This cannot be considered hardware but a platform for which we can build AR applications. Based on heavy research by companies such as Google, Niantic, OpenXR, and Mozilla, we have successfully accessed sensory data through web browsers to generate AR content on the web. Imagine an AR application that can run on your mobile device. By default, you have to install that application on your smartphone and launch it. Web XR allows anyone to view an AR experience through a mobile browser, not by installing different applications. This is game-changing since it allows any device with the necessary processing power and hardware to view AR content, regardless of the device or the operating system, and allows developers to build just for Web XR and deploy them to any operating system that can open a web link. Web XR currently supports desktop computers with VR hardware, standalone AR/VR headsets, as well as smartphone devices. WebXR uses WebGL 3d technology to view 3D content within the browser windows.

More information on Web XR can be found at **https://immersiveweb.dev/**.

Social AR

Social AR is one of the topics that have been emerging recently. One of the pain points of building Smartphone-based AR applications is that they have to be deployed to App stores, and the users must download them separately to experience the AR content. This is a hassle to build different applications for different AR experiences. Smartphone app stores have enforced restrictions in building similar applications and blocked apps with minimum functionality, such as viewing AR content, filters, etc.

People using social media apps like Facebook, Instagram, Snapchat, and TikTok can use their internal features to open AR filter cameras. Earlier, they used to face filters, but now with the native capabilities of smartphones, AR filters or social media AR applications have reached many content creators to build AR experiences using their authoring tools. Social media can also be considered a non-hardware platform to build AR applications on.

However, building AR filters on these platforms can be challenging. The content you create is limited to what the platform offers. There are limitations on resource usage, languages, review processes, etc., that can make a developer spend additional time optimizing and following the said processes to share the content. Considering the target market, people who do not use social media cannot be targeted through social AR filters and apps. Marketing-wise and engagement-wise, these platforms provide better capabilities and authoring tools for people to build content without a hassle.

AR development tools

Now that we have learned about different platforms that can run AR applications, this section will explore the tools that are available to build AR applications on different devices and platforms as discussed in the section, *AR platforms:*

Native

When we say Native, this depends on the platform that runs our AR applications. Android uses Java programming language and requires integrated development environments (IDEs, software used to code and build apps) such as **Android Studio** to develop AR applications. iOS (iPhone/iPad) applications can be developed using an IDE software, XCode (runs only on Apple Mac OS devices) with the Swift programming language. Both Android and iOS native AR application developments require additional tools to visualize the behaviors and simulate AR content in 3D and are time-consuming. However, the application performance will be higher since the apps developed directly use native **Application Programming Interfaces** (**APIs**). The interface for starting Native AR development with XCode is shown in the following figure:

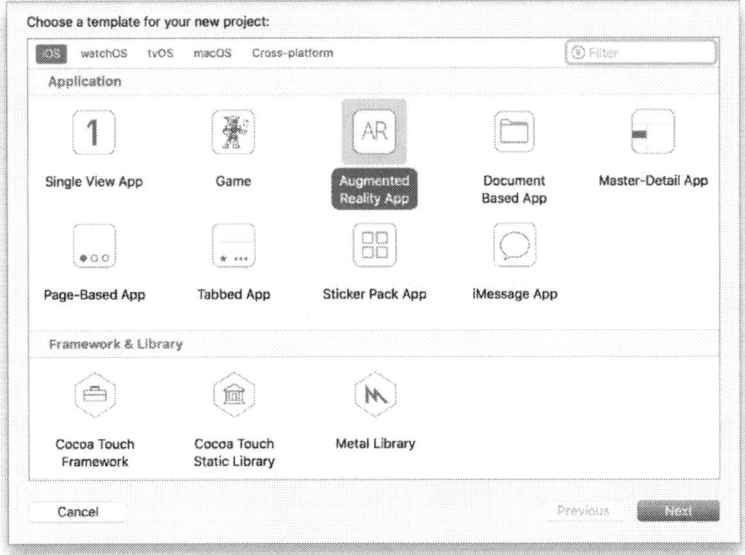

Figure 3.11: Choosing an AR app to start native development with XCode

Microsoft HoloLens requires Windows SDK, while many other AR wearables depend on the Android operating system. WebXR applications require HTML, JavaScript, and additional frameworks such as WebGL for 3D content rendering and visualization, WebXR to enable AR features and other APIs for platform capabilities.

Social AR- Spark AR, Snapchat Lens Studio, TikTok

As described in the previous section, social media uses their applications to distribute AR content among users, allowing developers and creators to design and develop AR applications using their authoring tools.

The first ever AR tool and the capability were built by Snap Inc. when they released front-cam face filters for the first time through their application. They added the ability to author AR content via their Snapchat Lens Studio application. Anybody with a Snapchat account can download the lens studio, develop AR content, and share with friends using the snap code (QR code specific for the AR content created). Lens Studio provides features such as face tracking, plane tracking, image tracking, body tracking, AR occlusion, wrist tracking, foot tracking, cloth simulations, and voice recognition. *Figure 3.12* features AR filter development with Lens Studio:

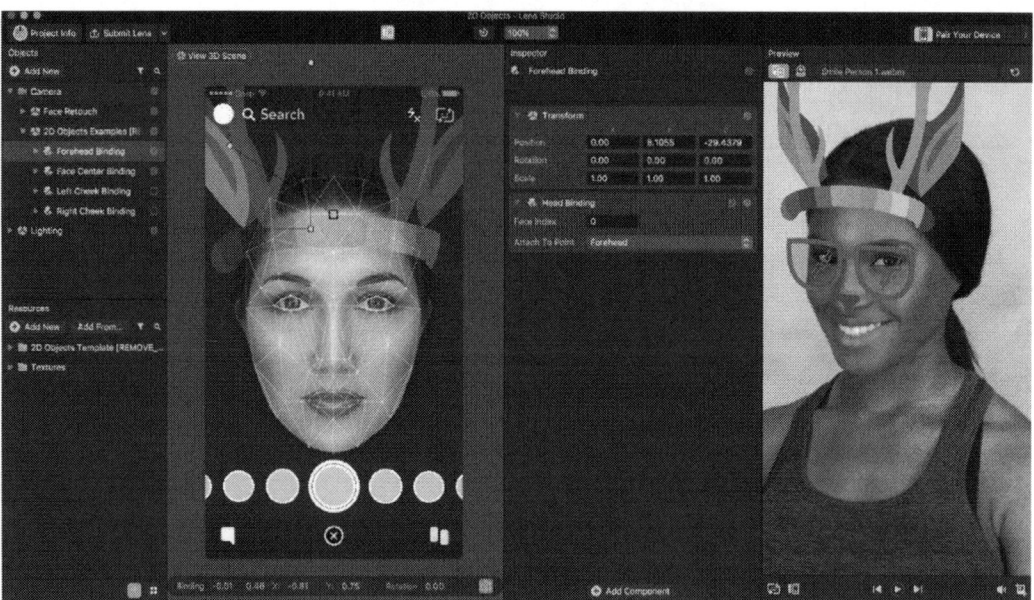

Figure 3.12: AR filter development with Lens Studio

Facebook followed the same and integrated AR filters into their Facebook and Instagram applications. They also released an authoring tool known as Spark AR, which provides similar capabilities to Snapchat. TikTok released their own version of the development tool, Effect House, and at the time of writing this book, their version is still in beta. However, the tool is as powerful as Spark AR and lens studio and provides similar capabilities through their platform.

Apple Reality Composer

iOS released its version of web/native AR Kit integration known as **AR Quick view**. This allows developers to upload 3D content using the USDZ (Universal Scene Description) format to web links and load them to Apple devices to view them in AR mode. This is a comparatively easier tool for anybody to develop AR content without writing logic using coding languages. Using this tool, designers can upload 3D models, animations, sound effects, music, and images to design an AR experience and convert everything to USDZ format. USDZ format can contain a 3D scene, including images and audio that can be used by Apple devices to load and render in an AR world. Reality composer supports horizontal and vertical plane, image, and face tracking. *Figure 3.13* shows the Apple Reality Composer window:

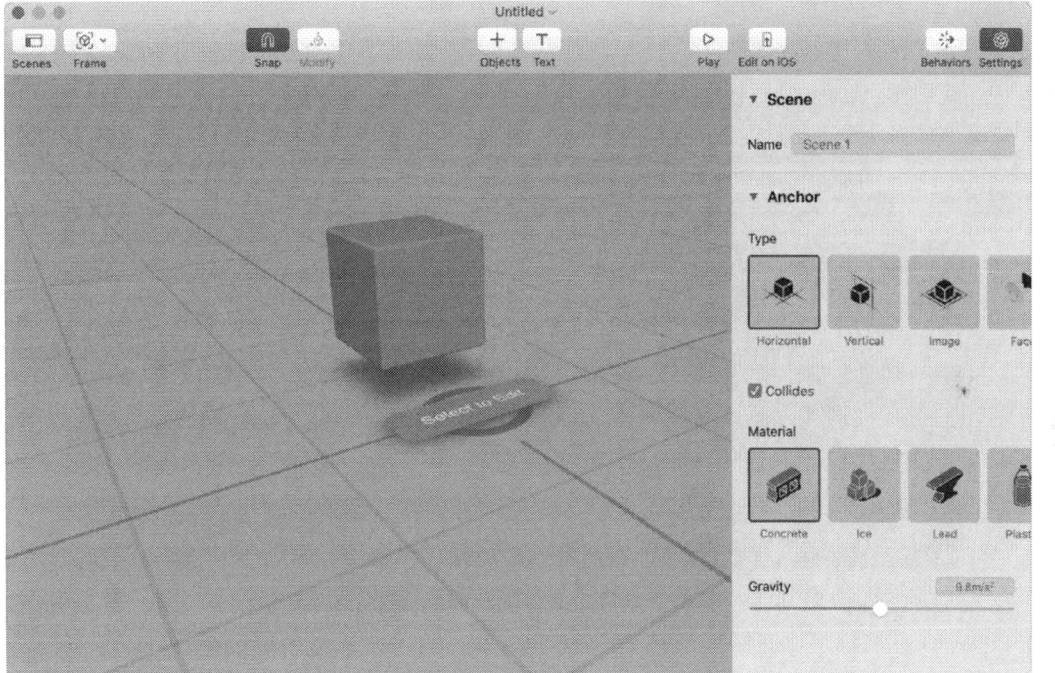

Figure 3.13: Apple Reality Composer

However, Reality Composer experiences come with limitations. Developing such an experience requires Apple MacOS devices. The experiences can only be viewed using Apple iPhones and iPads. Apart from trigger behaviors and action sequences, developing custom behaviors are limited compared to other AR development tools. However, this can be the tool for a beginner to learn AR, provided the necessary hardware is available.

8th Wall

8th Wall is a web-based AR development tool recently acquired by the AR research and development game development company Niantic. Currently, this is the largest web-based AR tool provider in the world and supports many capabilities for Web AR projects. The platform provides building AR content that uses plane tracking, image tracking, face tracking, light estimation, and many features. 8th Wall contains a scripting environment and a developing environment within their platform, and the projects are saved under their tenants. The platform also provides hosting for the developed AR content, and depending on the license, customizations can be made. This is a very straightforward tool for building web-based AR content, and it also has an internal IDE to script custom logic and behaviors. *Figure 3.14* shows some sample projects by the 8th Wall:

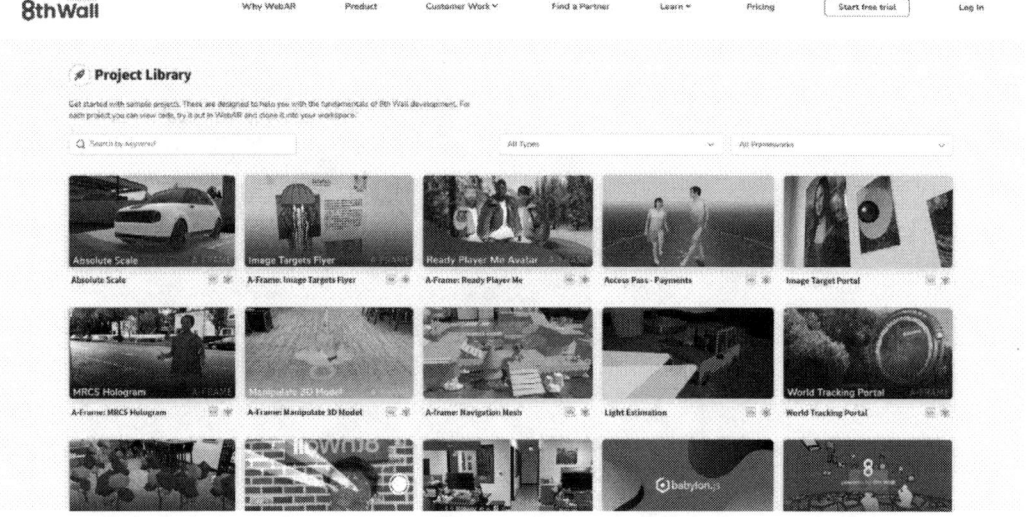

Figure 3.14: *Sample projects by the 8th wall*

8th wall provides the platform to build AR content for the web without the hassle of implementing Web XR and other 3D frameworks. Companies currently use this for their engagement campaigns since it allows users to quickly open the link and experience the AR content.

Unity 3D

Unity 3D can be recognized as one of the leading 3D Game Engines in the world. Not only it can build 3D games, but Unity has also been used in many use cases ranging from simple mobile apps to high-end 3D emulations in many industries around the world. Unity is cross-platform, meaning that its one project base can be used to build applications for many platforms, including Android, iOS, Windows,

Magic Leap, WegGL, and all the available gaming consoles. Because of its ability to provide support for many platforms and it being primarily a 3D engine, Unity has become the number one candidate to build VR and AR applications for many platforms.

Unity applications can be developed using C# programming language, and many AR and VR hardware manufacturers provide support for the Unity engine through their software development kits. Unity supports available headsets and smartphone devices for XR application development through their XR plugin management capability. Installing additional packages and modules extends the engine's capabilities for XR development.

Since AR is a cross-platform use case, as we studied in the previous sections, we will be using Unity 3D engine for the next chapters of the book to build AR applications. We will go through the steps of understanding the tool, polish our C# skills with Unity, and dive into AR development. In this book, our primary focus will be to develop applications for the majority. Therefore, we will focus on AR application development for iOS and Android smartphone devices.

AR software development kits

As mentioned in the previous section, our AR app development tool would be the Unity 3D engine. However, Unity alone cannot build AR applications on the provided platforms. Many SDKs support Unity, available for building AR apps. The following are the most popular and widely used AR SDKs for AR app development for AR hardware and smartphones.

Microsoft mixed reality toolkit

MRTK provides easier AR application development for Microsoft HoloLens. This provides a set of components and features that can be used to accelerate cross-platform mixed-reality application development with Unity. It runs on top of Microsoft Mixed Reality, Open XR, or Oculus XR frameworks. MRTK is incapable of AR meshing and tracking since it relies on the hardware capabilities of the wearable device. The kit provides many features, such as hand tracking, eye tracking, UI controls, spatial awareness, boundary system, speech recognition, and many more. The project is built and maintained by Microsoft, and currently, the latest version of it, MRTK 3, is in public preview at the time of writing this book.

ARToolkit

AR Toolkit is the oldest SDK available for AR development. Built in the 1990s, it has seen many iterations, thus providing capabilities for cross-platform development. After being made open source in 2001, it was available for Android and iOS app development around 2015. ARToolkit was developed further, and Unity SDK was released to the public by *Daqri*, the AR helmet manufacturer who took over the software rights. ARToolkit uses marker-based recognition mainly on fiducial markers with extended natural feature tracking capabilities. However, with Daqri company being out of business and many other reliable AR SDKs being available for the developers, AR Toolkit's popularity reduced over time. The open-source version of the kit is still available through its university website page: **http://www.hitl.washington.edu/artoolkit/**.

The Unity SDK for ARToolkit is currently available through ARToolkitX, supported by Realmax Inc, a Chinese-based AR company: **https://github.com/artoolkitx**.

Wikitude

Wikitude is an AR SDK that supports Android, iOS, and Windows platforms and provides a Unity SDK for cross-platform development. The first version of the SDK released in 2012 utilized Image recognition and tracking. In 2021, the company was acquired by Qualcomm. The SDK supports location-based AR, Image recognition, SLAM, Object, and scene recognition. They also support cloud AR detection, a system to update image targets through the cloud, which allows developers to provide AR content without app updates through app stores. Wikitude is primarily a commercial SDK, and its costs start with 290 Euros per year subscription fee.

Easy AR

Easy AR is an emerging AR SDK developed by VisionStar Information Technology (Shanghai) Co. Ltd. This is also primarily a commercial SDK, but they have provided a free version with almost all the AR-related features included. Their SDK provides image tracking, SLAM, spatial mapping, motion tracking, cloud tracking, and multiplayer modes. They also have a city-scale AR framework to detect and identify large objects for world-scale AR app development. Easy AR is a powerful SDK that uses its algorithms and supports native frameworks such as ARKit and ARCore.

Vuforia

Vuforia is one of the earliest and leading AR SDKs in the world. It was owned by Qualcomm in the beginning and was sold to an IoT company PTC in 2015. Since then, Vuforia has been leading the marker-based tracking AR world and partnered with Unity to provide its SDK as a part of Unity Modules. The latest versions of Vuforia feature plane tracking, world scale AR through cloud recognition and area targets, object, and 3D model detection. Compared to many commercial AR SDKs, Vuforia provides the most reliable tracking technology and has a stable version that supports native Android and iOS and Unity 3D engine. In this book, we will use Vuforia to build marker-based AR applications and a dynamic AR app with Vuforia cloud recognition service.

ARCore

ARCore is an in-built module built by Google for Android devices. The technology is in-built into any Android smartphone, providing marker less AR through plane tracking, image recognition, and face recognition. ARCore SDK is natively available for Android and iOS, as well as through the Unity Engine and Unreal Engine. ARCore uses positional tracking sensors for device tracking and light estimation to illuminate the 3D models to match the environment lighting.

ARKit

ARKit is Apple's Augmented Reality SDK, which was released in 2018. The technology is built on top of the work of Meta IO, an AR company acquired by Apple years before. ARKit primarily focused on marker-less AR, and the latest version of the SDK provides face recognition, body tracking, marker-based recognition, and plane detection and tracking. The SDK is used natively for Apple's measurement application, AR Quick Look, to visualize 3D models in physical space. The devices with Apple Lidar sensors allow the SDK to generate mesh data, increasing its tracking capabilities' accuracy. The SDK only supports iOS and can be used within their XCode development environment and Unity.

AR Foundation

Both ARCore and ARKit have released their versions for Unity. In addition to that, AR headset manufacturers such as HoloLens and Magic Leap have their own AR SDKs. This allows developers to freely use any SDK to develop apps that run on each platform. However, the development flow using each SDK is different, making developers use different ways to maintain a single project base. To overcome this issue, Unity released *ARFoundation*, a plugin that manages all the AR SDKs underneath and provides a single interface for the developers. This allowed developers to use just one project code for all the platforms provided with the native SDK support.

Figure 3.15 provides a feature comparison of what AR Foundation offers through the native SDKs:

Unity's AR Foundation
Supported Features

Functionality	ARCore	ARKit	Magic Leap	HoloLens
Device tracking	✓	✓	✓	✓
Plane tracking	✓	✓	✓	
Point clouds	✓	✓		
Anchors	✓	✓	✓	✓
Light estimation	✓	✓		
Environment probes	✓	✓		
Face tracking	✓	✓		
Meshing			✓	✓
2D Image tracking	✓	✓		
Raycast	✓	✓	✓	
Pass-through video	✓	✓		
Session management	✓	✓	✓	✓

Figure 3.15: AR Foundation feature comparison

Unity also released a commercial no-code AR framework, Unity MARS, allowing designers to leverage AR Foundation and build AR applications without coding. We will use AR Foundation to build a marker less AR application in the coming chapters.

Niantic Lightship

Augmented Reality became widely popular by the location-based smartphone game Pokémon Go. The developers of Pokémon Go, Niantic, acquired many AR companies, such as 6D.ai and 8th Wall, and released their public AR SDK for developers worldwide. Their SDK, known as Niantic Lightship ARDK, provides world-scale marker less AR capabilities to the devices regardless of ARCore and ARKit support. They primarily focus on visual positioning and 3D meshing without additional sensors like the Lidar sensor. Also, their ARDK provides network capabilities to develop shared AR experiences. They have a **Visual Positioning Service (VPS)** that crowdsources environmental data. Any developer who uses VPS can build applications that are world scale which can recognize public places to place AR content. *Figure 3.16* features AR apps built using Niantic Lightship AR Developer Kit:

Figure 3.16: Niantic Lightship offers world-scale multiplayer AR

Throughout this book, we will be going over the basics of Niantic Lightship to build an area-based AR application that can track a pre-defined location.

Conclusion

Through this chapter, we understood the platforms, tools, and SDKs that allow us to build AR applications. As an AR developer, you can now evaluate the requirements and choose the most suitable tool and framework, to build apps based on the target platforms. As many platforms support Unity and many SDKs are available for Unity engine, we will focus on building AR applications using the Unity engine with example use cases from the next chapter onwards.

Key points

- There are different platforms that can run AR applications.
- Wearable devices and Smartphones are the leading platforms.
- Developing AR apps that run on these platforms require tools and development kits.
- Unity Engine is a 3D engine that supports cross-platform development.
- Many Augmented Reality supported platforms have SDKs that support Unity 3D engine.

- This makes Unity 3D a suitable candidate for building AR applications across platforms.

Questions

From the following lists, choose the most suitable tool, platform, and SDK to build an AR application to cater to the scenarios provided here:

- **Tools**: Unity, Spark AR, Web Development, 8th Wall, XCode, Android Studio.
- **Platforms**: HoloLens, Magic Leap, Smart Phones, Web.
- **SDK**: AR Foundation, Windows SDK (and MRTK), Vuforia, Niantic Lightship, Web XR, 8th Wall, No separate SDK.

Scenarios

1. Build an enterprise on-site building inspection in AR.
2. Social media campaign with face tracking feature.
3. Multiplayer AR archery game in a shared physical space for school children.
4. AR Art Museum requests people to download an app to scan paintings and see them come to life.
5. A QR code that opens the camera to show tourist waypoints in AR.

Answers

1. Unity, HoloLens, Windows SDK
2. Spark AR, Smartphones, No separate SDK
3. Unity, Smartphones, Niantic Lightship
4. Unity, Smartphones, Vuforia
5. Web Development or 8th Wall, Web, Web XR, or 8th Wall.

Join our book's Discord space

Join the book's Discord Workspace for Latest updates, Offers, Tech happenings around the world, New Release and Sessions with the Authors:

https://discord.bpbonline.com

CHAPTER 4
Up and Running with Unity 3D

Introduction

Now that we have good knowledge about the tools and frameworks available to build **Augmented Reality** (**AR**) applications, the next chapters of this book, including this, will focus on building AR apps using the most popular and widely used tools from the ones explored. Unity 3D is one of the best 3D Game Engines in the world, which also expands its capabilities not just for Game Development, but any sort of interactive development. Allowing an easier interface to build custom components and having direct compatibility with C# (.Net framework), Unity has been picked up by many AR algorithm developers as a base platform. As discussed in the previous chapter, almost all the available AR SDKs support Unity. Moreover, Unity being cross-platform, makes it the best candidate to build AR applications that can run on many different operating systems and devices. In this chapter, we will go through the process of installing Unity, understand the basic elements of Unity, and build two projects to get started with 3D development.

Structure

In this chapter, we will discuss the following topics:

- Installing Unity 3D
    - Installing Android SDK, Java SDK

- Installing XCode (MacOS)
- Installing Visual Studio / Visual Studio Code
- Creating a project and setting up the target platform
- Unity Engine user interface
- Using the tools to create and manipulate primitive objects
- Understanding lights
- Creating materials
- Manipulating the virtual camera
- Using the Unity package manager
- Importing content into Unity
- Importing assets from the Unity asset store
- The structure of the GameObject
- Components of Unity
    - Transform
    - Mesh Renderer
    - Colliders
    - Rigid Body
- Creating Prefabs

Objectives

After completion of this chapter, you will be able to install the necessary tools required to build 3D applications, including Unity 3D and other supporting software. You will learn how to use Unity 3D engine to create 3D environments by using primitives, importing 3D models, using the Unity asset store, and an overview of the basic principles of 3D. You will also learn how to create a simple obstacle course by downloading assets from the asset store, creating custom components with C# language, and using the components to create a simple 3D clock.

Installing Unity 3D

Currently, Unity provides a manager application to install and manage different versions of Unity as well as manage the projects made in Unity on a local machine. This tool, known as **Unity Hub**, makes it easier for developers to manage Unity licenses, regardless of the version. It also helps manage different Unity versions and modules. Follow the given steps to install Unity Hub:

1. Go to **https://unity3d.com/get-unity/download**.
2. Click on **Download Unity Hub**, as shown in *Figure 4.1*:

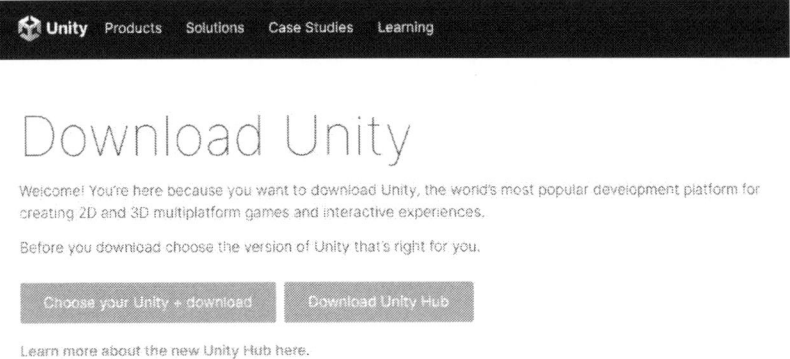

Figure 4.1: Unity Download web page

3. While Unity Hub is downloaded, sign up with Unity by creating a Unity ID. You may need to give your Email, name, username, and a password.
4. Install the downloaded Unity Hub software and launch it.
5. Click the profile picture icon and select **Sign in**, as shown in *Figure 4.2*. This will open a web page to sign into your Unity profile. Once signed in, it will redirect you back to Unity Hub and you will now be signed in.

Figure 4.2: Sign into Unity Hub with your Unity ID

6. Click the same profile icon again, go to **Manage Licenses**, and click the **Add** button to add a license. From here, you can activate a Unity Pro license key, or you can get a free personal license by selecting the free option. On agreeing to the license statement, your account will be bound with a free personal license.

7. Unity Window has two main sections: projects and installs. You can manage different versions of the Unity program by going to the **Installs** section. Go to the **Installs** tab and select the **Install Editor** option. This will give you a list of Unity versions to choose from. Unity, by default, provides you with three main editor versions. These versions are known as **Long Term Support** (**LTS**) versions, and Unity usually provides minor updates for a chosen version for up to 3 years. This book will focus on Unity 2021 LTS version (and the 2022 LTS version in some chapters). If you cannot see the 2021 LTS or 2022 LTS version, there may be changes in the flows of development that we discuss throughout this book. You can select the **Archive** option and navigate outside Unity Hub to download the 2021 or 2022 version. From the **Official releases** section, select **2021.3.xf1 (LTS)** version and click the **Install** button. Here, the x may be different based on the time you install it since Unity keeps incrementing it when updating the editor versions.

8. As Unity is a cross-platform development tool, you can choose different modules to install with the Unity Editor. For scripting in C#, Unity provides the community version of Microsoft Visual Studio by default. On the next screen, select **Visual Studio IDE** as the development or dev tool, Android Build Support if you are developing for Android, and iOS Build Support if you are developing for iPhones and iPads. Additionally, install **Windows Build Support** and **Mac Build Support**, depending on your computer operating system.

Installing Android SDK, Java SDK

Building Android devices requires Android and Java software development kits installed. The recommended option with Unity is to install them within Unity Hub. Make sure you have selected **Open JDK** and **Android SDK and NDK Tools** from the platform options. Continue with the following steps:

1. Click the **Install** button, and it will download and install the Unity version. Refer to *Figure 4.3*:

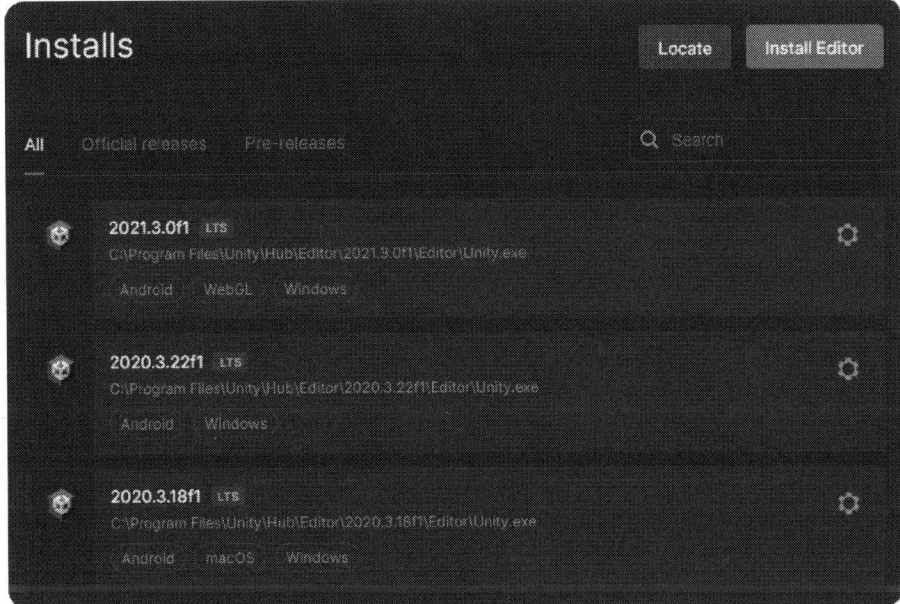

Figure 4.3: Installs section of Unity Hub to manage Unity versions.

If you were not able to install the said modules for a Unity version, you can click the **Settings** button and choose **Add modules** to add them to the editor.

Installing Xcode in MacOS

When developing iOS devices such as iPhones and iPads, Unity cannot directly manage the final export build. Instead, Unity will generate another project source file which can only be opened by **Xcode**. Xcode is the only development **Integrated Development Environment (IDE)** tallowed to develop Apple device-based applications.

To install XCode, follow the given steps:

1. Open Mac OS App (only on a Mac OS device) store and select **Develop** tab, as shown in *Figure 4.4*.

2. You will see XCode as an app. Click on **Get** to download the software. This is a large application that goes over 12 GB of your disk space. Therefore, make sure that you have enough space.

Refer to *Figure 4.4*:

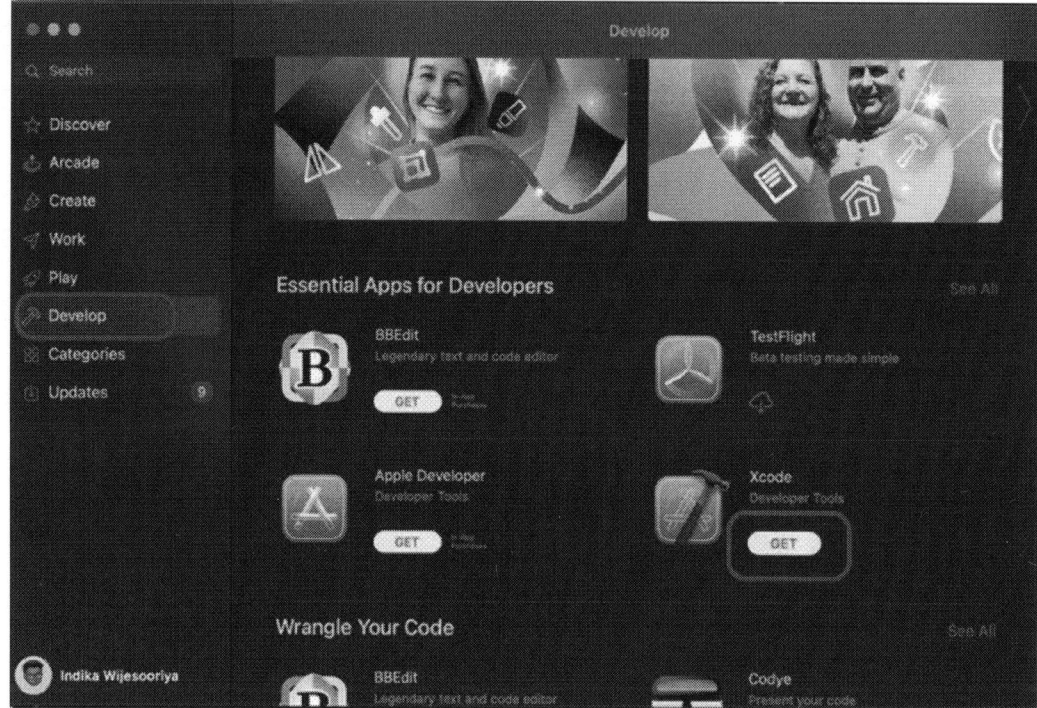

Figure 4.4: XCode installation from Apple App Store

Installing Visual Studio / Visual Studio Code

The recommended way to install Visual Studio is through the Unity Hub. If you want to use a separate Visual Studio version, you can go to the following link to download the latest community version of Visual Studio:

https://visualstudio.microsoft.com/downloads/

This will give you the Visual Studio installer to install the IDE.

Once the IDE is installed, open the installer again and click **Modify**. Select **Game Development with Unity** option from the pop-up window and click **Install while**

downloading. This will make sure that you have installed Unity support tools to work with Visual Studio. Refer to *Figure 4.5*:

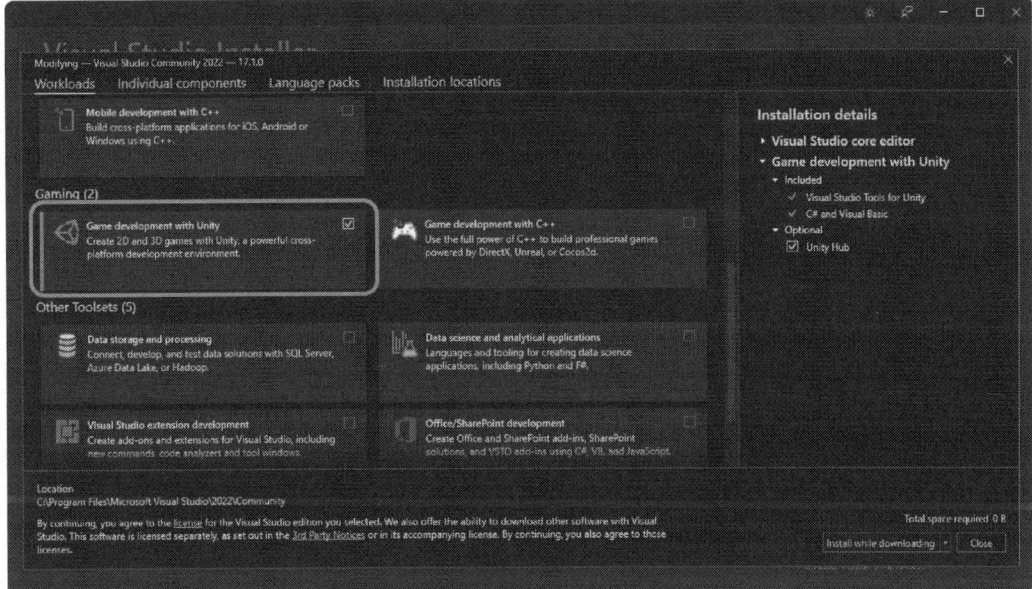

Figure 4.5: Installing Unity modules for Visual Studio using the VS Installer

You can also use Visual Studio Code instead of Visual Studio. However, VS Code is only a text editor with extended support and requires additional plugins and prerequisites to work with Unity.

To install VS Code, follow the given steps:

1. Install the .NET SDK. **https://dotnet.microsoft.com/download**.

2. For Windows machines, restart your computer. For MacOS computers, install the latest Mono release - **https://www.mono-project.com/download/**.

3. Install VS Code: **https://code.visualstudio.com/**.

4. Open **VS Code**, go to **Plugins** section, and install the C# plugin.

Refer to *Figure 4.6*:

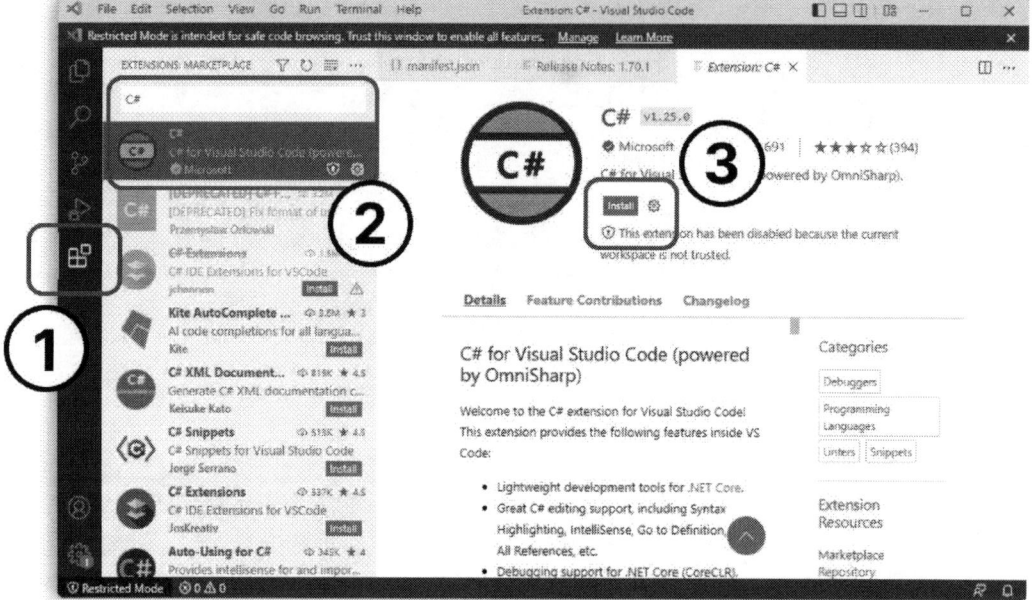

Figure 4.6: Steps to customize Visual Studio Code for Unity development

5. In VS Code, press *Ctrl* + (comma) to get the settings editor. Search for **Omnisharp: Use Modern Net** and uncheck the setting.

There are some additional settings that need to be changed within the Unity Editor, but that requires opening a project. Let us discuss it when we create our first C# script.

Creating a project and setting up the target platform

You can create new projects using the Unity Hub. To create a new project, go to the **Projects** tab and click **New Project**. This will open a new window to create a project which consists of different templates.

Throughout this book, we will be using the 3D **Universal Render Pipeline (URP)** template. This will create a new blank project for us, which uses Unity's URP. We will be using URP since the new render pipeline allows us to explore more effects provided by Unity. Moreover, performance-wise, it is better than the standard 3D render pipeline. If you are using Unity for the first time, you will be prompted to download the template before using it. Refer to *Figure 4.7*:

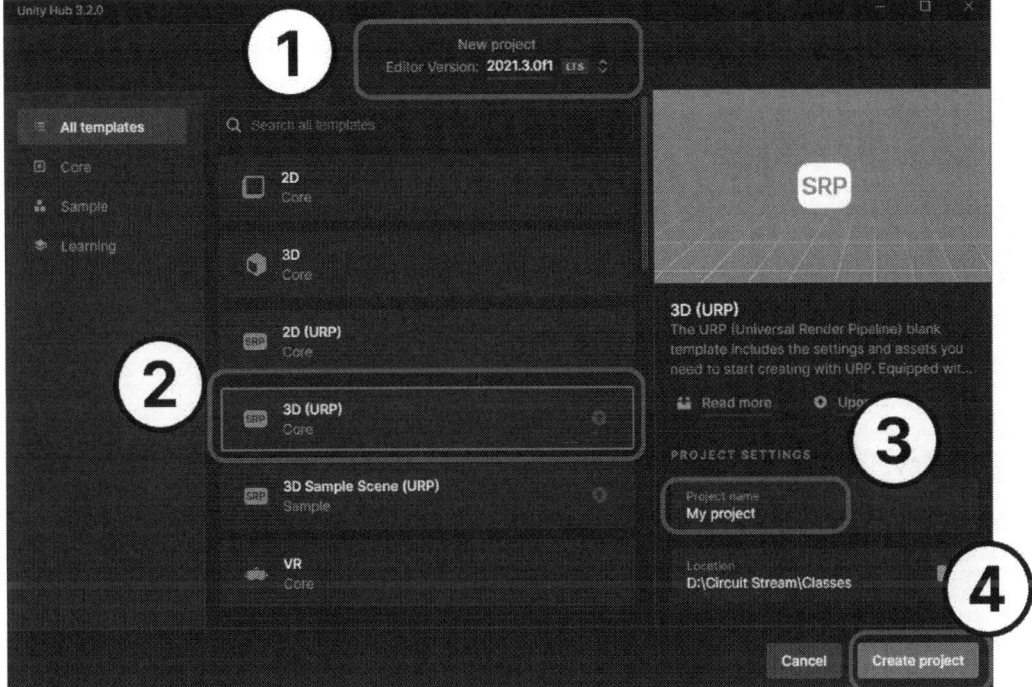

Figure 4.7: Steps to create a new URP project in Unity

At the top of the window displayed in *Figure 4.7*, make sure the editor version is selected as **2021.3.x**.

Select the **Project name** text field and change it to **Hello Unity**. Now choose a proper location to save the Unity Project and click **Create Project**.

This will create a new Unity Project for us in the given location. A Unity Project is a combination of files and folders and does not have a single file to launch the project. Unity Editor mainly looks for `Assets`, `Project Settings` and `Packages` folder within the project folder and opens the editor with the information within those folders.

Unity Engine user interface

The Unity interface consists of many windows. A 3D view in the Unity Editor shows the currently selected scene. A scene is an entity that holds 3D models, lights, script behaviors, and so on. By default, Unity has generated an empty scene with some content in it. This scene is saved as the `Sample Scene` in `Assets/Scenes` folder.

Figure 4.8 shows the default layout. An explanation of each window is as follows:

Figure 4.8: Unity Interface

1. **Scene View:** This window shows the currently opened 3D scene information. The default sample scene consists of a main camera (virtual camera), a directional light, and another global volume object.

2. **Hierarchy Window:** This window lists all the objects in the opened scene. Every object in this list is called `Game Objects`. A game object consists of `Components`. These components define the behavior of the game objects they are in. Selecting a game object will let you see its components.

3. **Inspector Window:** Once a game object is selected, all the components attached to the game object are listed in this window. Select the objects in the current scene through the hierarchy window and see how each object consists of different components in the inspector window.

4. **Project Window:** This will show you all the files and folders that are within the `Assets` folder of the project. There is also a `Package` folder in it. This folder content is managed by Unity and other libraries, and thus it is not recommended to modify the content in these folders.

5. **Game Window:** The virtual camera in the scene captures the scene content and projects it onto the game view. This is the camera point of view which you can see from the game window. When you export an application, what

you see through the final build will be what you ultimately see through the game window.

Using the tools to create and manipulate primitive objects

Right-click on an empty area of the hierarchy window or click the plus button at the top left corner of the window, as shown in *Figure 4.9*. This will open the **Create** menu. Select **3D** object and choose **Cube**:

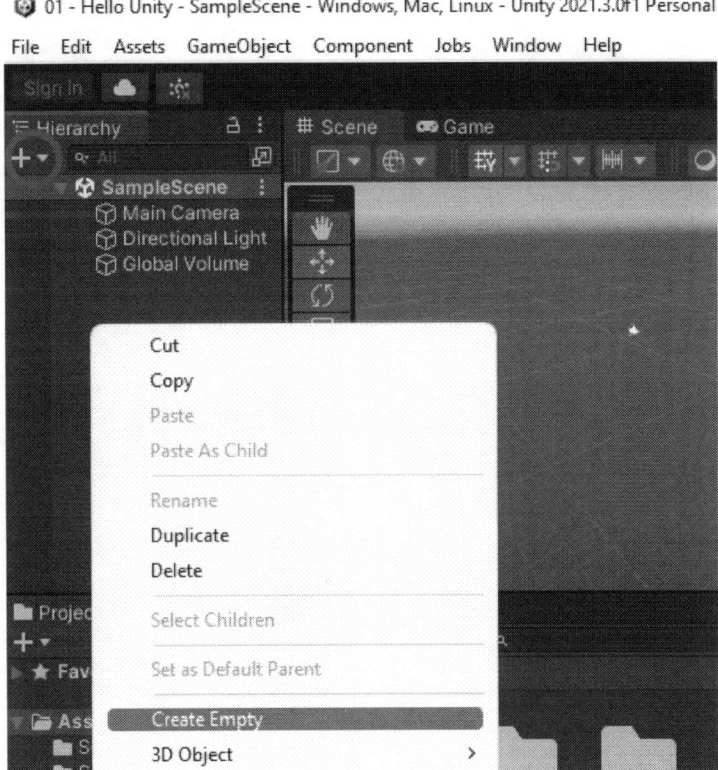

Figure 4.9: Create new objects in the scene using the hierarchy window

Navigating in the Unity Interface can be hard for a beginner but easy to master. The simplest way to move inside the scene is by holding the right click inside the editor and using *W, A, S, D* keys to move forward, backward, left, and right respectively. While moving, you can move the mouse (holding the right click) to look up and down, left, and right.

Another method is by selecting the 3D cube and pressing the *F* key to focus on the object. Now holding the *Alt* key / *Option* on Mac, you will be able to click and rotate around the cube. The right-click while holding the keyboard button will zoom in and out of the object selected.

You can manipulate the object transform by choosing the Move, Rotate, Scale, and Transform tools provided on the left side of the default scene window. You can switch these tools by pressing W, E, R, and Y, respectively, with your mouse within the Unity scene window. Each tool provides ways to handle gizmos to manipulate the object transform properties. Select each tool and see what you can get with each tool within the scene window.

Refer to *Figure 4.10* for a better understanding of basic transformation tools in Unity:

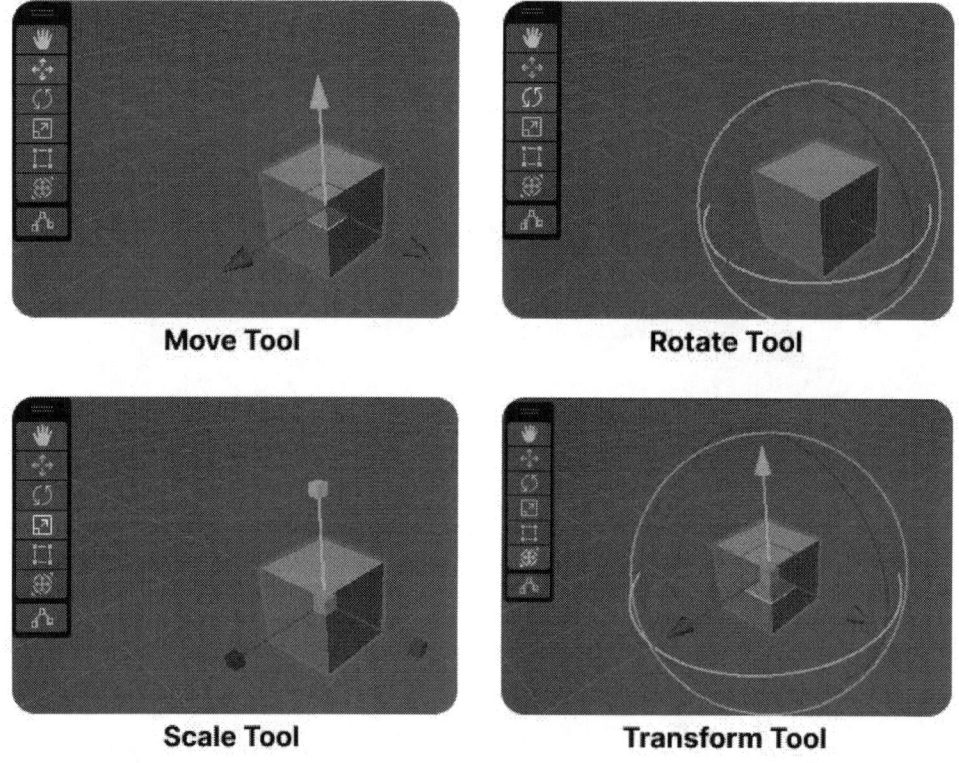

Figure 4.10: Basic transformation tools in Unity

At the top of the **Scene** view, there is a tool settings bar, as shown in *Figure 4.11*. Each button has configurations that can be changed to aid your 3D building scene:

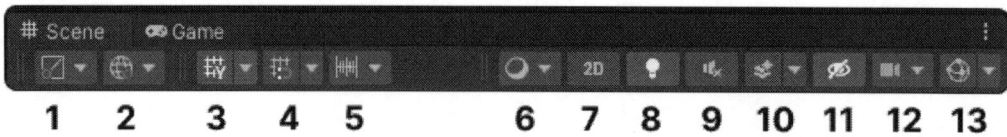

Figure 4.11: Unity scene view toolbar

1. **Toggle Tool handle position button:** This allows you to switch between the center point of the selected object or the pivot point of it. Usually, a 3D model has a defined point in its local space that defines the origin point of the model itself. The position of the 3D model is defined based on the pivot point. When the pivot is not exactly in the center, unity can estimate a center point if the tool position is selected to center.
2. **Toggle Tool handle rotation button:** This allows you to manipulate the object transform with respect to world space or the object's local space (check the previous chapter about different spaces). The scale tool only works with local space, as it cannot be scaled along a non-primitive axis.
3. **Toggle grid visibility:** You can also get X, Y, and Z grids to be visible.
4. **Toggle grid snapping:** You can also set the snapping parameters. Enabling this will allow you to snap objects to a grid.
5. **Snap increment:** Increase the snapping values. You can change the size of the snapping grid with this tool.
6. **Draw mode:** Choose a draw mode option from the list for 3D design and debugging of the scene details.
7. **2D mode:** Toggle between 2D and 3D mode.
8. **Toggle light:** Toggle the light check in the scene. Good for designing dark 3D environments.
9. **Toggle sound:** All the audio in runtime can be toggled.
10. **Toggle** different 3D scene options such as skybox, fog, post-processing, and so on.
11. **Toggle hidden objects.**
12. **Scene camera options:** This allows you to modify the virtual camera properties in the scene.
13. **Gizmos:** Allows you to toggle and modify the icons in the scene representing different objects such as lights, cameras, and so on. Gizmos are visible only in the scene view.

Try adding more objects to the scene and toggle the tools and manipulate them to practice moving around the scene. You can drag and move objects within objects to make groups. However, child objects scale and transform themselves with respect to their immediate parent object. Try dragging and dropping an object onto another object in the hierarchy window to make groups of objects. *Figure 4.12* features the hierarchy of game objects in a parent-child relationship:

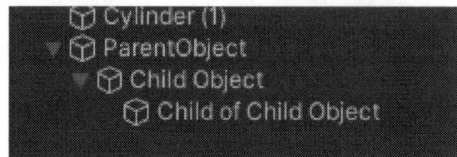

Figure 4.12: Hierarchy of Game objects in a parent-child relationship

You can build a simple character using primitive objects and transform tools. *Figure 4.13* is an example. Notice how the objects are created and placed inside other objects in the hierarchy. You can create a group of groups for easier manipulation of game objects in the scene.

Refer to *Figure 4.13*:

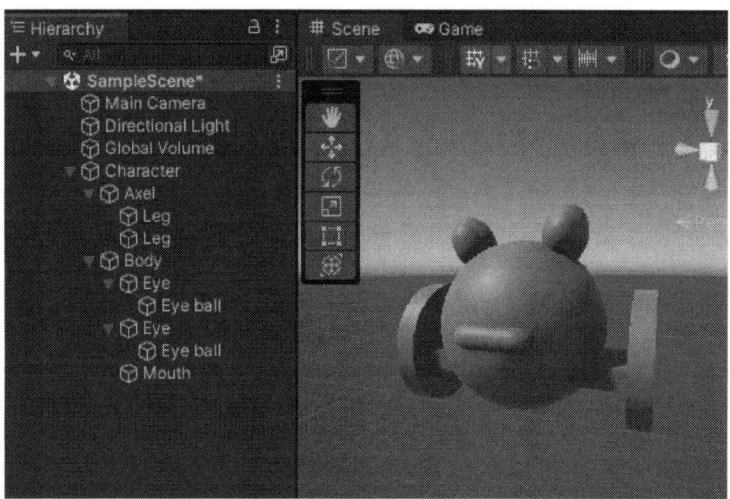

Figure 4.13: Simple 3D character using primitive objects

Understanding lights

In Unity, the whole scene shades rely on the virtual lights. Without an ambiance and a light object, you will not be able to see the 3D models in the scene. By default, and Unity scene is lit by an ambiance light from the skybox. A skybox is the surrounding colors in the infinite space of the 3D scene.

1. Go to **Window** | **Rendering** | **Lighting** to open the lighting window.
2. Go to the **Environment** tab.
3. Under **Environment Lighting**, select **Color** as the **Source**.

4. Now click on the **Ambient Color** bar and choose a different color. Notice how changing the color manipulates the 3D object colors by adding shading. This is the basic light that sets up the scene ambiance.

Refer to *Figure 4.14*:

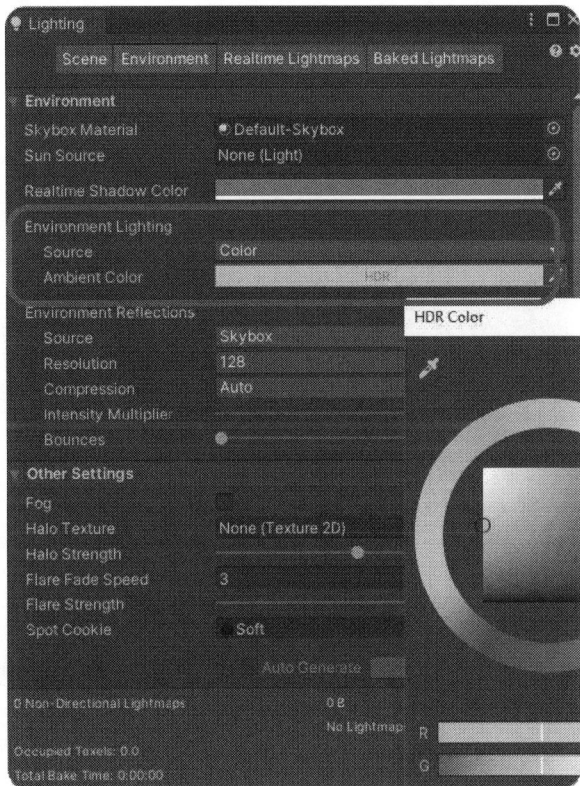

Figure 4.14: Ambient lighting settings in the Lighting window

Apart from the ambient lights, the directional light acts as a parallel light to the whole scene. Every time you create a new scene, a directional light will be there by default. This is managed by a **Light** component provided by Unity, which is attached to an empty game object. Let us talk about components in a later section of this chapter.

Let us carry out the following experiment:

1. Add a plane object to the bottom of your character such that it looks like it sits on the floor.

2. Select the **Directional Light** in the scene. Look at the Inspector window.

3. Change the intensity to 10 and see how the scene brightens up. Change it back to 2.

76 ■ *Mastering Augmented Reality Development with Unity*

4. Change the **Shadow type** to hard shadows, soft shadows, or no shadows, and see how the shadows on the plane change accordingly.

5. At the top of the inspector window, change the Rotation values under **Transform** and notice how the direction of the light affects the shadows and the shading of your character.

Refer to *Figure 4.15*:

Figure 4.15: Impact of the directional light in the scene

6. Move the directional light closer to your character.

7. Now change the light type from **General** to **Point**. Move the light around and notice how the total scene light changed to a simple point light. You can also modify the Light color by providing color in the **Inspector** window.

8. Similarly, change the light type to spot and notice how the light acts as a flashlight. Try changing the **Inner / Outer Spot** angle and modify the spotlight area. You can also use the rotational tool to rotate the direction of the light.

9. The name of the game object **Directional Light** is independent of the light type configured in the inspector window.

Figure 4.16 features the difference between the point light (left) and spotlight (right):

Figure 4.16: *Difference between the point light (left) and the spotlight (right)*

Creating materials

If you are familiar with 3D modeling tools, you may know the term **materials**. If you are new to this, consider the material as a **paint bucket**. Each 3D mesh can have one or more materials to define the colors of the 3D model. Materials can contain textures to wrap images around 3D models. The textures are known as maps, and based on the material configuration, different maps make materials get different looks.

Materials are defined by a computer program called shaders. Shaders run in your computer's **Graphical Processing Unit (GPU)** and run parallelly for each screen pixel. For this chapter, we will use a shader known as **Lit** under the Universal Render Pipeline given by Unity.

As a start, let us start coloring our character.

1. Go to your project window and right-click on the **Assets** folder. Choose **Create** and select **Folder**. Now name it as **Materials**. You can name it with anything you like; it is always better to be organized since your project folder can be messy with various files and folders.

2. Now go into the **Materials** folder and right-click on an empty area.

3. Go to **Create | Material**.

4. This will give you a new file that has an *orb* icon. You can rename it to anything. For this example, name it **Yellow**.

5. Now, select the material you created and look in the Inspector window. There you may see a list of options under the material. Go to the base map under Surface inputs.

6. Click on the white color bar and choose a yellow color. Notice how it changes the color of the material preview in the project window as well.

7. Now drag and drop the material onto the body of your character. Notice how it changes the color of the object to yellow. Now, changing the color of the original material will change the colors of the objects they are attached to as well. Select the material and change the options in the Inspector window. Try changing the surface type and options in surface inputs, such as the Metallic map value, Smoothness, Emission, and so on. We can manipulate these values to generate physical-based materials such as metal, rubber, plastic, and so on.

8. You can now create multiple materials and assign different colors. Try adding different colors to your character meshes and complete them. This is our character in colors in *Figure 4.17*.

Note: If you are reading the paperback, you may not see it in color. Please download the digital content provided with this book to view them in colors.

Refer to *Figure 4.17*:

***Figure 4.17**: Coloring the character with materials*

9. Now, create a new **Sphere** in the scene and a new material in the **Materials** folder. Rename it to `tiled yellow`. Change the color of the material to **yellow**.

10. Now, click the small dot on the left side of the color bar and select **Default-Checker-Gray**.

11. Change the **Tiling** to 10 for both X and Y. Notice how the image we selected has wrapped around the sphere as a tile. This is how we can use images (textures) and align them onto 3D models using materials.

Refer to *Figure 4.18*:

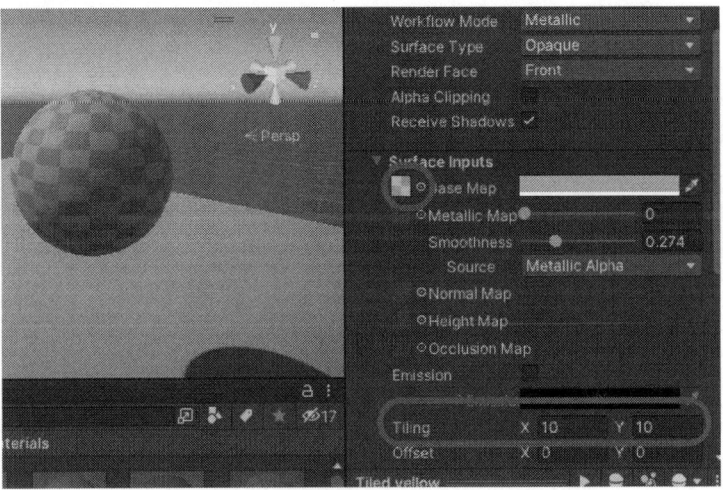

Figure 4.18: Assigning a texture for a material

Manipulating the virtual camera

Virtual Camera is the only component that captures the objects in the scene with its point of view to render the final output. The output is given through the Game window in Unity Editor. Once exported as an application, it can be through your PC screen, mobile screen, a HoloLens projection, or a VR headset.

By default, Unity provides us a **Main Camera** game object which has a **Camera** component attached to it.

To try how the Camera works with Unity, follow these steps:

1. Dock your Game view by the side of the Unity window. You can do that by dragging from the **Game window** tab.

2. Now select the **Main Camera** and look at the Inspector window.

3. Change the position, rotation values of the camera and notice how the view through the game window changes, as shown in *Figure 4.19*:

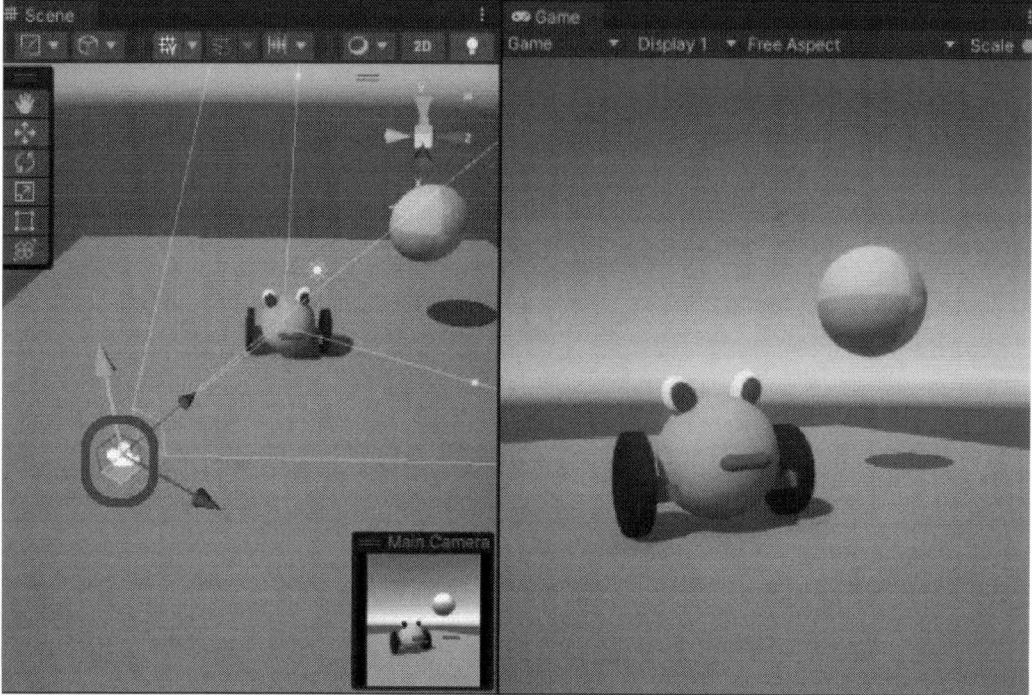

Figure 4.19: How we see the camera and how the camera sees the world

In AR development, we will use this virtual camera to move and rotate within the 3D space with respect to the movement of your AR device. All the AR SDKs, we are learning throughout this book, have custom components that help the cameras do it. The cameras will replace the background sky with the device camera input (actual world capture).

There are many options in the camera component to modify:

- Try changing the clipping plane near the value from 0.3 to 4 and moving the camera.

- Also, change the far value to a smaller value, such as 10, and notice how your objects cut through the game view output.

- Clipping plane filters only the objects that should be visible in the final view based on the distance from the camera.

- Also, go to the **Culling mask** under **Rendering** options and change the value to none. Now, click other values and notice how all the objects are gone from the game view except the sky, and selecting **default** shows all of them again.

This is known as a layer mask, where you can enable and disable objects being captured from the virtual camera based on the layer that the object is given. There are many use cases for using a layer mask, and filtering objects through the camera is one of those common uses.

Using the Unity package manager

Unity is a tool that is capable of many things. By default, Unity Editor comes with the basics needed to develop a 3D application. However, there are extensions and packages that can extend the capabilities of the editor. For that, unity has a package manager which works as an extension repository.

1. Click **Window | Package Manager**.

2. There are many ways how a package can be installed to your current project:

    a. **Unity Registry:** Packages that are already available by Unity.

    b. **Asset Store:** Packages you download from the asset store.

    c. **External sources:** Sources like GitHub, local packages, and so on.

You can switch between different options by clicking on the package option dropdown at the top, as highlighted in *Figure 4.20*:

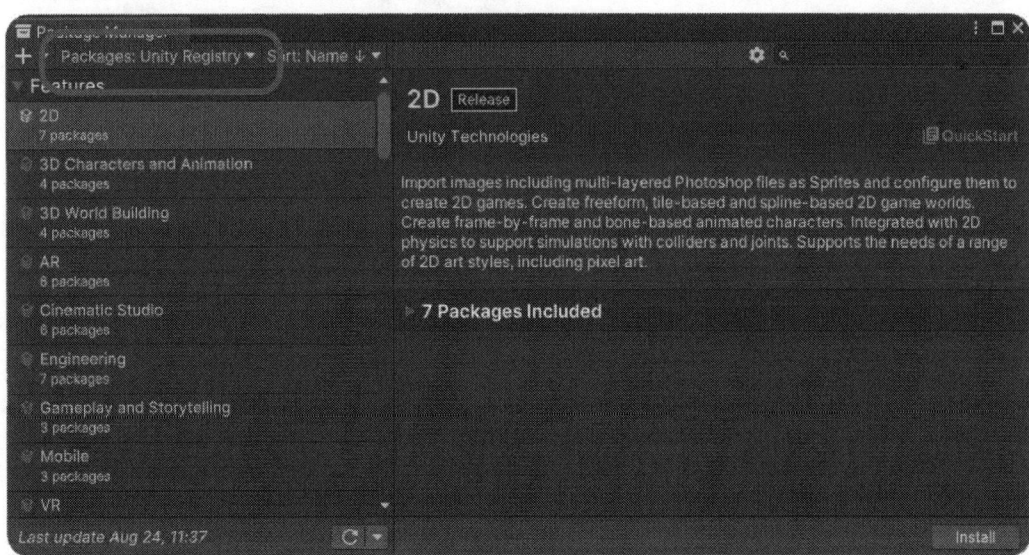

Figure 4.20: Selecting the package repository from the package manager

This window lists the packages that can be installed into your project. If you scroll down, you may see that some packages, such as the universal render pipeline, are already installed.

To install any package, select the package and click the **Install** button at the bottom right corner.

Importing content into Unity

There are many ways in which we can import assets into Unity. Importing assets into Unity creates a copy of the assets we imported within the `Assets` folder of the project. Based on the project target platform, it also generates metafiles related to conversions and other metadata.

1. If you have downloaded the project files associated with this book, go to **Assets | Chapter 4** and open the `Smiley` folder.
2. In Unity Editor, create a new folder and name it **Textures**. Double-click and go into the folder.
3. Now, go to **Assets | Import New Asset...**
4. This will open a new window. Navigate to the `Smiley` folder and select all three images. Click **Import**, as shown in *Figure 4.21*.

This will convert and import 3 new images into your project `Assets` folder. Now we can use them as textures in our materials:

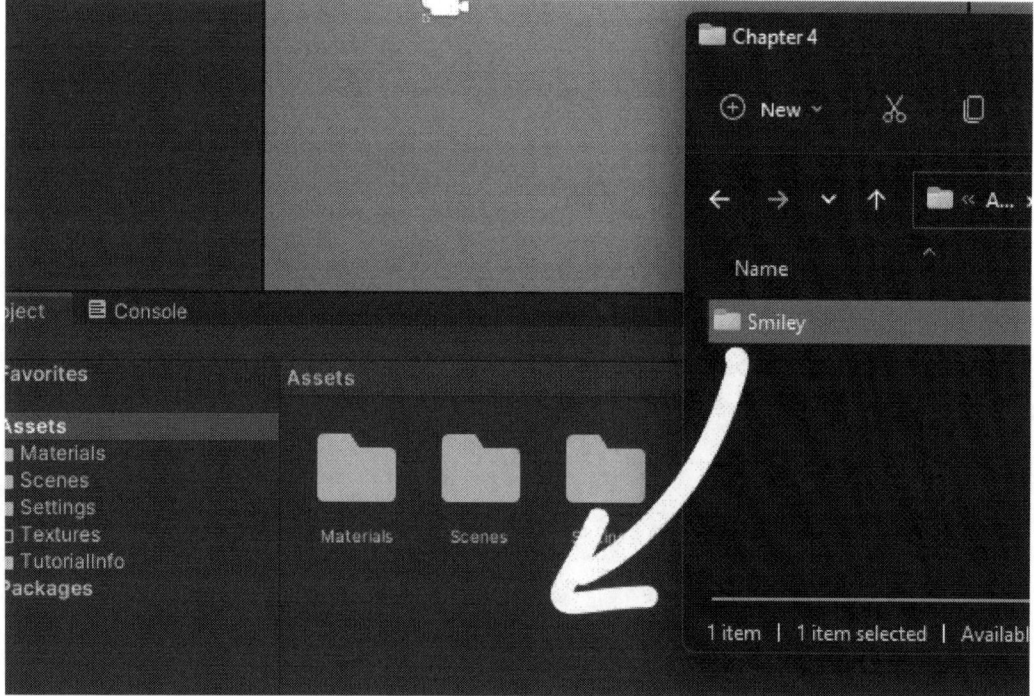

Figure 4.21: Importing files into Unity by dragging and dropping them

You can also drag and drop the whole folder into Unity's project window. Additionally, you can use the textures that we imported to create a new material. Name the material as **Smiley**. The material parameters can be as follows:

- **Base map** | Use the Texture image.
- **Metallic Map** | Use the **Metallic Map**. Increase smoothness to 1.
- **Enable Emission** and add the Emission map. Change the emission color to white.

Apply the material to a sphere and notice how each map works with different areas of the sphere. Refer to the following *Figure 4.22*:

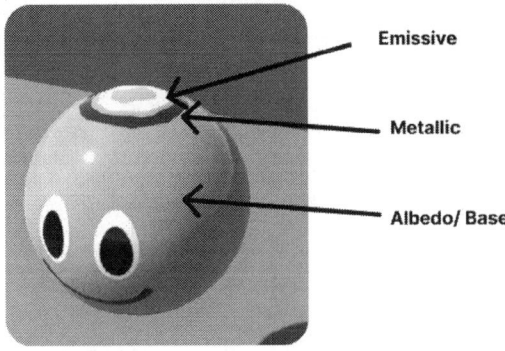

Figure 4.22: Impact of the different maps attached to a material

Importing assets from the Unity asset store

Unity also has a crowdsourced asset store with millions of assets containing 3D models, animations, custom components, audio, video effects, and so on. Currently, you can use the package manager to download the asset into your project. However, you have to log in to the asset store to purchase assets to your Unity ID. Follow the given steps:

1. Head over to the following link and log in:

   http://assetstore.unity.com

2. Search for any free asset available.

3. Click **Add to My Assets**. If you see a license agreement, read it, and click **Agree**.

4. Now, go to the package manager window (**Window** | **Package Manager**). Choose **My Assets** from the dropdown and search for the asset you added to your library.

5. Click **Download**. Once downloaded, click **Import** button again. This will show you a list of all the files that will be added to your project. Click **Import**.

The structure of the GameObject

As you know, a unity scene is made of lighting settings and Game objects that fill the scene. A game object, by default, is an empty entity. Game objects can contain many components. These components define the behavior of the game object. The application logic is scripted into the components, and the components will manage the interactions. Unity has provided a list of components to prototype a 3D environment quickly. Refer to *Figure 4.23* for a hierarchy of a Unity application:

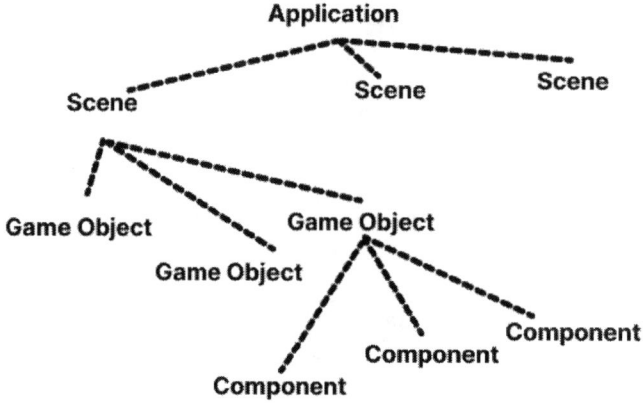

Figure 4.23: Hierarchy of a unity application

Let us go through some of the most used components in Unity.

Components of Unity

In our scene, create an empty game object (right-click the hierarchy | **Create Empty**) and name it **Component Test**, as shown in *Figure 4.24*. Now select the game object and look at the Inspector window. At the top of it, you will see the name of it with a tick box. This tick defines the activate/deactivate status of the game object. If a game object is inactive, it will neither be visible in the scene nor run any component logic attached. You can also provide a layer to the game object and a tag that can be used in segmenting game objects in a scene:

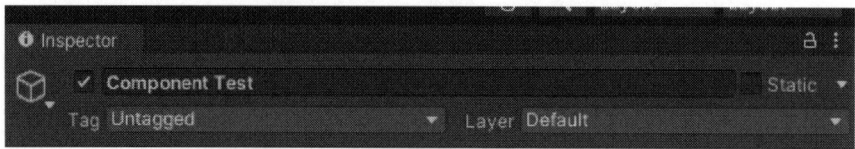

Figure 4.24: Game object properties in the inspector window

Transform

This is the base component for any game object. Without a transform, there cannot be a game object in existence. The transform component defines the position, rotation, and scale of a game object. Moreover, this component provides useful functions (methods) to move, rotate, translate, and scale objects in local and world spaces. Additionally, a transform component can be used to change the parent of a game object as the transform component keeps a list of all the child game objects within its transform.

Mesh Renderer

Any game object, by default, can be considered an empty object with just a transform. A Mesh renderer can use a 3D mesh and materials to draw a 3D model in the 3D space. A mesh renderer is an inherited component from the *renderer* component. If a 3D model is non-deformable, you may always see a mesh renderer component attached to any 3D model in the scene.

In 2021 URP, the mesh renderer is divided into materials, lighting, probes, and other additional settings. Mainly, we will be using the materials section to change the material of a 3D model. You may also notice that with the mesh renderer, another mesh filter component is attached to it. This component passes the 3D mesh to the renderer, as the renderer and the mesh are independent. Try changing the Mesh of the mesh filter component and notice how the game object changes its appearance without changing the color/material. The lighting sections of the component also define whether the 3D model should receive and cast shadows. Let us carry out the following steps:

1. Add a **Mesh Filter** and a **Mesh Renderer** component to the **Component Test** game object.
2. Click the *dot* next to **Mesh input** and select any mesh you like from the list. Notice how the object appears in pink. This is because the mesh renderer draws the mesh but does not have a material attached to it.
3. Drag a material to the 3D model or choose a material from the inspector window. Notice how the material now colors the model with your material color.

Colliders

In 3D development, we may need collisions in various situations. To identify interactions, detect physics-based collisions to move objects naturally under simulated forces, to trigger events are some of the use cases of colliders. They work as a virtual boundary for a game object. The task of a collider is to detect if the boundary of the collision area is inside another collision boundary and pass that information to other components attached to the game object. Usually, a collision can be used as a collider or a trigger. Triggers can detect collisions but would not restrict another collider from entering the trigger area. Unity has provided us with basic collider shapes for 3D. Those are the sphere collider, box collider, capsule collider, and mesh collider. The number of faces of a boundary area increases the mathematical calculations Unity must do to detect a collision. Usually, a sphere collider uses the least amount of computational power, while a mesh collider can have the highest based on the complexity of the collider. Let us carry out the following steps:

1. Click the component test game object.

2. Add a **Box collider** and notice how it generated a green color boundary gizmo that resembles the boundary areas of the collider. Base collider components have a button to configure the boundaries visually, known as **Edit collider**. You can use it to change the boundary parameters, which can also be modified using the inspector UI.

Figure 4.25 shows how different colliders attached to empty game objects:

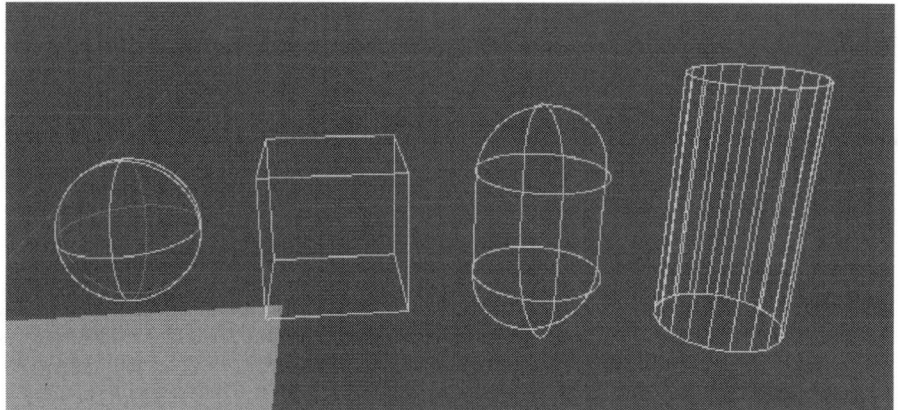

Figure 4.25: Different colliders provided by Unity. The Cylinder is a mesh collider

Rigid body

If your 3D application requires built-in physics by the Unity engine, it will be managed by the Rigid body component. Adding a rigid body component to any game object makes it responsive to external forces. The forces can be applied to the object at any given point in any direction. However, without a collider, the engine cannot recognize the external collision-based forces. You can also use a rigid body to apply torques (rotational forces), set the velocity of a game object, detect physics-based collisions, and apply gravity. Let us carry out the following steps:

1. Select the test game object and add a rigid body. Now click the *Play* button in the editor. Notice how it falls. If you have a plane at the bottom of it, it will collide with the floor and stop there.

2. Stop the play mode, and attach a sphere collider instead of the box collider. Move the object on a plane and click *Play*. Notice how the object rolls despite the mesh resembling another shape. Create a duplicate of the same and try to collide them both together.

Rigid body, by default, responds to a gravity value and will fall towards a negative Y direction. You can disable this to simulate gravity less space. There is another option to enable and disable the *kinematic* feature of a rigid body. Enabling this will make the object immovable with any external force but will result in collisions. Try changing the values with many duplicates of the game objects in your scene and test them in play mode.

During this section, we went through very few components that Unity offers by default. We can use C# to build custom components for the object and other components to provide custom interactions. A game object can contain as much as components as the child objects of it. However, having many game objects in the scene with many components can be chaotic when we need to change the property of a component in a range of game objects. There needs to be a reusable approach to manage game objects.

Creating prefabs

Imagine you have a character game object to duplicate and place around a 3D scene. Their behavior needs to be the same with slight variations. By default, you can create a game object with all the necessary components and custom components, make duplicates of the same object and place it everywhere.

Now imagine that you need to change some values of the parameters of all the character copies. This will be a nightmare if you have many changes to make. Creating prefabs allows you to create a game object with any child object or any component and convert it in a way that lets you easily reuse and update the components as much as you want. The changes will resemble all the instances (copies) right away.

In Unity, a prefab can also be referred to as a game object. A prefab consists of the same components as a game object. When you have a prefab in the scene view, that is an instance of the prefab.

To create a prefab, follow these steps:

1. Drag and drop a game object from the scene view to the project view.
2. Create a new folder called **Prefabs**.
3. Now drag and drop the **Character** game object into the **Prefabs** folder.

Refer to *Figure 4.26*:

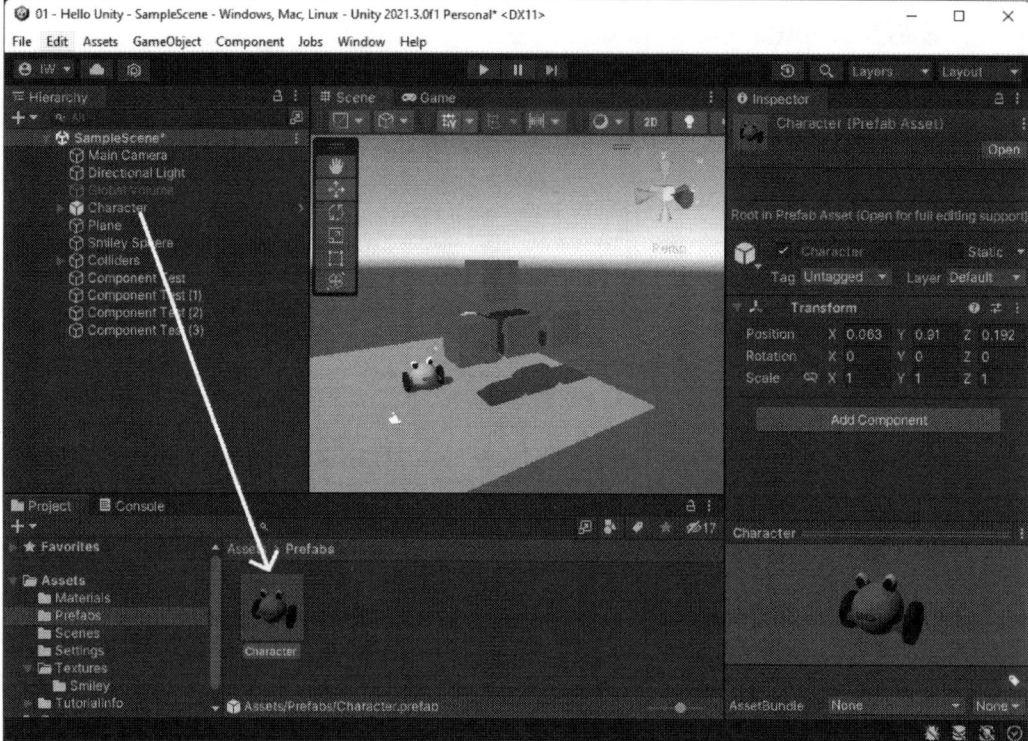

Figure 4.26: *Creating a prefab by dragging and dropping a game object from the hierarchy to project view*

Now you can see how the character is converted into a prefab by changing its icon to a blue cube.

You can delete the character from the scene but drag and drop again into the scene view just like you are adding a 3D model from the project. The prefab consists of all the child objects and components attached to the original game object.

You can also open the prefab in its own local space to modify it by double-clicking it or choosing the open function in its right-click menu. Any prefab instance can be modified, but the changes need to be applied for the main prefab to be updated. Since the prefabs are defined objects, you cannot delete or remove any objects or components by an instance of the prefab. However, you can append and modify the instance by adding components and game objects to the end of it.

Conclusion

In this chapter, we not only went through the basics of Unity installation but also learned the interface, basic 3D concepts and how components work with each other, properties of different components, and the concepts of creating prefabs. In our next chapter, we will be taking an introduction to C# with Unity and learning to create our first custom component.

Key points

- Unity uses Unity Hub to manage projects and versions.
- Unity is a cross-platform tool, and supportive modules must be installed to enable the platform capabilities.
- You can use Visual Studio or Visual Studio code to write C# scripts for Unity Projects.
- iOS applications can only be built using XCode, an IDE only available for Mac OS devices.
- A Unity Project can have multiple scenes. A unity scene consists of game objects. Components define game objects.

Multiple choice questions

1. **Which of the following is not true regarding Unity 3D engine?**
    a. Unity engine is a cross-platform tool and supports multiple platforms, including Android, iOS, Hololens, and Magic Leap.
    b. Unity Hub is an authorizing tool that provides you with the Unity license and manages Unity Projects and versions installed.
    c. Unity uses a `MonoManager` component written in C# language to allow developers to inherit and build custom components.
    d. Unity uses native core language capabilities integrated with .NET runtime.

2. **What is a transformation tool out of the following?**
    a. Rect Tool
    b. Tool handle position
    c. View Tool
    d. Gizmo Tool

3. What is the most appropriate definition for a prefab?

   a. A Prefab is a group of `GameObjects` with transform, renderer, and collider components.

   b. A Prefab is a 3D model with materials combined to provide a complex 3D shape.

   c. A Prefab is an Asset downloaded from the asset store, imported using the package manager.

   d. A Prefab is a reusable `GameObject` created in a Scene and saved in the project assets.

4. Which of the following is not true regarding different components in Unity?

   a. Collider components use a boundary to check whether it is inside another boundary.

   b. Transform component is the base component that allows any object to enable physics.

   c. Renderer components use the material and the GPU to draw the graphics in the 3D scene.

   d. Light component adds illumination in different shapes to all the objects with lit materials in the Unity scene.

Answers

1. c
2. a
3. d
4. b

Join our book's Discord space

Join the book's Discord Workspace for Latest updates, Offers, Tech happenings around the world, New Release and Sessions with the Authors:

https://discord.bpbonline.com

CHAPTER 5
Creating Your First Custom Component

Introduction

C# is a language developed by Microsoft that runs on the .NET framework. This language is primarily used to build Windows applications, but lately, it has also been used for web, mobile, and game development.

This book is for designers and developers with basic knowledge of C# including the basic syntax, variables, methods, loops, and conditional statements. If you are very new to programming and C#, it is recommended to go over the C# tutorials provided by Microsoft. Go to the following link to learn more about C#:

https://docs.microsoft.com/en-us/dotnet/csharp/

In this chapter, we take a quick peek at C# within Unity, and see how we can use it to create a custom component. We will also see how to communicate with other components and manipulate their values using C#.

Structure

In this chapter, we will discuss the following topics:

- Introduction to C# in Unity
- Exploring the **MonoBehaviour**

- Serialized variables
- Debug class of Unity
- Time in Unity
- `GetComponent()`
- Building a simple 3D clock

Objectives

After completing this chapter, the reader will be able to understand how C# scripts work with Unity, while also understanding some core features of the syntax with Unity, by creating custom components with C# language and using the components to create a simple 3D clock.

Introduction to C# in Unity

In Unity, a base script is considered as a *component*. Components are defined by Unity based on another C# class file. A basic component script is a class file derived from **MonoBehaviour** class created by Unity.

In order to create a C# component, we can use the project window to generate a C# class file for us. Instead of a blank C# class, unity will generate a class inherited from the **MonoBehaviour** class. Due to that, the script now works like a blueprint for a custom component that can be attached to any game object in the scene.

Now, let us create our first component by following the given steps:

1. Go to our sample scene with the character and the smiley face sphere.
2. Create a new folder called **Scripts** in the **Assets** folder.
3. Inside the scripts folder, right-click and click **Create | C# Script**.
4. This will generate a default script for us. We have to immediately rename it. Change the name to **Spinner**. If you click somewhere else, Unity will generate a component called **NewBehaviourScript**. This should not be renamed from the Unity editor, as the name of the C# file should be the same as the **MonoBehaviour** class name.
5. Previously, we talked about setting up Visual studio and visual studio code (*Chapter 4: Up and Running with Unity 3D*) to script in Unity, and we paused the last step to set it up with Unity. Let us also continue that.
6. Go to **Edit | Preferences**.

7. Select **External tools** from the window that appears.
8. For the **External Script** editor, choose the IDE that you prefer. This IDE should support C# development (such as VS and VS Code).
9. If you do not see the editor in the list, you can browse and choose the location of the editor application.
10. Click on the **Regenerate Project files** button. Now, the Unity editor is configured with the IDE. This is only a one-time process and there is no need for it to be done for every project.
11. Close the window, go to the `scripts` folder, and double-click on the script to launch it through the editor.

Exploring the MonoBehaviour

As soon as you open the new C# script, this will be the template code you get:

```
1.  using System.Collections;
2.  using System.Collections.Generic;
3.  using UnityEngine;
4.
5.  public class Spinner : MonoBehaviour
6.  {
7.      // Start is called before the first frame update
8.      void Start()
9.      {
10.
11.     }
12.
13.     // Update is called once per frame
14.     void Update()
15.     {
16.
17.     }
18. }
```

In Unity, the script must be attached to an active game object in the runtime to execute it. There are some imports made by Unity to use Unity-based methods and C# system collection APIs. The class name is similar to the file name and is inherited from the **MonoBehaviour** component. There are two primary methods in any C# template script:

- **start()**: This method is executed by Unity if this component is attached to an active game object. This method always executes only once at the very moment the game is started. Usually, this method is used to initialize things in the scripts.
- **update()**: This method is also executed by Unity as long as the application is running. This is a loop method and executes once every frame. The **update** method can be used for any continuous checks, input detection, movement of objects, and so on.

There are other standard methods that Unity executes, such as **Awake()**, **FixedUpdate()**, **OnTriggerEnter()**, and so on. However, we will not delve into them in this chapter.

Serialized variables

Follow the given steps for serialized variables:

1. Before utilizing the **start()** method, create a simple public **float** variable named as **spinnerSpeed** as follows:

    public float spinnerSpeed;

2. Now save the script and go back to Unity.
3. Select the smiley sphere we created before, and click **Add component**.
4. Type **Spinner** in the search bar and click on the **Spinner** C# component.
5. Now you may see that a new custom component **Spinner** got attached to the sphere, along with a text field to input the spinner speed value.

    This is a **public** variable. Unity can use its interface to access the public variables and change them, just as other scripts. Sometimes we do not need the variable to be public and must have proper access modifiers. As in this case, the spinner speed can be a **private** variable.

6. Go back to the code, change **public** to **private**, save the script, and go back to Unity.

7. Select the sphere and notice that the variable input is gone. This is because the access modifier is private; Unity cannot access or modify it through the interface anymore.

8. However, being developers, we can use the **[SerializeField]** attribute in order to ask Unity to serialize it. This allows the unity interface to show and modify the value. However, being a private variable, other scripts do not have the permission to access the variable directly.

9. Change the variable to a serialized field by adding the attribute. It should now be like this:

    [SerializeField] private float spinnerSpeed;

10. Save the script and go back to Unity. Notice that the field for **SpinnerSpeed** is now back. Refer to *Figure 5.1*:

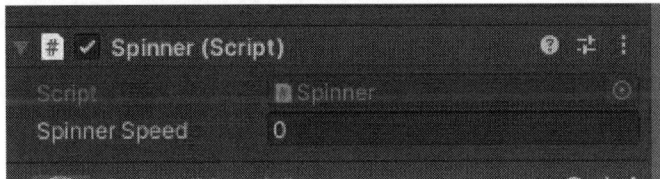

Figure 5.1: How a script component appears in the inspector window, with placeholders for serialized variables

Debug class of Unity

In Unity, you can use the debug class to print messages in the console and draw editor-only gizmos in the scene at runtime. This allows us to use graphics and text to debug our code properly.

The most used method of the **Debug** class is the **Log()** method. This is similar to **Console.PrintLine()** method provided by core C#.

Open the **Spinner** script, and add the following line into the **start** method:

    Debug.Log("Hello Unity!");

Add this to the **update** method:

    Debug.Log("Hello Update!");

Save the script and run the game. Open the console window at the bottom, as shown in *Figure 5.2*, and see how it prints **Hello Unity** at once and **Hello Update** infinitely (until you stop playing):

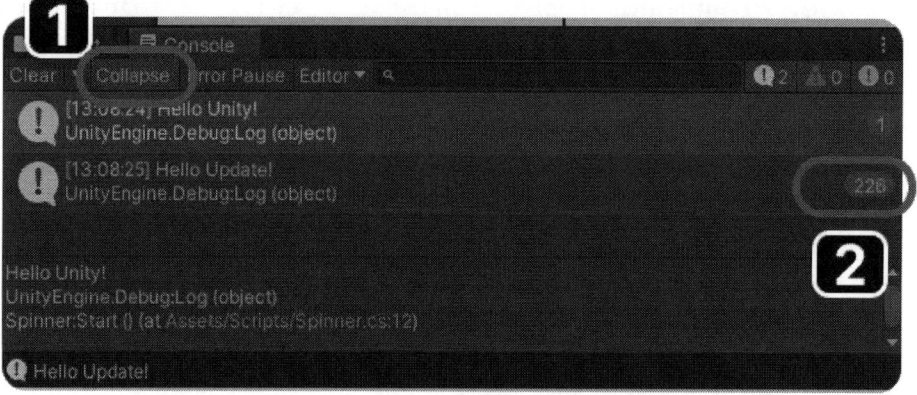

Figure 5.2: Console window of Unity

1. Press the **Collapse** button to collapse duplicate logs.
2. It will show the number of iterations that it is logged.

Throughout this book, we will be using **Debug.Log()** method to debug our code executions. You can go to **https://docs.unity3d.com/ScriptReference/Debug.html** to learn more about the **Debug** class and the methods it offers.

Time in Unity

Unity uses the clock speed of the computer that it is running in order to perform frame-based calculations. Also, Unity uses the internal clock to determine the real time using the **Time** module.

As we learned before, the **Update** method executes once per clock cycle assigned to Unity by the processor. This is variable due to the number of processes running in the computer, as the operating system schedules and allocates time to run the Unity app. By default, a good computer can run around 200-300 frames per second, and it totally relies on how your application performs as well.

So how do we calculate real times in the **update** method?

This can be achieved by using a variable provided by unity known as **Time.deltaTime**. This is a **float** value, and it varies between each frame, as it gives the time between two frame updates. Therefore, if we keep appending **Time.deltaTime** to **0** in the **update** method, the resultant value would be the number of seconds that have taken, since the start of the play mode.

Change the inside of the **Spinner** class to the following, save it, and run:

```
1.    float timeSinceStart = 0;
2.
3.    void Update()
4.    {
5.        timeSinceStart += Time.deltaTime;
6.        Debug.Log(timeSinceStart);
7.    }
```

Notice how the console window prints the time after each iteration and how it matches the real-time. The **Time** module in Unity offers various time-related values, such as the current time since level load, frame rate, frame count, and so on.

We can also use the **DateTime** module from the C# System core module and use that within Unity. One of the best features of Unity is the ability to use .NET core modules within the custom components we build. In the next section, let us use the **DateTime** method to create a simple 3D clock.

GetComponent

Out of all the methods that Unity provides, the **GetComponent** can be considered an important method to be used within components. This method can be used anywhere in a component script to access other components of the game object that this script is attached to.

By default, Unity provides access to the **gameObject** and the **transform** component of the attached game object by using the same keywords. In order to get access to other components, we must use **GetComponent<T>()**. Here, the **T** stands for the component generic, that is, the class name of the component we are referring to. **Get** component method is costly. Unity iterates through all of the components attached to the game object to look for the needed component. Instead of using the **GetComponent** in the **update** method, we can use it just once in the **Start** method and cache the value to reuse it

Modify the **spinner** script to the following, change the spinner speed to 100, and play to test it:

```
1.  using UnityEngine;
2.
3.  public class Spinner : MonoBehaviour
4.  {
```

```
5.      [SerializeField] private float spinnerSpeed;
6.
7.      private MeshRenderer rend;
8.      float timeSinceStart = 0;
9.
10.     void Start()
11.     {
12.         rend = GetComponent<MeshRenderer>();
13.     }
14.
15.     void Update()
16.     {
17.         transform.Rotate(0, spinnerSpeed * Time.deltaTime, 0);
18.
19.         timeSinceStart += Time.deltaTime;
20.         if(timeSinceStart > 0)
21.         {
22.             timeSinceStart = 0;
23.             rend.material.color = Random.ColorHSV();
24.         }
25.     }
26. }
```

You may notice that the smiley sphere starts rotating around its Y axis while changing its color tint to a random color every second. A description for the above code is as follows:

- **Line 7:** We create a **MeshRenderer** reference variable.
- **Line 12:** In the **Start()** method, we cache the attached mesh renderer component of the smiley sphere as the **rend** variable. Now we have access to the mesh renderers' methods and variables.
- **Line 17:** We call the transform component of the sphere to rotate around itself by using the Rotate method with **x, y,** and **z** parameter values.

- **Line 19 to 24:** We increment the `timeSinceStart` by `Time.deltaTime`, and every time it goes beyond 1, we pull it back to 0. This way, we can execute anything with a 1-second interval.

- **Line 23:** We access the material of the mesh renderer and change the color of it to a random color using `Random.ColorHSV()` method. This is a method provided by Unity under `UnityEngine.Random` module.

As you can see, we are given a sandbox of methods and components to play with scripts to build any computer graphics visualization. It is always better to follow the C# documentation by Microsoft as well as Unity's own documentation, to learn more about the components and supporting methods provided by Unity.

Building a simple 3D clock

Using the content we learned in the previous sections, let us now try to build a simple 3D clock. Refer to the following steps:

1. Create a new Scene in the **Scenes** folder and rename it to 3DClock.

2. Open the scene and create a cylinder 3D object. Remove the **Capsule collider** component from it by clicking on the **three dots** button on the top right end of the component.

3. Scale the cylinder in such a way that it looks like a clock face.

4. Now inside the clock, add three empty game objects and rename them as **Hours**, **Minutes**, and **Seconds**. These objects will hold the clock handles inside them separately. We can reference the transform components of these empty game objects to rotate based on the current system time.

5. Now, add another cylinder inside the main clock face and rename it as **knob**. This will be a good reference game object to know the center of the clock face.

6. Inside each empty game object, create a cube, and scale it in such a way that it looks like a proper clock handle. Because the cubes use the center of them as the pivot point, we may have to move it away from its parent's origin to *look like* it starts from the knob position.

7. You can use different materials to color each cube inside each empty game object.

8. Finally, you should have a clock model with the time perfectly set to 12:00:00. All the **hours**, **minutes**, **seconds**, and **knob** game objects should be at 0,0,0 position with 0,0,0 rotation. If we select any handle game object and rotate it around the Y axis, you can see that it goes around the clock face.

Figure 5.3 shows how the clock, and the handles must be set up:

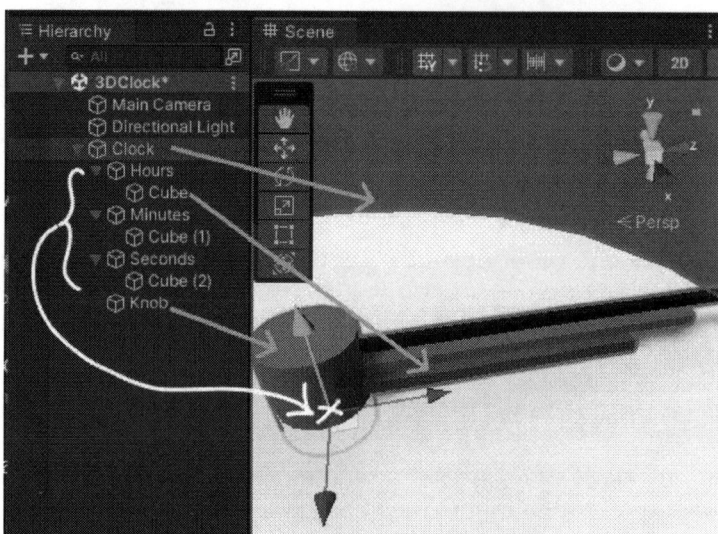

Figure 5.3: *Clock created using primitive objects*

9. Save the scene.

10. Go to the **Scripts** folder and create a new C# Script. Rename it as **Clock** and press *Enter*.

11. Open the script and change it as follows:

    1. using UnityEngine;
    2. using System;
    3.
    4. public class Clock : MonoBehaviour
    5. {
    6.   [SerializeField] private Transform hoursHandle;
    7.   [SerializeField] private Transform minutesHandle;
    8.   [SerializeField] private Transform secondsHandle;
    9.
    10.   DateTime currentTime;
    11.   Vector3 hours, mins, secs;
    12.
    13.

```
14.     void Update()
15.     {
16.         currentTime = DateTime.Now;
17.
18.         hours = new Vector3(0,(360/12) * currentTime.Hour, 0);
19.         mins  = new Vector3(0,(360/60) * currentTime.Minute, 0);
20.         secs  = new Vector3(0,(360/60) * currentTime.Second, 0);
21.
22.         hoursHandle.localEulerAngles = hours;
23.         minutesHandle.localEulerAngles = mins;
24.         secondsHandle.localEulerAngles = secs;
25.     }
26. }
```

The following is an explanation of the code:

- **Line 6 to 7:** We added transform references for the empty game objects that are holding the handles.

- **Line 10:** Cached variable to hold and update the current time.

- **Line 11: Vector3** values to hold the rotation of the handles in Euler angles (**x,y,z** values).

- **Line 16:** Assign the current time to the **currentTime** variable using **DateTime.Now**.

- **Line 18 to 20:** We use the **hour**, **minute**, and **second** values from the current time, divide the full 360 circle by the number of segments and multiply that value to convert the time values to degrees. Here, we applied the rotation only to the y-axis; the other two axes are kept at 0. We calculate these vectors and hold them temporarily in variables we created in line 11.

- **Line 22 to 24:** We use the **localEulerAngles** variable of the transform component to assign the rotation directly to its local space. This way, the rotation of the handles will only be with respect to the **Clock** game object. Therefore, rotating the parent game object will not impact the rotation of the handles.

12. Save the script and go back to Unity.

13. Select the **Clock** object, click **Add Component**, and choose the **Clock** script.

14. Now it has 3 placeholders to assign **Transform** components. In Unity, we can do that by dragging and dropping the associated game object onto the placeholder. Drag and drop **Hours**, **Minutes** and **Seconds** game objects onto the relevant placeholders. *Figure 5.4* shows what it should look like after the assignment.

15. Now, click play and see how the clock ticks based on your actual computer time:

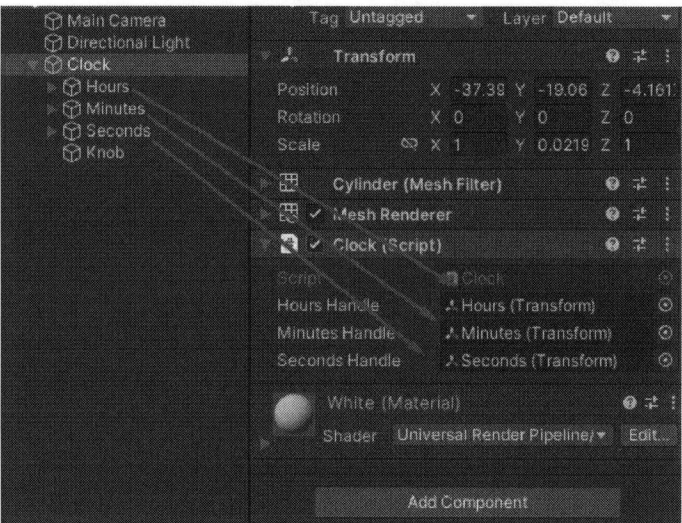

Figure 5.4: Assigning reference components by dragging and dropping the game object

Conclusion

In this chapter, we took an introduction to C# with Unity and understood how it works with other components. In our next chapter, we will dive deeper into C# with Unity and learn how to create components that can talk to each other to build a complete interactive application. As Unity and C#, both contain a large number of modules to discuss, this book will only limit it to the scope of building AR applications. Therefore, it is highly recommended to read the C# documentation and Unity documentation to understand how scripting can be used effectively in your projects.

Key points

- C# scripts are inherited from a **MonoBehaviour** class, which makes it a blueprint for a component.

- A **MonoBehaviour** class has default methods, such as **start**, **update**, **awake**, **FixedUpdate**, executed (if available within components) by Unity, as a part of the program's runtime process.

- A script can use **Get** component to get access to other components and manipulate their values to create logic and implement interactions.

Multiple choice questions

1. **Which of the following variables cannot be modified using the inspector window?**

    a. `[SerializeField] public int health;`

    b. `[SerializeField] private string name;`

    c. `private bool useGravity;`

    d. `public float gravity;`

2. **What is the difference between the start and the update methods?**

    a. The **start** method runs before enabling the component as soon as it enters runtime. The **update** method runs once every second.

    b. The **start** method runs when the component becomes available in play mode. The **update** method runs once per frame.

    c. The **start** method runs once every second, and the **update** method runs per every frame.

    d. The **start** and **update** methods both get executed once, one after the other.

3. **What is the use of the GetComponent<T>() method?**

    a. It goes through all the objects in the scene to find the **T** component and returns it.

    b. It goes through all the components in child objects to find the **T** component and returns it.

    c. It returns the transform (**T**) component attached to the game object to which the script is attached.

    d. It returns the component of **T** type attached to the game object to which the script is attached.

Answers

1. c
2. b
3. d

Join our book's Discord space

Join the book's Discord Workspace for Latest updates, Offers, Tech happenings around the world, New Release and Sessions with the Authors:

https://discord.bpbonline.com

CHAPTER 6
Refreshing C# Concepts with Unity

Introduction

Our goal is to develop 3D applications that can run in an AR world. Before that, understanding C# concepts with Unity and the capabilities of different components will allow us to build any interaction that can be done within an AR world. In the previous chapters, we got a thorough introduction to Unity's ecosystem and a simple implementation of a custom component using C#.

This chapter of the book goes through all the essential components we discussed before and attempts to manipulate the values to build a simple top-down shooter game. We will be using this game to understand a simple structure of a 3D application, moving through different scenes, using physics, coded animation, audio, and particle effects. There will also be a lot of coding in this chapter.

Structure

In this chapter, we will discuss the following topics:
- Setting up the scene
- Movement of the player
- Creating a bullet for the player to shoot
- Shooting bullets

- Setting up the enemy
- Setting up the player
- Spawning and destroying enemies
- Game UI
    - Game manager
- Adding audio and polishing
    - Adding the main menu
    - Switching scenes
    - The next steps

Objectives

After the completion of this chapter, you will be able to understand how to use different components for different system behaviors, use design patterns to access your code, use cases of different components, and finally polish an application, making it ready to be published as a first prototype.

Setting up the scene

Our requirement is to build a simple top-down shooter game that is similar to the Capcom legend 1942 game. We will be creating a straightforward version of it but in 3D. The idea is straightforward. You will be controlling a spaceship that shoots bullets in timely intervals and keeps shooting at the enemy spaceships that are coming at you from the opposite side, as shown in *Figure 6.1*. Occasionally, the enemy ships will also shoot at you, and you can block the bullets by shooting at them. There will be different enemy ships with different levels of difficulty. The goal is to get the highest score possible during a single run. Let us get started. Refer to *Figure 6.1*:

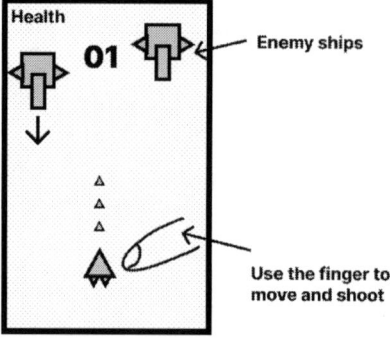

Figure 6.1: *Simple sketch of the final output of the game*

Let us create a new URP project in Unity and load up the sample scene. It is recommended to download all the asset files provided with the book before trying out this chapter. Import the *Top-Down Shooter* unity package within the **chapter 6** folder of the assets. This has all the necessary assets and prefabs that are required for the completion of the project.

For the project, we need a player, enemies, bullets, and an enemy spawner to generate enemies. For the moment, we can use primitives to set up the basic scene. Create a sphere for the enemy with a scale of a unit vector (1,1,1), another sphere for the player, a small cube for the bullet, and a big cube in front of the player. We will be using the collider bounds of this cube to randomly generate and spawn enemies that fly toward the player's direction. Also, the main camera should be moved to the top of the scene, looking down at the player. The arrangement of the setup should be as shown in *Figure 6.2*:

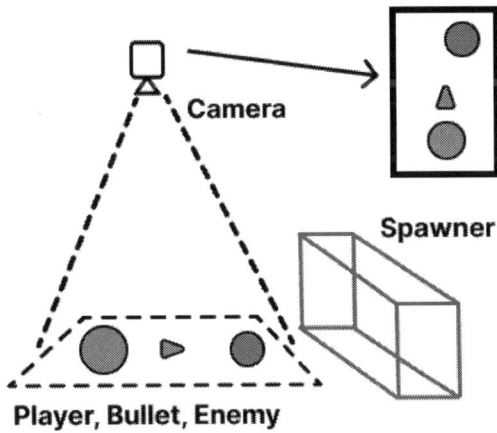

Figure 6.2: Sketch of the Scene setup

Make sure that the player's forward direction is towards the enemy and the enemy's is towards the player. In this game, we are going to keep the player's position within the screen space and move the enemies and the background to visually mimic the movement of the player along an endless path forward.

Movement of the player

Add a rigid body to the player. This allows us to use physics to move the player's object. Change the sphere collider radius to 0.5 since 1 meter seems too big. Eventually, we are going to remove the mesh filter and mesh renderer from it but keep that for now.

Create a C# script and name it **PlayerMovement.cs**. This class is going to capture your touch input and move the player. Open the script and update the script as follows. The descriptions of the major lines will be given after the code:

```csharp
1.  public class PlayerMovement : MonoBehaviour
2.  {
3.      [Range(0,.3f)]
4.      [SerializeField] private float touchSpeed = 0.5f;
5.      [SerializeField] private Camera cam;
6.
7.      private Rigidbody playerBody;
8.      private Vector3 worldPos;
9.      private Vector3 touchPos;
10.     private float playerZ;
11.
12.     void Start()
13.     {
14.         playerBody = GetComponent<Rigidbody>();
15.         playerZ = cam.transform.position.y - playerBody.transform.position.y;
16.     }
17.
18.     void FixedUpdate()
19.     {
20.         if (!cam || !playerBody)
21.             return;
22.
23.         if(Input.touchCount>0)
24.         {
25.             touchPos = Input.GetTouch(0).position;
26.             touchPos.z = playerZ;
27.             worldPos = cam.ScreenToWorldPoint(touchPos);
28.
29.             MovePlayer(worldPos);
```

```
30.        }
31.    }
32.
33.    void MovePlayer(Vector3 target)
34.    {
35.        playerBody.MovePosition(Vector3.Lerp(playerBody.position, target, touchSpeed));
36.    }
37. }
```

Here, we are using linear interpolation to slowly move the player toward the touch position using **Vector2.Lerp** method. A linear interpolation running in the update method moves the player towards a given point by a provided fraction, which is a variable that can span between **0** and **1**.

Here, in line number 4, we referenced that as **touchSpeed** and have given a restriction range to be within 0 and 0.3. In order to move the player, we use the **rigidbody** object's **MovePosition** method instead of the **transform** component. This way, the movement will give priority to any physics-based movements, such as collisions. We also cache the **rigidbody** of the players game object by using **GetComponent** in the **start** method.

We also need the *Camera* reference. Since the touch point is in screen space, we use the camera to convert that point to one in world space. However, this will give you a position too close to the camera. Therefore, we need to get a distance from the camera, and usually, it is better to have the distance that you have set up by default in the scene. Therefore, we calculate a **z** value to position the player with a **z** offset with respect to the camera. This is captured in line 15, and the value is stored in a variable.

Now select the player game object and attach a **Rigidbody** and the **PlayerMovement** script. In the **rigidbody** component, enable rotation constraints for all **x**, **y**, and **z** under the constraints section. This will restrict the player from rotating due to external forces.

Creating a bullet for the player to shoot

Now that we have the players' movement ready, we need to create another component to shoot bullets while the screen is being touched. However, first of all, we need to create a bullet.

Select the cube we created for the bullet and attach a **Rigidbody** component to that. We need the bullet to be instantiated by both the player and the enemy. Therefore, the bullet should be given damage and information on the initiator of the bullet (whether it is the player or the enemy who owns the bullet). Create a new C# script and name it **Bullet.cs**:

```
1.  public class Bullet : MonoBehaviour
2.  {
3.      [SerializeField] private GameObject bulletHitParticle;
4.      [SerializeField] private int bulletDamage = 20;
5.      [SerializeField] private Material bulletMaterialEnemy;
6.      [SerializeField] private Material bulletMaterialPlayer;
7.      [SerializeField] private MeshRenderer bulletMeshRenderer;
8.
9.      public enum BulletInitiator
10.     {
11.         ENEMY,
12.         PLAYER
13.     }
14.
15.     private BulletInitiator initiator;
16.
17.     public void SetBullet(BulletInitiator bulletInitiator, int damage)
18.     {
19.         bulletDamage = damage;
20.         initiator = bulletInitiator;
21.         bulletMeshRenderer.material = initiator == BulletInitiator.ENEMY ? bulletMaterialEnemy : bulletMaterialPlayer;
22.     }
23.
24.     private void OnTriggerEnter(Collider other)
25.     {
26.             if(other.CompareTag("Enemy") && initiator.Equals(BulletInitiator.PLAYER))
27.         {
28.             //destroy the enemy
```

```
29.             other.GetComponent<Enemy>().ReduceHealth(bulletDamage);
        //add score
30.             GameManager.instance.AppendScore(1);
31.         }
32.         else if(other.gameObject.CompareTag("Player") && initiator.Equals(BulletInitiator.ENEMY))
33.         {
34.             //reduce health or game over
35.             other.GetComponent<Player>().ReduceHealth(bulletDamage);
36.
37.         }
38.
39.         // Initiate a simple puff particle
40.         Instantiate(bulletHitParticle, transform.position, transform.rotation);
41.         Destroy(gameObject);
42.     }
43. }
```

The bullet manages the following tasks:

- **Keeps track of the initiator of the bullet**: This is done using an **enum** called **BulletInitator** and a variable of the same **enum** type **initiator**. The **public** method **SetBullet** requests a **BulletInitiator** parameter to assign a value to the initiator.

- **Changes the material based on the initiator**: The **SetBullet** method will check what the initiator is and assign different materials. We can create a blue and a red material such that the enemy will spawn red bullets while the player would spawn blue.

- **Checks the collision**: We use **OnTriggerEnter** method in line 24, which is executed by Unity when there is a collision with triggers. Here, we check the **tag** associated with the other game object that the bullet collides with. Based on the **tag**, we specify whether it is the player or the enemy and provides damage by calling **ReduceHealth()** methods in both **Player** and **Enemy** components. However, we have not made those components yet. Let us talk about those methods when we get there.

- **Adds the score**: Every time the bullet hits an enemy, the script will call a function in a **GameManager** component to append the score by one. In line 31, we directly call the **GameManager().instance** and call its method instead of a direct drag-and-drop reference. We will talk about this in the *Game manager* section.

- **Spawns a particle prefab at the time of collision**: We use the **Instantiate** method to instantiate a bullet particle when the bullet collides with anything. Once done, the bullet will destroy itself.

Now attach the script to the bullet. You should probably see errors since we reference scripts that are not available yet. For the moment, you can comment on the lines in the script that contain calls to components that are not created.

In the inspector window, assign a bullet hit particle from the project window (**Asset package | Prefabs | BulletHit**), two materials for the player, and the enemy bullets (**Asset package | Materials | Enemy_Bullet/Player_Bullet**). Set the **Bullet** damage to 20 and assign the mesh renderer component of the bullet as the **Bullet** Mesh Renderer. The component should look as shown in *Figure 6.3*:

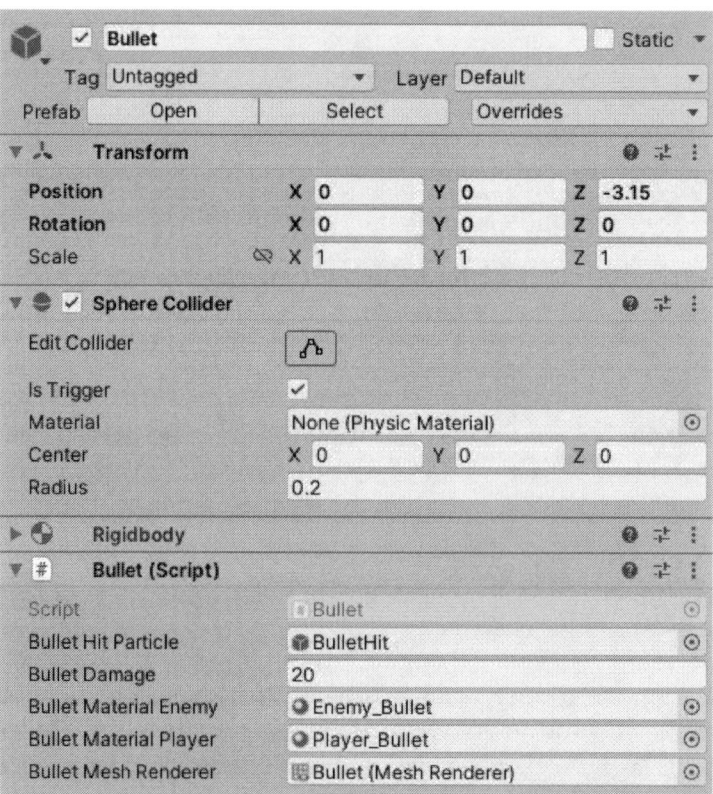

Figure 6.3: Bullet component attached to the bullet object

Additionally, select the collider of the bullet and tick **Is Trigger**.

Shooting bullets

As explained before, the bullets can be shot by two objects: the player and the enemy. For this section, let us see how to instantiate bullets and shoot at the enemy:

1. Before creating a new component for this, we need to convert the bullet into a **prefab**. Once done, you can remove the bullet from the scene.

2. Now create an empty game object within the player and move in front of the player. This is going to be a reference point for the bullet to be instantiated. Because the object is inside the **Player** as a child, it moves with the player.

3. Rotate the game object in a way that its local forward direction is pointing forward. The following *Figure 6.4* shows how the spawn point is added inside the player game object:

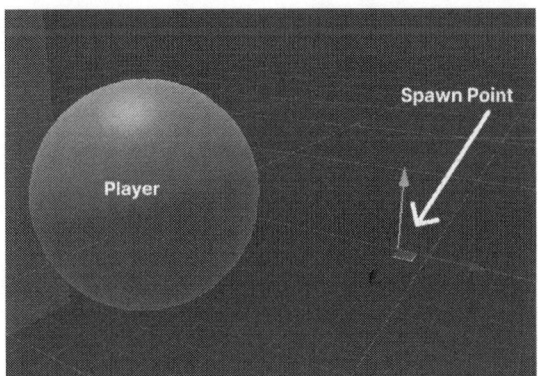

Figure 6.4: Player and the spawn point

4. Create a new C# script and name it **PlayerShoot.cs**. This component will instantiate and shoot bullets with a given frequency while the screen is being touched:

   1. `public class PlayerShoot : MonoBehaviour`
   2. `{`
   3. `    [SerializeField] private GameObject bulletPrefab;`
   4. `    [SerializeField] private Transform spawnPoint;`
   5. `    [SerializeField] private float shootFrequency;`
   6. `    [SerializeField] private float shootForce;`
   7.
   8. `    private float timer = 0;`

```
9.      private GameObject tempBullet;
10.
11.     void Update()
12.     {
13.         if(Input.touchCount>0)
14.         {
15.             Shoot();
16.         }
17.     }
18.
19.     void Shoot()
20.     {
21.         if (shootFrequency <= 0)
22.             return;
23.
24.         timer += Time.deltaTime;
25.         if(timer>= 1/shootFrequency)
26.         {
27.             tempBullet = Instantiate(bulletPrefab, spawnPoint.position, spawnPoint.rotation);
28.         tempBullet.GetComponent<Rigidbody>().AddForce(spawnPoint.forward * shootForce);
29.             tempBullet.GetComponent<Bullet>().SetBullet(Bullet.BulletInitiator.PLAYER, 20);
30.
31.             AudioManager.instance.PlaySFX("fire");
32.
33.             Destroy(tempBullet, 5);
34.
35.             timer = 0;
36.         }
37.     }
38. }
```

This component will check for the touch input and run a **Shoot()** method in the update loop. The shoot method contains a timer that increments and resets to 0 after each **1/shootFrequency** second. If the shot frequency is 2, the timer will reset every 0.5 seconds, and every time the timer resets, it shoots a bullet. Line 21 to 25 is used for the time increment and frequency check.

From line 27 to 29, we instantiate a bullet on the spawn point (transform reference variable) and add a force on the **rigidbody** component of it by getting the forward direction of the spawn point and multiplying it by the shoot force variable value. Finally, we get access to the **Bullet** component of the spawned object and set its values: the initiator and the damage.

In line 31, we have called an **AudioManager** to play a sound effect. We will talk about it at the end of the chapter. For the moment, we can comment out the line.

5. Before resetting the timer to zero, we register the bullet to be destroyed after 5 seconds. If we do not destroy it and if the bullet does not hit an enemy, it will be loaded into memory, which will increase memory usage and hinder the performance of the game. Therefore, we use the **Destroy** method with the temp bullet and the number of seconds as parameters.

6. Go back to Unity and assign this component to the **Player**. Drag and drop the **Bullet** prefab from the project window onto the **Bullet Prefab** option and the **BulletSpawn** game object onto the **Spawn Point** option. The following *Figure 6.5* shows a sample configuration to spawn 13 bullets per 10 seconds and a shoot force of 400:

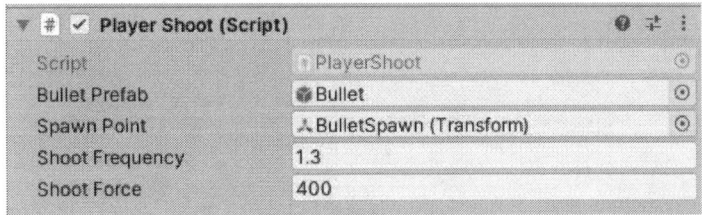

Figure 6.5: Player shoot component attached to the player

Setting up the enemy

We will set up the enemy with the most basic setup. Once the enemy is spawned, it will move in the forward direction with a given speed and shoot a bullet in random time frequencies. The enemy will have a health value that will be reduced when it collides with a bullet. If the health goes below 0, the enemy will explode and destroy. In order to indicate the enemy's health, we are going to use a simple world space canvas with a tiny health bar attached to the top of the enemy:

116 ■ *Mastering Augmented Reality Development with Unity*

1. Select the enemy game object we created before. Right-click and **Add UI | Canvas**. This will add a fairly big 2D element inside the enemy.

2. Change the scale of the canvas to 0.01. In the canvas component, change the render mode to `World Space`.

3. We will be adding two Image game objects in the canvas by using **UI | Image**. Name one as `HealthBarBackground` and `HealthBar`. For both images, set all the left, right, top, and bottom to 0 in the **Rect** transform component, 0 for Min and 1 for Max, while keeping the pivot to 0.

4. Now select the `HealthBar` and make sure that it is at the bottom. Select the **Image** component of it and change the **Source Image** to **HealthBar** sprite from the assets package (**UI Images | HealthBar**). Refer to *Figure 6.6*.

5. Set the **Color** to red and **Image** type to **Filled**. Change the **Fill Method** to **Horizontal**. Now if we change the **Fill amount** of the component, we will be able to see a small progress bar that would look like a mini health bar.

6. Position the canvas on top of the enemy in a way that it is visible from the top camera.

Refer to *Figure 6.6* to see the setting up of the health bar:

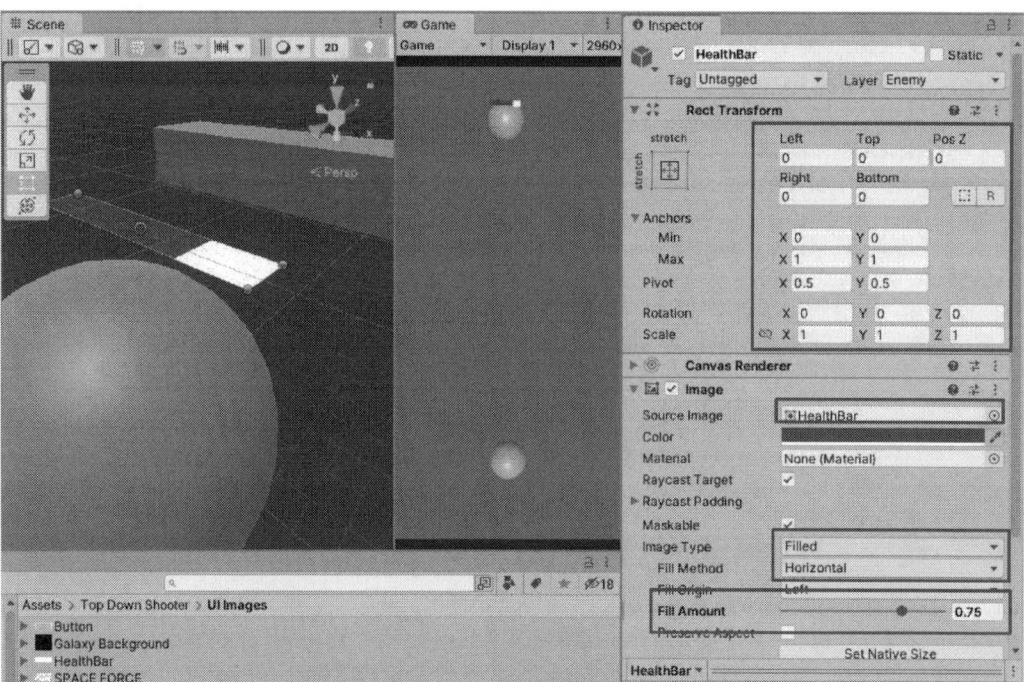

Figure 6.6: Setting up the health bar with filling UI image

7. Now like the player's spawn point, add an empty game object inside the enemy as well, and make sure that it is rotated towards the forward direction of the enemy. However, the enemy can look in the opposite direction as the player.

8. Create a new C# script and name it **EnemyMovement.cs**. Open it and add the following:

```
1.  public class EnemyMovement : MonoBehaviour
2.  {
3.      [SerializeField] private float enemySpeed;
4.
5.      private Rigidbody enemyBody;
6.      private Vector3 nextPosition;
7.
8.      public void SetSpeed(float speed)
9.      {
10.         enemySpeed = speed;
11.     }
12.
13.     public float GetSpeed()
14.     {
15.         return enemySpeed;
16.     }
17.
18.     void Start()
19.     {
20.         enemyBody = GetComponent<Rigidbody>();
21.     }
22.
23.     void Update()
24.     {
25.         nextPosition = enemyBody.position + enemyBody.transform.forward * enemySpeed * Time.deltaTime;
26.         Move(nextPosition);
```

```
27.        }
28.
29.        void Move(Vector3 target)
30.        {
31.            enemyBody.MovePosition(target);
32.        }
33. }
```

This script will capture a given speed and move the player in the forward direction. The next position of the enemy is calculated in line 25, where it adds a forward position multiplied by the enemy's speed.

9. We also add a couple of **set** and **get** methods to manage the **speed** variable. The rigid body added to the enemy will be cached at the **start** method using the **GetComponent** method.

10. In order to manage the rest of the enemy functions, create another C# script and name it **Enemy.cs**. Add the following:

```
1.  using UnityEngine.UI;
2.  public class Enemy : MonoBehaviour
3.  {
4.      [SerializeField] private int enemyHealth;
5.      [SerializeField] private GameObject bulletPrefab;
6.      [SerializeField] private Transform spawnPoint;
7.      [SerializeField] private GameObject destroyParticle;
8.      [SerializeField] private Vector2 bulletTime;
9.      [SerializeField] private Image healthUI;
10.
11.     private GameObject tempBullet;
12.     private EnemyMovement enemyMove;
13.     private float startHealth;
14.
15.     private void Start()
16.     {
17.         enemyMove = GetComponent<EnemyMovement>();
18.         StartCoroutine(ShootBullets());
```

```
19.      }
20.
21.      public void SetHealth(int value)
22.      {
23.          enemyHealth = value;
24.          startHealth = enemyHealth;
25.          UpdateHealthUI(1);
26.      }
27.
28.      public void ReduceHealth(int reductionAmount)
29.      {
30.          enemyHealth -= reductionAmount;
31.          UpdateHealthUI((float)enemyHealth / (float)startHealth);
32.          if(enemyHealth <= 0)
33.          {
34.              Instantiate(destroyParticle, transform.position, transform.rotation);
35.              AudioManager.instance.PlaySFX("explode");
36.              Destroy(gameObject);
37.          }
38.      }
39.
40.      private IEnumerator ShootBullets()
41.      {
42.          while (gameObject.activeSelf)
43.          {
44.              yield return new WaitForSeconds(Random.Range(bulletTime.x, bulletTime.y));
45.              tempBullet = Instantiate(bulletPrefab, spawnPoint.position, spawnPoint.rotation);
46.              tempBullet.GetComponent<Bullet>().SetBullet(Bullet.BulletInitiator.ENEMY, 20);
47.              tempBullet.GetComponent<Rigidbody>().AddForce(
48.                  spawnPoint.forward * enemyMove.GetSpeed() * 2,
```

```
                ForceMode.VelocityChange
49.                 );
50.                 Destroy(tempBullet, 5);
51.         }
52.     }
53.
54.     void UpdateHealthUI(float value)
55.     {
56.         healthUI.fillAmount = value;
57.     }
58.
59. }
```

In this script, we will be using **UnityEngine.UI** to manipulate the fill amount of the health bar. For initializing the health value of the enemy, the **SetHealth** method is added with a parameter. This will reset the start health of the enemy, as well as reset the health bar.

The **ReduceHealth** method in line 28 will take any amount as a parameter and reduce that amount from the current health of the enemy. If the current health is below 0, the enemy will be destroyed while instantiating an exploding particle and playing an audio effect. We can comment the line 35 for the moment. This method also will call the **UpdateHealthUI** method to change the health bar values.

UpdateHealthUI method changes the fill amount by getting the fraction of the current health from the start health of the enemy. This will give a value between 0 and 1 and will be used as the fill amount of the health bar.

ShootBullet() is an **IEnumerator** method that returns a yield. The yield can be represented as a wait. It can be dynamic or configured. Inside the **IEnumerator**, the loop will work indefinitely until the enemy is active. The loop returns a yield wait time which is a random number between the **x** and **y** values of the **bulletTime Vector2** method. We used a **Vector2** here to store two values in one variable.

Once the wait time is over, similar to the player, it will shoot a bullet by instantiating and adding force to the bullet while setting the damage and the initiator. The force of the bullet is calculated by doubling the speed of the enemy. **ForceMode.VelocityChange** will apply a force in a way that the starting velocity matches the value in the first parameter of **AddForce** method. We call this **IEnumerator** to run by initiating a coroutine, as in line 18.

11. Now select the enemy and add both **EnemyMovement** and **Enemy** components. Assign all the necessary references to the **enemy** component, as shown in *Figure 6.7*:

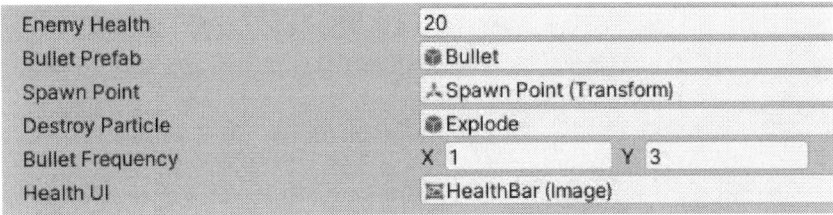

Figure 6.7: Enemy component

The **Bullet Prefab** is the same as players; **Spawn Point** is the empty game object within the enemy, and **Destroy Particle** as **Explode**, which can be found from the **asset package** | **Prefabs** | **Explode**, and the **Healthbar** is the **Image** game object added inside the health bar canvas.

Setting up the player

Now, let us finalize the player object by adding a new **Player.cs** script. Similar to the enemy component, this method will take care of the health of the player and end the game once the player gets destroyed. The player will immediately destroy if it collides with an enemy. Open the C# script and add the following:

```
1.  public class Player : MonoBehaviour
2.  {
3.      [SerializeField] private int playerHealth = 100;
4.      [SerializeField] private GameObject destroyParticle;
5.
6.      private void Start()
7.      {
8.          GameManager.instance.DisplayHealth(playerHealth);
9.      }
10.
11.     public void ReduceHealth(int reductionAmount)
12.     {
13.         playerHealth -= reductionAmount;
```

```
14.
15.          if (playerHealth <= 0)
16.          {
17.              Instantiate(destroyParticle, transform.position, transform.rotation);
18.              Destroy(gameObject);
19.
20.              // Game Over
21.              GameManager.instance.GameOver();
22.          }
23.          else
24.          {
25.              GameManager.instance.DisplayHealth(playerHealth);
26.          }
27.      }
28.
29.      private void OnCollisionEnter(Collision collision)
30.      {
31.          if(collision.gameObject.CompareTag("Enemy"))
32.          {
33.              // Reduce max health
34.              ReduceHealth(100);
35.          }
36.      }
37. }
```

In this component, we use the **GameManager** to set the display health in the UI and end the game. We will come to that later; for the moment, we can comment on the lines. Like the enemy component, the **ReduceHealth** method deducts the health from the player and destroys it once it reaches the 0-health limit. The **OnCollisionEnter** method will check if the player collides with the enemy and reduces the max health amount to immediately end the game.

Assign the player component to the player and assign the destroy particle (choose **Asset pack | Prefabs | Explode**). Now, we can uncomment lines 29 and 36 from the Bullet C# script.

Since all the base components are set up, we can convert the enemy into a prefab and remove it from the scene.

Spawning and destroying enemies

Now that we have the base enemy setup, we will be spawning and destroying the enemies. Create a new C# script and name it **EnemySpawner.cs** and open it:

```csharp
public class EnemySpawner : MonoBehaviour
{
    [SerializeField] private GameObject enemyPrefab;
    public bool isPlaying = true;

    private BoxCollider spawnArea;
    GameObject enemy;

    void Start()
    {
        spawnArea = GetComponent<BoxCollider>();
    }

    public void StartSpawning()
    {
        isPlaying = true;
        StartCoroutine(Spawner());
    }

    private IEnumerator Spawner()
    {
        yield return new WaitForSeconds(3);
        while(isPlaying)
        {
            SpawnEnemy();
            yield return new WaitForSeconds(Random.Range(1, 3));
        }
```

```
27.     }
28.
29.     void SpawnEnemy()
30.     {
31.         enemy = Instantiate(enemyPrefab, GetRandomPosition(), transform.rotation);
32.         enemy.GetComponent<EnemyMovement>().SetSpeed(Random.Range(1f, 10f));
33.     }
34.
35.     private Vector3 GetRandomPosition()
36.     {
37.         return new Vector3(
38.             Random.Range(spawnArea.bounds.min.x, spawnArea.bounds.max.x),
39.             Random.Range(spawnArea.bounds.min.y, spawnArea.bounds.max.y),
40.             Random.Range(spawnArea.bounds.min.z, spawnArea.bounds.max.z)
41.             );
42.     }
43. }
```

We are using the spawner cube we created earlier, and its box collider is bound to generate a random position to spawn the enemy. In line 36, we will create a **GetRandomPosition** method to generate a random **vector3** that values inside the collider bounds. We cache the box collider as the **spawnArea** from the **start** method.

Just like the enemy bullet shoot, we are using an **IEnumerator** here to initiate a coroutine. The **IEnumerator** will run while the **isPlaying** variable is **true**. **isPlaying** is a public variable that can be modified by a game manager component. The coroutine will spawn an enemy with a random speed, as stated in line 32 and 33. After every enemy spawn, the coroutine will wait for a random period before instantiating the next enemy.

Now attach the component to the spawner cube that we placed. Make sure that the box collider of the spawner is a **Trigger (Is Trigger | Ticked)**

Now that we can spawn enemies, there is a high chance that the enemies can bypass the player and be in the scene, even outside the camera bounds. Therefore, we need to destroy the enemies that go beyond the player. Just like the spawner, let us create another cube that is placed behind the player.

Create a new C# script and name it as **DestroyBounds.cs**:

```
1. public class DestroyBounds : MonoBehaviour
2. {
3.     private void OnCollisionEnter(Collision collision)
4.     {
5.         Destroy(collision.gameObject);
6.     }
7. }
```

This component will destroy any game object that it collides with. Add this component to the cube that we created.

Game UI

Now that we have all the game elements ready, it is time to put everything together to work. Before setting up the game manager, let us set up additional game objects in the scene.

1. Create a new **Canvas** object. In the **Canvas Scaler** component, change the UI scale mode to Scale with **Screen Size**. Inside the canvas, create two **Text-TextMeshPro** UI game objects. Import any additional packages if Unity requests to do so.

2. Now using the 2D mode and the **Rect** transform tool, place the text objects on top of the screen. These two text objects are going to show the current health and the score of the player.

3. Inside the canvas, create a UI panel and add a **Button** and a text object into the panel. Change the text to **GameOver**. You can also change the color of the panel to be semi-transparent black. Change the colors of the text objects as

required. *Figure 6.8* shows a sample configuration of the UI; in our case, a custom font was used for the sample project.

Figure 6.8: *UI of the game scene including the game over overlay*

Now deactivate the panel in the inspector window.

Game manager

Create a new C# script and name it as **GameManager.cs**. You may notice that it takes a new icon. Open it and add the following script:

```
1.  using TMPro;
2.
3.  public class GameManager : MonoBehaviour
4.  {
5.      public static GameManager instance;
6.
7.      [SerializeField] private TMP_Text scoreText;
8.      [SerializeField] private TMP_Text healthText;
9.      [SerializeField] private GameObject GameOverUI;
10.     [SerializeField] private EnemySpawner enemySpawner;
11.
12.     private bool isRunning = false;
13.     private int score = 0;
14.
15.     private void Awake()
16.     {
```

```
17.         if(instance != null && instance != this)
18.         {
19.             Destroy(this);
20.         }
21.
22.         instance = this;
23.     }
24.
25.     private void Start()
26.     {
27.         StartGame();
28.     }
29.
30.     public void StartGame()
31.     {
32.         isRunning = true;
33.         score = 0;
34.         enemySpawner.StartSpawning();
35.     }
36.
37.     public void AppendScore(int value)
38.     {
39.         score += value;
40.         scoreText.text = score.ToString();
41.     }
42.
43.     public void DisplayHealth(int value)
44.     {
45.         healthText.text = value.ToString();
46.     }
47.
48.     public void GameOver()
49.     {
```

```
50.          isRunning = false;
51.          GameOverUI.SetActive(true);
52.          AudioManager.instance.PlaySFX("gameOver");
53.      }
54.
55.      public bool IsRunning()
56.      {
57.          return isRunning;
58.      }
59. }
```

Game manager should be a component that can be referenced by any other component without assigning it manually. And also, there can only be one game manager in the scene. In order to overcome this, we can use a *Singleton* design pattern along with public access to its methods. In line number 5, we added a blank static object of the same **GameManager** variable called **instance**. Since this is a **static** variable, there can only be one variable as **instance** of type game manager, and any object can directly reference the instance by calling **GameManager.instance**. In the **Awake** method, we check if the instance has been assigned, and if so, any other duplicated game objects will be destroyed. If now, the only available **GameManager** instance in the scene will be referred to by the **instance** variable (line 22).

We are using TMPro since we use text mesh pro to update our health and score. The game manager can perform the following tasks:

- **Start the game**: In line 30, the **StartGame()** method resets the score, sets the **isRunning** variable to true, and requests the **enemySpawner** to start spawning enemies.

- **Append and display the score**: In line 37, the **AppendScore()** method requests an integer parameter and adds that value to the score. Also, it displays the score by changing the text of the **scoreText** Text Mesh pro referenced component.

- **Display the health of the player**: The player can call this method to update the current health of the player.

- **Ends the game**: Once the player is destroyed, the player can request the Game manager to end the game. In line 48, the **GameOver()** method sets **isRunning** to false, plays a Game over sound, and activates the **GameOver** UI panel that we deactivated in the scene.

Once the script is complete, attach that to a new empty game object in the scene. Rename the game object as **GameManager**. Drag and drop the necessary UI components from the scene view to the game manager.

Now that the game manager is ready, the game would still not work without adding proper tags. Select the **Layers** dropdown at the top right corner of the Unity editor window, and select **Edit Layers**, as shown in *Figure 6.9*. Now from the tree view, expand **Tag** and add the **Enemy** tag by clicking the plus button:

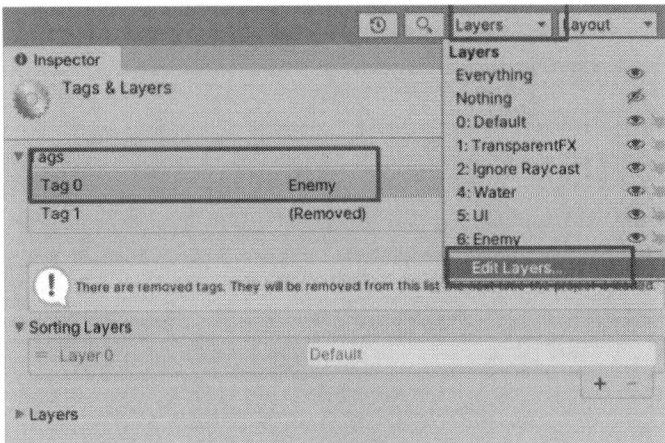

Figure 6.9: Adding new layers

Select the **player** object and assign the **Player** tag from the top of the inspector window. It is a dropdown right under the name of the game object. Similarly, select the **Enemy** prefab from the project window and assign the **Enemy** tag we previously created.

Finally, revisit the previous scripts and uncomment all the places where we commented the **GameManager** reference lines.

Adding audio and polishing

As you may have noticed, we have been calling a Singleton instance of the **AudioManager** and its **PlaySFX()** method from different other components. It is time to create that component and the relevant methods. Create a new C# script and name it as **AudioManager.cs**. Open it and add the following:

```
1.  public class AudioManager : MonoBehaviour
2.  {
3.      [SerializeField] private AudioSource foregroundAudioSource;
4.      [SerializeField] private AudioClip shootSFX, explodeSFX, buttonClick, gameover;
```

```
5.
6.      public static AudioManager instance;
7.
8.      private void Awake()
9.      {
10.         DontDestroyOnLoad(gameObject);
11.
12.         if (instance == null)
13.         {
              instance = this;
14.         }
15.         else
16.         {
17.             Destroy(gameObject);
18.         }
19.     }
20.
21.     public void PlaySFX(string name)
22.     {
23.         switch (name)
24.         {
25.             case "button":
26.                 foregroundAudioSource.PlayOneShot(buttonClick);
27.                 break;
28.             case "fire":
29.                 foregroundAudioSource.PlayOneShot(shootSFX);
30.                 break;
31.             case "explode":
32.                 foregroundAudioSource.PlayOneShot(explodeSFX);
33.                 break;
34.             case "gameOver":
35.                 foregroundAudioSource.PlayOneShot(gameover);
36.                 break;
```

```
37.                default:
38.                    break;
39.            }
40.        }
41. }
```

Similar to the game manager, the **Audio** manager also can be referenced by other components without a manual drag and drop of any other methods. However, this component awake method is a little bit different, as it is a **DontDestroyOnLoad()** method. This will keep the game object without destroying it, even if we change the scene. This will become handy for us in the next stage.

Moreover, instead of checking whether the instance is assigned, here we check whether it is not assigned and immediately assign it. Any other **AudioManager**s in the scene will be destroyed immediately this way, as well as prevent this from duplicating when you keep coming back to the first scene. Loading the same scene will duplicate the **AudioManager** object's game object due to **DontDestroyOnLoad()**.

In order to play the audio, we need an **AudioSource** component and references to a set of **AudioClips**. Since this is a small game, we use 4 different sound effects, as you can see in line 4.

The **PlaySFX()** method takes a string as the parameter, and based on the value, it plays the selected audio clip just once by using **PlayOneShot()** method.

We will not be attaching this to our **Game** scene. Instead, we are going to create a new scene for the main menu and have it there.

Adding the main menu

In your scenes folder of the project window, right-click and select scene to create a new scene. Rename it as **MainMenu**. Also, rename your game scene as **Game**. Now follow the given steps:

1. Double-click and open the **MainMenu** scene.
2. This scene will only use a canvas with the name of the game and a button to load the game. Create a new **Overlay** canvas and change the UI Scale mode of this to **Scale with Screen Size**.
3. Inside the canvas, add a UI Image. Use the **rect** tool to scale the image to cover the whole canvas. You can use the **Galaxy Background** image from the asset pack as the background.

4. Now add a new **Image** object inside the canvas. Use the **SPACE FORCE** image in the UI **Images** folder of the `asset` package. You can use the anchoring points to anchor the title image to the center.

5. Similarly, add a button and change the text inside the button to **PLAY**. You can also use the **Button** image in the asset back as the button background button. Once done, change the image type of the button's **Image** component to Slice. Once everything is set up, the final result should be as shown in *Figure 6.10*:

Figure 6.10: Main menu setup with images and other manager game objects

Now, it is time to set up the audio manager. To set up the audio manager, follow the given steps:

1. As in the preceding figure, create an **Empty game** object for the **Audio Manager**, and add two more empty game objects to play the background music and the SFX.

2. Select the background game object and do the following in the inspector window:

   a. Add an `AudioSource` component.

   b. Assign the `BackgroundMusic` audio clip from the asset pack as this `AudioClip`.

c. Enable **Play on Awake and Loop**.

d. Select the SFX game object and add an **AudioSource**—Disable **Play on Awake**. We will be using this audio source to play all the SFX.

3. Now select the main **AudioManager** game object and add our **AudioManager** script component.

4. Assign the SFX game object's audio source as the **Foreground Audio Source**. Now you can assign other audio clips as per the component references. The Asset pack contains sound effects for shooting, explosions, button clicks, and game over.

Switching scenes

Finally, we need a way to switch from one scene to another. This is to be performed by the **PLAY** button in the main menu and the **MENU** button in the game scene. To be generic, let us create a C# script and name it **SceneChanger.cs**:

```
1.  using UnityEngine.SceneManagement;
2.
3.  public class SceneChanger : MonoBehaviour
4.  {
5.      public void ChangeScene(string sceneName)
6.      {
7.          SceneManager.LoadScene(sceneName);
8.          AudioManager.instance.PlaySFX("button");
9.      }
10. }
```

Once the script is created, follow the given steps:

1. We will be using the **SceneManager** by Unity to switch the scene by the name of the scene. Additionally, we call the **Audiomanager** to play the button sound effect.

2. Go back to unity, attach this component to a **Manager** empty game object, and select the Play button.

3. In the button component under **OnClick()** event, click the **+** (plus) button and drag and drop the **Manager game** object on top of **None(Object)** prompt.

To the right of the event, the drop-down list will show all the components attached to the **Manager** object, including the `SceneChanger` component. Select it and choose the `ChangeScene()` method.

4. Now since the parameter requests a string, the UI will show a text box to add the name of the scene. Since we want to switch to the Game scene, type **Game** in the text box. The event should be as shown in *Figure 6.11*:

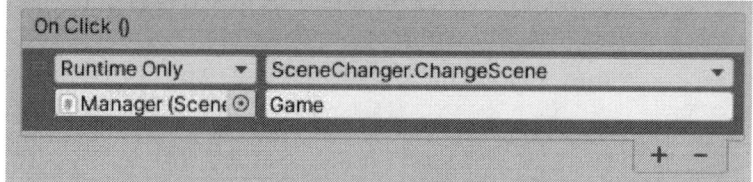

Figure 6.11: Using OnClick unity event

5. Now go to the **Game scene**, select the **Menu** button in the game over panel, and assign the same with a manager game object in the **Game scene**.

6. The `SceneManager` uses the scenes listed in the build settings in order to switch from one to another. Therefore, we need to add both scenes to build settings.

7. Click **File | Build Settings**.

8. From your project window, drag and drop the Game and the `MainMenu` scene into the Scenes in the **Build** panel. Make sure to keep the `MainMenu` scene on top of the list.

The next steps

Now we are almost ready. We can click play from the main menu and play the game. However, the models do not look nice, and the liveliness of the game is not yet achieved. The final finished project comes with the book has additional features added to the game, such as:

- Auto-scrolling background in the game view.
- 3D models for enemies and the player.
- Adding difficulty by increasing the health of enemies over time.
- Spawning different enemies with different strengths.

Refer to *Figure 6.12*:

Figure 6.12: Final completed project gameplay

Conclusion

In this chapter, we went through the process of adding game objects, developing C# scripts that work with each other, design patterns, using prefabs with collisions, simple scoring mechanisms as well as touch input. In our next chapter, we will learn to build the game on Android and Apple devices and to play properly with the touch input. From the next chapter onwards, this book will not prioritize Unity editor interactions and instead focus more on AR integrations with Unity.

Key points

- Instantiate method is used to spawn game objects in the scene.
- **OnCollisionEnter** method detect collisions if a **rigidbody** and a collider are present in both objects.
- **OnTriggerEnter** detects triggers that do not have a force impact.
- Any game object can be converted to a prefab and can be instantiated from the project window during run time.

- Input-based methods can be used in update methods to capture mouse and touch inputs.
- **IEnumerators** can be used to run coroutines within Unity which works similarly to parallel processes alongside the main application.
- Game UI can be an overlay or world space. Overlay UI's render in screen space, while the world space UI uses the 3D scene to render the UI elements.
- The audio source can play one audio clip at a time.
- Buttons in unity use `UnityEvents,` such as `OnClick,` to capture events and execute methods directly from the inspector window.
- Unity UI images can use filled, tiles, stretched, and sliced methods to present the final texture.

Multiple choice questions

1. **What is the purpose of using the `[SerializeField]` attribute in Unity scripts?**
   a. It allows a variable to be visible in the inspector window and be editable.
   b. It makes a variable private and inaccessible from other scripts.
   c. It automatically initializes a variable with a predefined value.
   d. It forces a variable to be updated every frame.

2. **In Unity's Image component, what does the fill amount property represent?**
   a. The current opacity level of the image.
   b. The percentage of the image's visibility on the screen.
   c. The amount of memory used by the image asset.
   d. The fill level or progress displayed within the image.

3. **Which Unity function is used to detect collisions between two `GameObjects` with colliders?**
   a. `OnTriggerEnter`
   b. `OnTriggerExit`
   c. `OnCollisionEnter`
   d. `OnCollisionExit`

4. In Unity, how can you play an audio clip only once using the `AudioSource` component attached to a `GameObject`?
   a. Call the `PlayOneShot()` method on the `AudioSource` component.
   b. Attach an `AudioListener` component to the `GameObject`.
   c. Call the `PlayOnce()` method on the `AudioSource` component.
   d. Instantiate the audio clip and attach it to the `GameObject`.

5. What is the purpose of Unity's Scene Management system?
   a. To manage the rendering of objects in the scene.
   b. To control the lighting and shading of the scene.
   c. To handle interactions between different scenes in the game.
   d. To manage the physics simulations within a scene.

Answers

1. a
2. d
3. c
4. a
5. c

Join our book's Discord space

Join the book's Discord Workspace for Latest updates, Offers, Tech happenings around the world, New Release and Sessions with the Authors:

https://discord.bpbonline.com

CHAPTER 7
Trying Out First 3D Mobile App Development

Introduction

In the previous chapter, we learned how to develop a simple mobile game using the Unity engine. Further, we covered the basic components and the steps of creating custom C# components. However, we did not test the game on a mobile device to check the touch input. In **Augmented Reality** (**AR**) application development, one of the major steps is to iteratively test the application on actual devices for usability as well as optimization. The way the app features in the development environment will never be the same as on an actual mobile device.

In this chapter, we are going to go over the steps of building the mobile application on Android and iOS devices. We will be going through the necessary tools we discussed during *Chapter 4: Up and Running with Unity 3D* prior to development. Furthermore, the debugging steps required to check the status of the app while running on mobile devices will be discussed as well. Since our game was not an AR application, there are some additional steps required for such builds, which we will go over in other chapters.

Structure

In this chapter, we will discuss the following topics:

- Unity build settings

- Android build settings
- iOS build settings
- Building unity apps
  - Building for Android
  - Building for iOS
- Unity script debugging with Visual studio
- Debugging the app for both platforms

Objectives

After completion of this chapter, you will be able to optimize and build for mobile devices that run on Android and iOS operating systems. You will also be able to connect your devices to the computer and debug your code and test for complications. Additionally, you will be able to connect script debugging tools to Unity directly to test your code more effectively.

Unity Build settings

Let us now discuss Android build settings as well as iOS build settings. These settings are used to customize the build such as the build tools, icon and splash screen information, scaling information, rendering, operating systems and devices-based features.

Android build settings

In *Chapter 4: Up and Running with Unity 3D*, we discussed installing the necessary tools to build Android apps using Unity. The Android development architecture allows the **Software Development Kit (SDK)** and the **Native Development Kit (NDK)** to be used by other applications, such as Unity, to build the app from within. In the previous chapter, we opened the build settings folder to add the necessary scenes for the scene manager.

Go to **File | Build Settings**.

From here, you must switch to the platform you want to build the app for. However, switching is not necessary to set up the build settings. For this section, select **Android** and check the settings. However, before moving to the settings in this window, we need to click the **Player Settings** button at the bottom left corner of it.

You can also open this window by going to **Edit | Project Settings** and choosing the **Player** tab from the left sidebar.

The player settings consist of shared settings across all the platforms, such as the name of the app, the version, the developer's name, and the icon. You can add the information you prefer, including the icon. If you can access the shared assets, use the **ICON** texture in the `Textures` folder.

Underneath the shared settings, you can see the icon tabs of the platform modules you have installed with Unity. Click the **Android** tab and check the settings for Android, as shown in *Figure 7.1*:

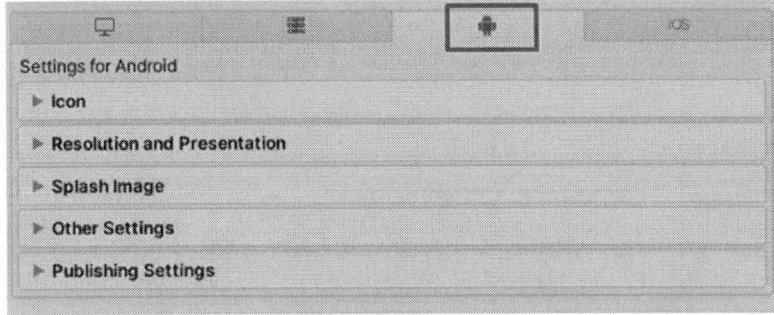

Figure 7.1: Android tab of the Build settings window

Icon

This is important if you need different icons for different devices with various screen sizes. Like the shared settings icon, you can upload different icons that match several resolutions, as requested by the interface.

Resolution and presentation

This defines how your screen should be when you build it on an Android device. There are various options to enable and disable full-screen window mode, hide the navigation bar, and forced aspect ratios. You may need to keep the default settings except for the **Orientation** and allowed orientation. Usually, it is better to lock the orientation of AR apps to portrait, as it allows users to view a large AR viewport through the screen. This also depends on your application. In this scenario, we need to enable only portrait rotation. You can lock this to just one orientation or allow auto-rotation and tick only **Portrait** and **Portrait Upside Down** options. Refer to *Figure 7.2*:

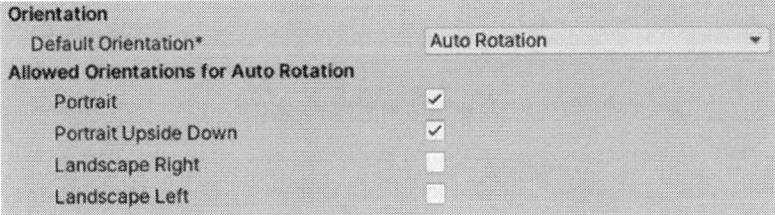

Figure 7.2: Resolution and Presentation section of Build settings

Splash image

Unity has a default splash with its logo. You can remove it if you have a paid Unity license. However, there are a few customizations that you can make to add your logo alongside Unity, as well as to change the background colors. We can leave them on default settings for now.

Other settings

This is the most important section when it comes to building AR applications. Many settings can be left as default, but this section will point out the necessary settings required to build AR apps for Android.OS Choose the following for the options under **Other settings**:

- **Rendering | Color Space:** Set this option to Linear color space.
- **Rendering | Graphics APIs:** Currently, many Android-based AR SDKs do not support Vulkan or OpenGLES2 graphics API since they are upgraded to the latest. Select them and click the "-" button underneath to remove it. Only keep OpenGLES3 available. If you do not see any of these options, untick **Auto Graphics API** over it to make them visible.
- **Identification | Package Name:** This is the unique package name for your project. When you upload it to any app store, it is going to use this to uniquely identify your app. There cannot be two apps under the same package name. Therefore, enter a unique value here. Usually, it is recommended to use `com.companyname.appnickname` to make it unique easily. A sample identifier we can use is `com.indikawijesooriya.spaceforce`.
- **Identification | Versions:** If you need to update the app for the next versions, you can use this to add the version as a meta value. This will help you recognize the latest build version of your app.
- **Identification | Minimum API level:** Android keeps on updating its operating systems, and each operating system has its own API level. Depending on the hardware and software capabilities, different OS versions do not support AR applications. Some APIs discontinue their support for newer features. Currently, the minimum API required to build an AR app is limited to API Level 25 (Android 7.1 Nougat). If your app is not an AR one, you can choose the default version to build the app. However, devices with a low OS version will not be able to run your app.
- **Configuration | Scripting backend:** Many recent Android devices now support the 64-bit architecture. In order to support the 64-bit hardware, the compiling must be done by a backend that supports it. The default Mono can be used only to create Armv7 architecture-based apps for Android. Therefore, change it to **IL2CPP**.

- **Configuration | Target Architectures:** When you switch to IL2CPP, you will get the option to choose the target architecture. Only select **ARM64** since AR apps will not work with any other architecture.

- If the app does not require any AR capabilities, we can use Mono and Arm v7 as the scripting backend and the target architecture.

Publishing settings

Android uses a *keystore* to sign the app when building. The signing binds a certificate made by the developer, which can be used to recognize who built the final executable file. This is used by the app stores to verify the developer. Currently, the Google Play store has the capability to manage the key stores within its developer console. Once an app is signed with a certificate, every new update should be signed using the same certificate.

You can leave this as it is if we are just testing the app on our phone. This uses a debug key and a certificate which is already there in your computer. If you use a different computer to build the app, the debug key certificate would be different, and the app cannot be considered as an update even if it is the same project.

You need to make a new key if you want to upload this app to the app store. For Android, Unity has created the necessary interfaces to create our own keystore for an app.

If you are hoping to publish the build in an app store, click the **Keystore Manager** button to launch the keystore window, as shown in *Figure 7.3*. Here, you can load an existing keystore file or create a new one. It is recommended to use one key per application within a keystore and save it securely within your secure repositories. You can also password-protect the keystore. Once the keystore is saved, you can add keys to the store. These keys can then be used to sign your app. Refer to *Figure 7.3*:

Figure 7.3: Steps to create and setup an Android sign key

In *Figure 7.3*:

1. **Keystore Manager** is used to create a new keystore and a key.
2. Choose an existing keystore with its passkey.
3. Add the password to authenticate the key loaded from the keystore.

Add new key values and load them to sign your app. Always keep in mind that once an app is saved using a key, the same key must be used for further updates. Once the keystore is loaded, you can use the loaded key under the **Project Key** section. Select the key and add the password to authenticate the signature.

Additionally, more settings may help you customize the manifest of your Android app. Since Unity manages the manifest of your application, we can leave the settings as default for now.

If your app size is large, you can **Split application binary** to build the app in multiple parts. This allows app stores to distribute an app in chunks rather than streaming a large app file. If you plan to build a large AR app that could be uploaded to the Google play store, it is recommended to enable **Split application Binary** at the bottom of the **Player settings** section.

iOS build settings

Compared with Android, iOS build settings are different. Apple has not provided an SDK to use their APIs to build the iOS app on their behalf. Instead, Apple requests the final build as an XCode project to build and deploy to devices. All the settings for icon, resolution, and splash image is similar for Android. Therefore, let us look at the other settings section in the iOS tab of the player settings.

Identification | Bundle Identifier

This property is similar to the Package name property in Android. You can use the same identifier here since it is the same app on different platforms. For iOS, each version can have multiple build numbers for testing purposes. Usually, a developer build is given a unity incrementing number for a specific version.

Identification | Provisioning profile and Signing team ID

Apple manages the keys and certificates in the device keychain. This is similar to Android Keystore, but it cannot be made within Unity. For development purposes, you can use your Apple ID to test the app on your devices. But if you need to publish your app in the app store, a developer account with a team ID should be obtained from Apple developer connect. Since that is out of the scope of this book, we will leave that option for now.

Configuration | Target Device, SDK and minimum iOS version

Currently, any AR app that uses ARKit must be over iOS 11.0. AR apps cannot be run on an iOS simulator. Therefore, it is good to keep *Device SDK*. If you want the app to be installed only on several device types, such as the iPhone and the iPad, you can select the target device option here as well. For the moment, we can keep them as default.

Configuration | Camera Usage Description

Any app that uses the camera must add a camera request message to request the user to allow camera usage. Similarly, it goes to location usage as well as microphone usage. Since AR app requires the camera to work, we must add a camera usage description to show the message to the user. We do not need to add anything for the space force project, but a similar message for the description can be, *we are using your camera to enable Augmented Reality support.*

Configuration | Requires AR Kit support

This is not needed for any app that does not require AR Kit. For the Space force project, we can leave it. But when we go through the AR Foundation section, we must enable AR kit support to allow the camera to work in our app.

These are the necessary settings that we can set up from the Unity side. However, for iOS, some changes can be made after building the XCode project. We can explore that in the next section of this chapter.

Building Unity apps

Now that we understand the different necessary settings required to build Android and iOS applications let us go through the process of building and loading the app on your devices. Both devices use different methods for the build process. Let us start with Android.

Building for Android

When building for Android, it creates an Android package file, also known as an **APK file**, which can be loaded and installed on your Android device. You can also use the

146   ■   *Mastering Augmented Reality Development with Unity*

Build and run method, which uses the **Android Device Bridge** (**ADB**) to connect to your device over a cable or Wi-Fi, to install and launch the app without touching the APK file by ourselves. For the purpose of understanding both the options, let us built it in both ways.

Building for Android without ADB

Open the build settings window. Make sure that your current target platform is Android. If not, select **Android** and click **Switch Platform** at the bottom of the window. After a while, your project will be ready to be built.

Ensure that the scenes in build are properly listed and ticked in the window, and click the **Build** button at the bottom with default settings. Now this will ask for a folder location to save the APK file. Choose a location and a name (the name here is not important; it can be anything like **build.apk** and so on) and click **Save**, as shown in *Figure 7.4*:

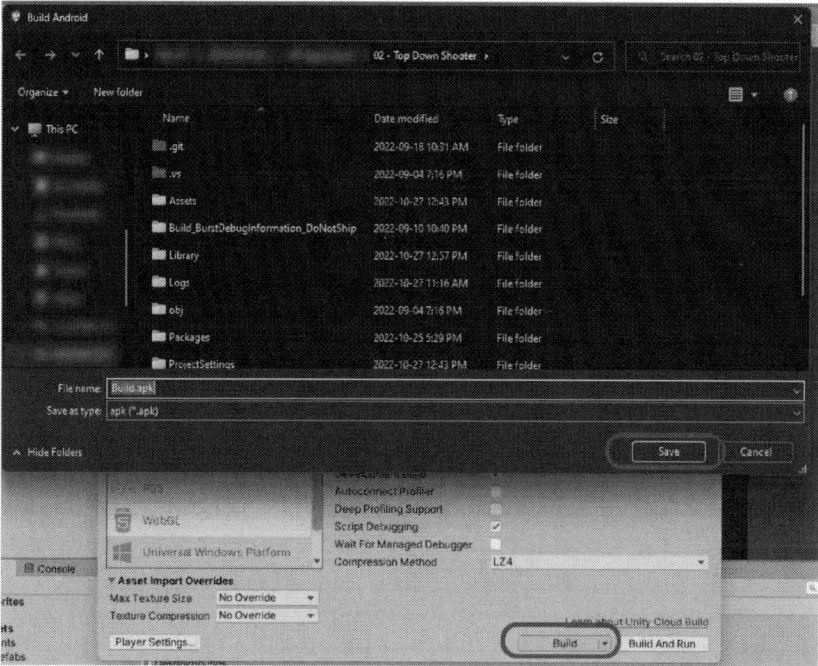

Figure 7.4: Saving an Android build APK

If you are building this app for the first time, Unity may take some time to compile your assets and scripts. Once the process is completed, you will have a **build.apk** file saved at the location you gave before.

Now, connect your Android device, copy the APK file into it, and open it in a file browser. By default, Android has locked the capability to install apps from third parties. Therefore, you will be redirected to enable **Unknown Sources** to install this application on your device.

Figure 7.5 shows how to enable unknown sources and the prompt you get when you tap on the `build.apk` from within your file manager:

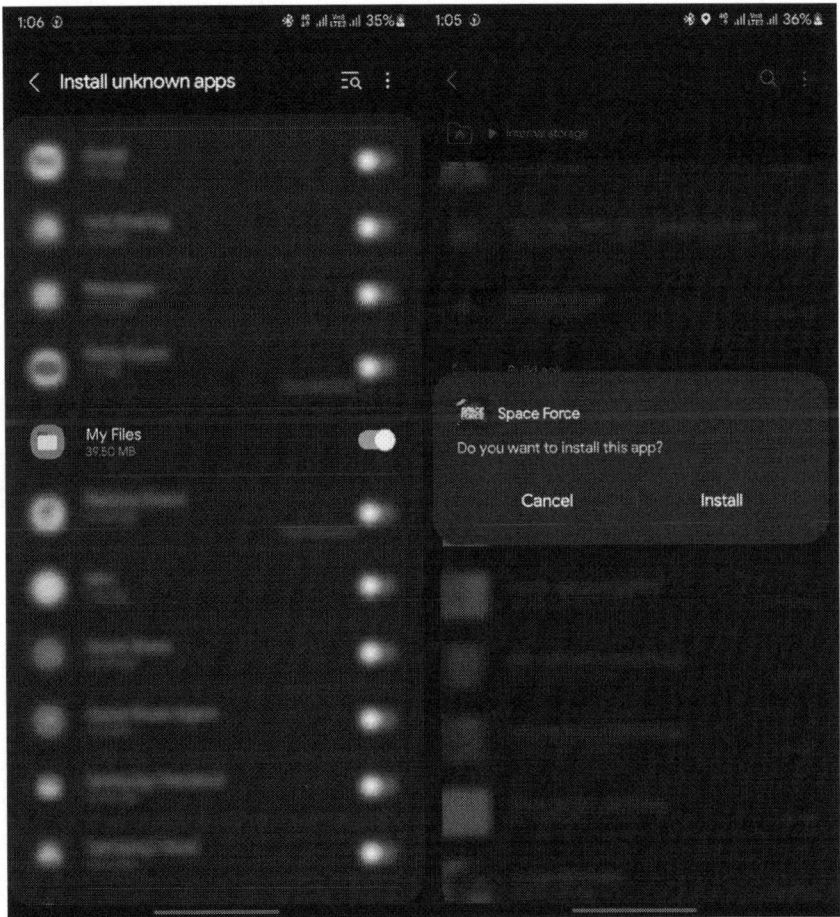

Figure 7.5: Enabling USB Debugging on Android

Now, this process will be overwhelming when we want to iteratively test the app on our device. Therefore, a quick way is to directly build and install the app on our device. In order to enable this, we need to enable the developer settings of our device. To do this, check the following steps. These steps, however, can be slightly different based on the Android device manufacturer and the model:

1. In your Android device, go to **Settings** and find the **About Phone** section.
2. Find something that says, **Build Number**. This can be inside the **About Phone** section or inside another menu, such as software information.

3. Now tap on the build number 5, 6 times until you see a small message at the bottom which says **Developer mode enabled**.

4. Now, go back to settings, and you will see the **Developer** options at the bottom. Open it and enable **USB Debugging**. Make sure that you turn it off when you are not developing since it can lead to security issues if your device is lost.

5. Now, connect your device using a USB cable. It will show a message on your mobile screen to allow USB debugging with the computer. Allow it and click the refresh button in the build settings window, right next to the **Run Device** drop-down.

6. Now select **Build and Run**. Choose the location to save your APK file and click **Save**. This will take the same build process, but it will launch the app directly on your device, and you will be able to test it seamlessly. Refer to *Figure 7.6*:

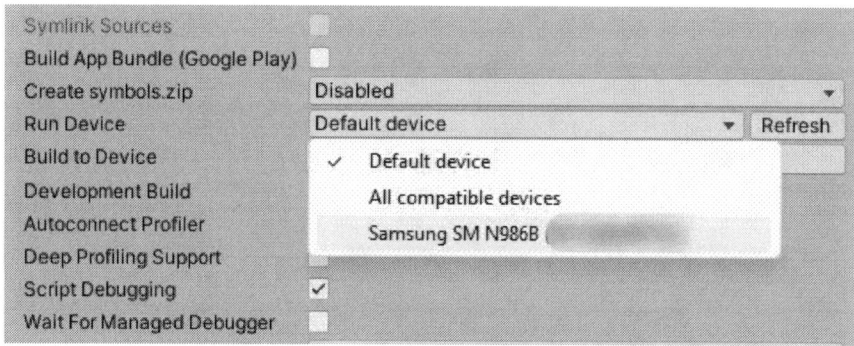

Figure 7.6: Choosing the connected Android device to build and run

If you are building to test iteratively, you can directly select **Build and Run** from the **File** menu without opening the build settings window.

Building for iOS

Unlike Android, building for iOS requires a Mac OS device and XCode installed along with it. Depending on the plugins we install in Unity, we may require installing additional packages into XCode as well. Fortunately, the AR SDKs we use throughout this book will not require additional Xcode-based pod packages.

1. Similar to Android, open up **Build settings** and switch the platform to iOS for building. We can also select **Build and Run** here, but it is safe to do a manual build once to set up the build certificates using XCode.

2. Select the **Build** button to initiate the build process. You can choose a new folder to export the build. Unlike Android, this will not give a single executable file to install. Instead, it will generate the XCode project to build the app another time to run on a device/emulator.

3. Once the build process is completed, go to the build folder and open **Unity-iPhone.xcodeproj** XCode project file, as shown in *Figure 7.7*. This will open the XCode project generated by Unity:

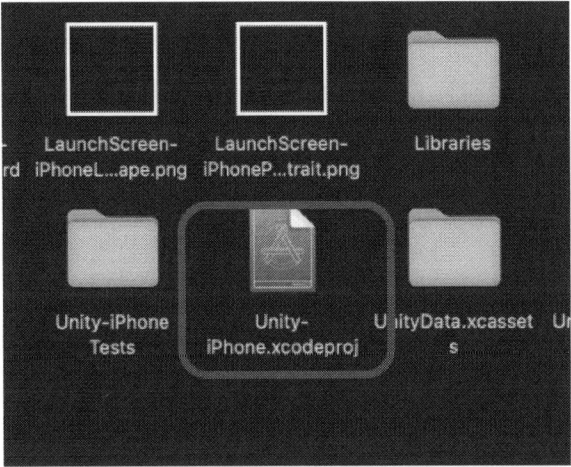

Figure 7.7: *The XCode project built by Unity*

4. Once the XCode project is open, head over to the **Unity-iPhone** in the left side tab, as shown in *Figure 7.8*. Select **Signing & Capabilities** tab in the middle view and select **All** from the window underneath.

5. Now tick on the **Automatically manage signing** option and enable automatic signing. Make sure the bundle identifier is correct. Once you have enabled the tick box, select a team. If you are logged in to XCode with your Apple account, you will be able to see your name and **(Personal Team)** right next to it. Refer to *Figure 7.8* to verify the flow:

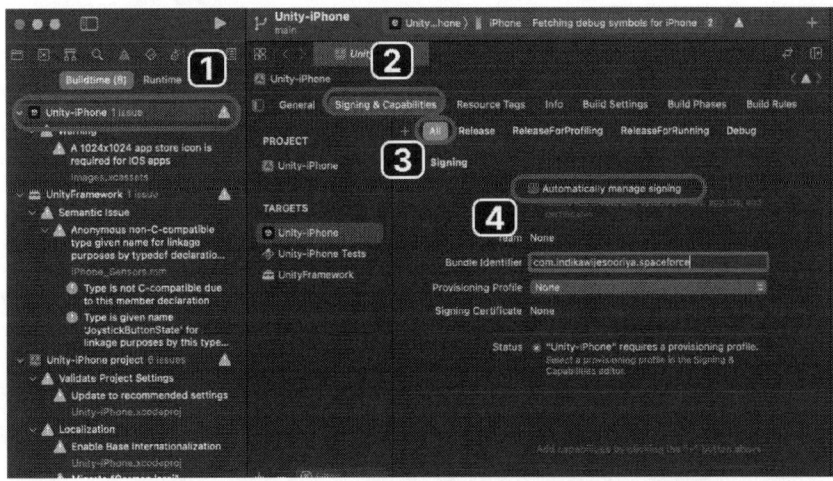

Figure 7.8: *Signing an iOS app with a certificate before building*

6. Once you select this for the first time, XCode will generate a certificate for you. Now, connect the iOS device to your MacBook using the cable.

7. Select your device from the top breadcrumbs bar, as shown in *Figure 7.9*:

Figure 7.9: Breadcrumbs bar

8. Then, click on the **Play** button, as shown in *Figure 7.10*:

Figure 7.10: Play button

This will initiate a secondary build process, which generates an IPA file, which will be automatically installed on your Apple device. Launch it, and once launched, you can see the Debug log within XCode itself. Let us discuss it in the next section.

Unity script debugging with Visual studio

Now that we know how to build and run an app on your mobile devices that you developed using Unity, let us take a step back and look at how to properly debug your codes with Unity and Visual Studio. Script debugging allows us to check for issues in our code and the status of the variables properly. This can be done in development time using both Windows and Mac environments. Follow the given steps:

1. For this exercise, let us use the **Game Manager** script and check the `AppendScore(int)` method we created in the previous chapter.

2. Double-click and open the **Game Manager** script.

3. In order to check and debug a certain line of code, we need to create a `breakpoint`. Click on the leftmost column on the `score+=value` line of `AppendScore` method until you see a circle under the mouse pointer. Click it, and it will make a breakpoint. Now, when the game is running, and it reaches this point, the game will pause, and you will be able to analyze the code and variable values in that line.

4. Once you make the breakpoint, select **Attach to Unity** from the top panel. This will initiate debugging and connect to Unity (in macOS, you need to click the play button in Visual Studio). Now go back to Unity and click the **Play** button.

5. *Figure 7.9* and *Figure 7.11* show below how to add breakpoints and attach them to Unity:

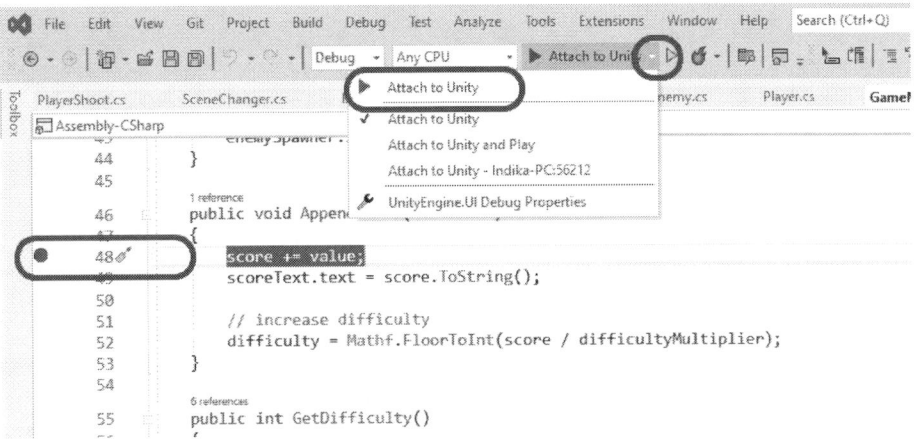

Figure 7.11: Script debugging on Visual Studio – Windows

Refer to *Figure 7.12*:

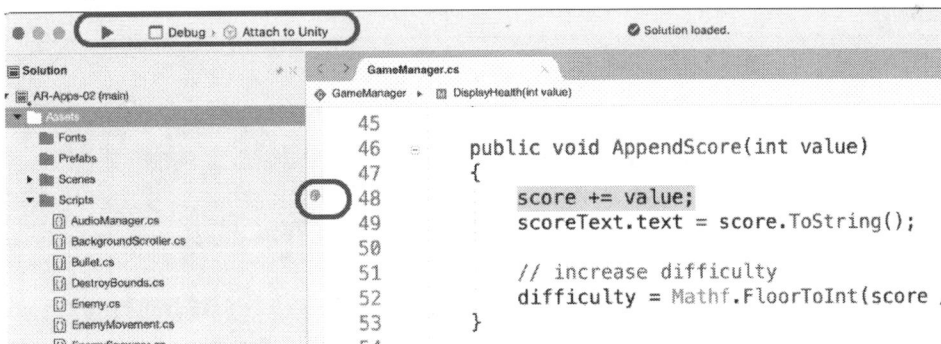

Figure 7.12: Script Debugging in Visual Studio – MacOS

Now when you take a score, the game will pause and will launch Visual Studio with the current status of the game at that point. You will be able to see all the components attached to the game object and the values of each variable.

This will become very useful when your project has scaled, and you need to understand how the scripts behave. *Figure 7.13* shows how the debug view is represented in Visual Studio when the game hits a breakpoint:

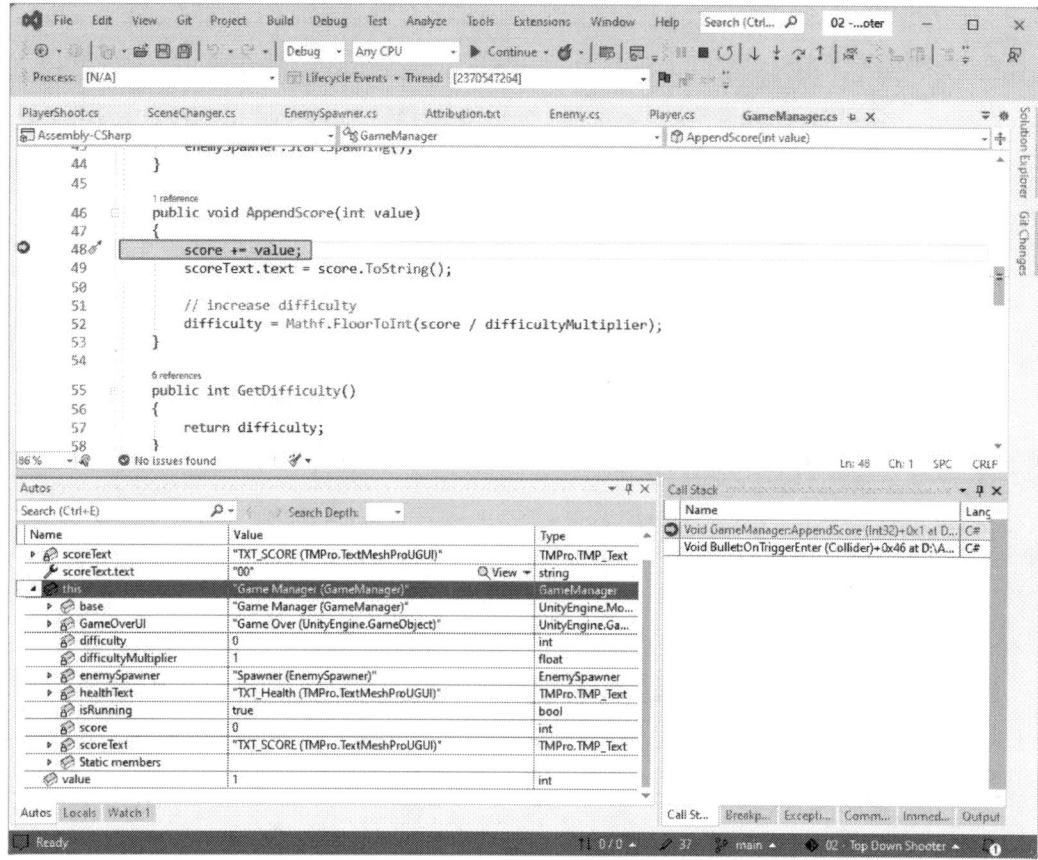

Figure 7.13: Debugging a Breakpoint at Runtime

Debugging the app for both platforms

One of the challenges in developing mobile applications is the limited ability to debug what happens when the app runs off the development environment. In this section, let us go through some of the tools that are available for both iOS and Android platforms to view the console log while the app is running on the device.

Using the ADB console for Android

Unity comes bundled with the Android SDK, which includes the Android device bridge tool to connect and push data into the device. We can use the same to open the console log, also known as the logcat, which logs details of every process on the device. However, we can use certain parameters to filter the data log, only to show any log from our app. Follow these steps:

1. Connect your Android device running the Unity app we created to your computer.

2. In Unity, go to **Edit | Preferences** (in MacOS, it is **Unity | Preferences**). Select External tools and scroll down to the **Android SDK path**. Click **Copy path.**

3. Now open the Windows terminal or MacOS Terminal. Open the path you copied by this command. Make sure to add **\platform-tools** to the end of the copied path:

    cd <<The path you copied>>\platform-tools

4. Now type the following:

    ./ adb logcat -s Unity ActivityManager PackageManager dalvikvm DEBUG

This will show a complete real-time log of your device and only log lines containing the above-mentioned keywords. Whenever your game prints something on the console, you can view it through the log.

Using the XCode Console for iOS

Compared to Android, XCode provides a cleaner log-checking system by immediately opening the console within XCode as soon as it starts running on the device. When you connect your device and click the play button to build the app onto the device, you can see the filtered console log on XCode until you click the stop button.

Conclusion

In this chapter, we discussed the fundamentals of building and testing your mobile application on your mobile phone, which runs either Android or iOS. We also went through debugging basics and explored the console log out of the Unity editor. This will help us easily look for issues that you may encounter when the AR apps run on your mobile phones.

Key points

- There are different build settings requirements for different operating systems.
- Unity used the Android SDK directly to build and install the app on a mobile phone.

- Unity exports an XCode project which can be later customized, signed, and deployed on an iOS device.
- Visual Studio debugger can be connected with Unity to test and debug the code at runtime.
- Console log can be viewed using the ADB logcat and XCode runtime console

Questions

1. What is the tool used by Unity to build for Android?
2. What should be enabled in an Android device to seamlessly deploy the app directly from Unity?
3. What is a necessary step in XCode before building the app on an iOS device?
4. What should be placed in Visual Studio to check a certain script line in scrip debugging?

Answers

1. Android SDK.
2. Developer options and USB Debugging.
3. Sign it with a certificate.
4. A breakpoint.

Join our book's Discord space

Join the book's Discord Workspace for Latest updates, Offers, Tech happenings around the world, New Release and Sessions with the Authors:

https://discord.bpbonline.com

CHAPTER 8
Building Marker-based AR Apps with Vuforia

Introduction

In the previous chapters, we were introduced to AR, 3D development concepts, Unity 3D, C# development with Unity, and debugging and building applications for mobile platforms. This will be the first chapter to introduce core AR development concepts throughout the book.

In this chapter, we will be building AR projects which use the *Vuforia Software Development Kit*. We had a quick introduction to Vuforia in *Chapter 3: Exploring Tools and Development Platforms*, but in this chapter, we dive into marker-based AR app development with Vuforia, considering different kinds of markers, identification-based events and finally, building a simple AR treasure hunt game which involves physical marker-based tracking for clues.

Structure

In this chapter, we will discuss the following topics:

- Introduction to Vuforia
- Using image targets
- Using cylinder targets

- Using multi targets
- Development of an AR treasure hunt game

Objectives

After completing this chapter, you will be able to design and develop marker-based AR apps for mobile devices. Not only will this allow the users to scan, but it will also help you learn to develop logic around marker-based AR recognition, such as tracking and losing events. Additionally, you will learn different tricks to design illusions around augmented reality.

Introduction to Vuforia

As mentioned in *Chapter 3: Exploring Tools and Development Platforms*, Vuforia is one of the leading and oldest marker-based AR SDK providers in the world. Their SDK supports both iOS and Android, as well as any other device with a web camera, and it does not rely on hardware limitations. Therefore, we are able to test and run any AR application within the development environment just by using a webcam.

Create a Vuforia developer account and login

Vuforia is a third-party library. Therefore, it allows developers to develop and publish applications without paying for the SDK, but charges for commercial and industry-related applications. Vuforia offers different license categories, which vary with their business goals. However, any AR application that uses Vuforia should register and obtain a license key to authenticate it for use. This requires registering on their platform. Follow the given steps:

1. Go to **https://developer.vuforia.com/**.
2. Click **Register** and create a new account using your email address. You can use the same link to log in to the license dashboard.
3. Once logged in, you will be redirected to the **License Manager**. This is the page you need to use to buy premium licenses or get a basic developer license.
4. Click the **Get Basic** button to create a new license key.
5. Now add a name for your license key, tick the developer agreement box, and click **Confirm**.
6. Once done, you will be able to choose the selected license and copy the license key. Depending on the Vuforia version, the services they offer for the basic license could differ. However, always allows standalone AR tracking for unlimited number of markers.

Downloading and installing the SDK

To download and install the SDK, follow the given steps:

1. Now, click on the **Downloads** tab and download the Unity Vuforia package. As of writing this book, the latest version of the SDK is 10.11.

2. Create a new Unity URP 3D project.

3. Import the Unity SDK package by either double-clicking or dragging the Unity package into your project or choosing the **Assets | Import Package** menu.

4. This will install Vuforia SDK in your packages folder. If you are using Git version controlling for your projects, you may have to add the SDK archive to your `.gitignore` file or enable **Git Large File Storage (Git LFS)** or; otherwise, there will be problems in pushing your updates to the repository. This archive is over 250MBb and may not be compatible directly with Git.

5. Once the package is installed, go to **Window | Vuforia configuration**.

Figure 8.1 shows the configuration page for Vuforia. Under the **Global** category, you will be able to see an input for **App License Key**. Copy the license key we created from the developer account and paste it here. Now your application is ready to work with AR:

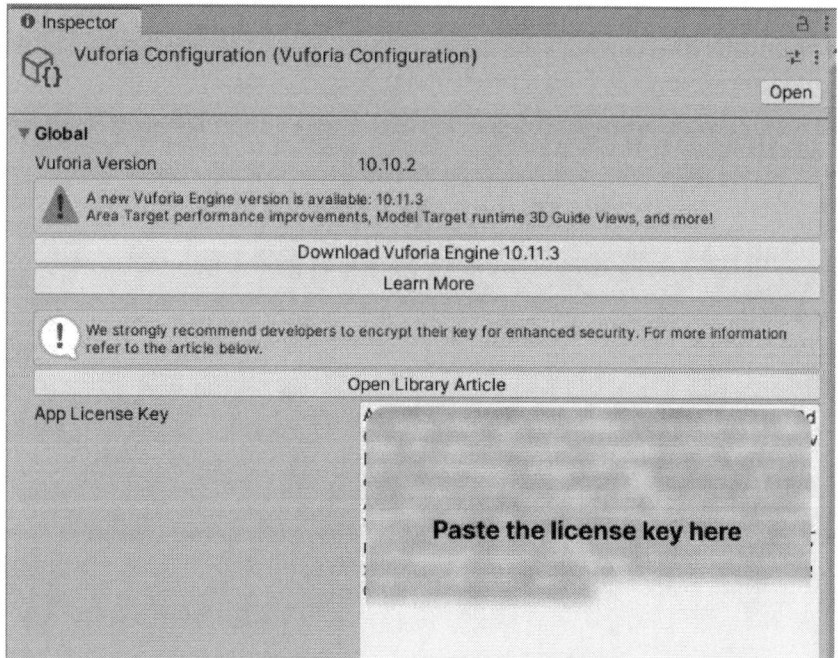

Figure 8.1: Adding the Vuforia license key

If you are paying for a license key, adding the key to this window is not secure. Moreover, if you are hosting the project in a shared repository, sharing keys will exploit them, and therefore, they must be kept outside of your project. You can use C# to load the key from an external file and load it before the runtime in order to avoid any of your keys being exposed to unauthorized access.

You can create a script as follows to load the license key from an external source securely and add it in an **Awake** method:

1. `void Awake()`
2. `{`
3. `  VuforiaConfiguration.Instance.Vuforia.LicenseKey = "MyLicenseKey";`
4. `}`

Setting up a basic AR scene

There are two main game objects required to set up the most basic AR scene:

- AR camera
- A trackable to track something in the space

To set up a basic AR scene, follow the given steps:

1. Create a new scene and remove the **Main Camera**. We will be replacing that with an AR camera, which is the same main camera but with additional components.
2. Right-click an empty area in the hierarchy and select **Vuforia Engine | AR Camera**.
3. This will create a new AR camera in your scene.
4. Now right click again and choose **Vuforia Engine | Image Target**.
5. Now, you have a basic blank AR setup with an **Image Target**. You can click **Run** to play, and this should open up your webcam in the game view as the background. If you get a black screen, make sure that you have given proper access to the webcam by selecting the **Camera Device** in the **Play Mode** section of **Vuforia Configuration** window, as shown in *Figure 8.2*:

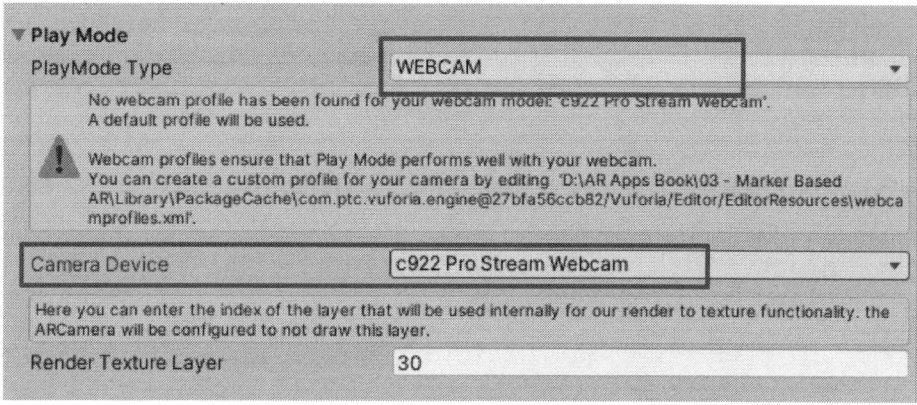

Figure 8.2: Changing the camera to run Vuforia in the editor

Using Image Targets

There are multiple ways how an image target can be loaded into the project:

- Database method
- Image method

If you need to quickly prototype with any image target, you can choose the **From image** option when you add a Vuforia image target `GameObject` into your scene. However, you will not know the number of features and the tracking ability of the image. The database method is relevant to generating pre-trained targets that have proven tracking ability.

To get an AR marker running with a 3D model, follow the given steps:

1. Import an image into your project. This figure also should be printed and be with you physically to test it. Usually, a book cover with an image works well. For this section, we will be using the following *Figure 8.3* as the target:

Figure 8.3: Image Target (plane marker)

2. Select your **Image Target** in the hierarchy, drag and drop the image from the project window onto the **Image** property in **Image Target Behaviour** component. You can also specify a unique name for the target name. Now, you will see the Image target representing the same image you added.

3. Now, right click the **Image Target** and add any 3D object. For this exercise, we will be adding a sphere with a scale of 0.1. Move the sphere above the image target so that it looks as if it is on top of the figure.

4. Once everything is set up, the configuration is as shown in *Figure 8.4*:

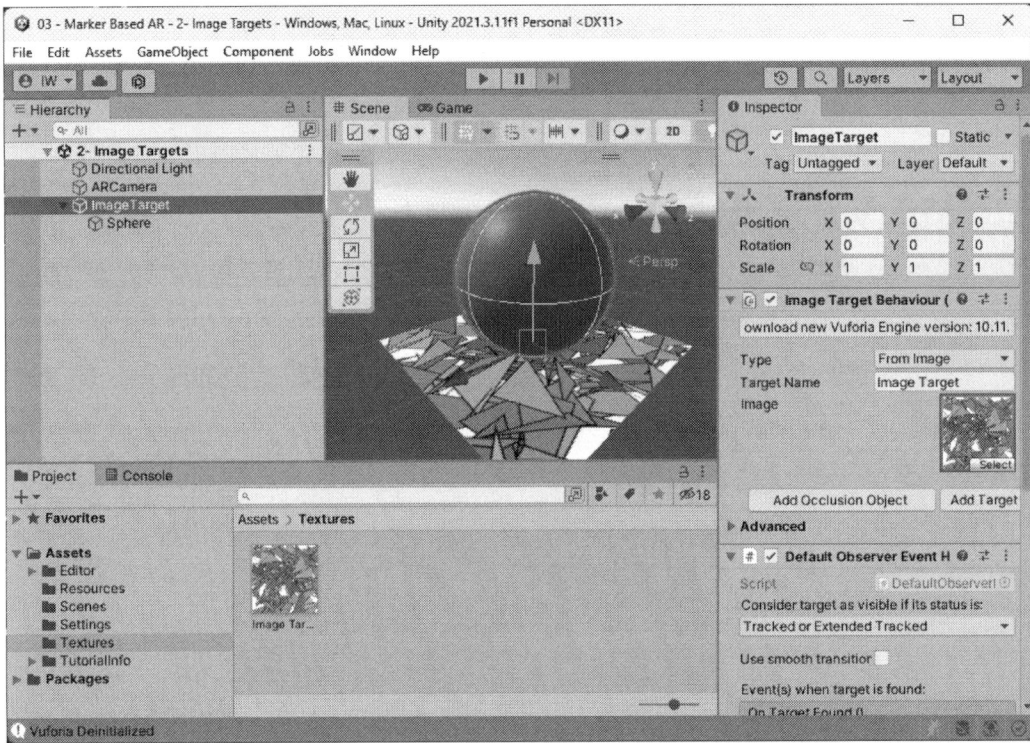

Figure 8.4: Vuforia Image Target implementation

5. With Vuforia, this is all you have to do in order to get an AR marker running with a 3D model. Click the **Play** button, and show the same marker physically to the camera, and you will see a sphere appearing on top of the figure, as depicted in *Figure 8.5*:

Building Marker-based AR Apps with Vuforia ■ 161

Figure 8.5: Result of Vuforia Image Target

Now, let us see how to use the database method to add an image target. Follow the given steps:

1. Go to your Vuforia console and select the **Target manager** tab.

2. In this tab, we can create marker databases. In this chapter, let us create a new database by pressing the **Add Database** button.

3. Once pressed, add a name to your database without spaces and choose **Device**. A device database will generate a list of images that can be integrated into the application. We will further discuss Cloud and VuMark in the next chapter.

4. Now select the database you created. Here, we can upload different types of targets alongside Image targets. Click on the **Add Target** button.

5. Make sure that the **Image** option is selected. Browse and choose the image target, add the width of the target (in meters), add a name, and click the

Add button. For this section, we will be using two different image targets, as shown in *Figure 8.6*:

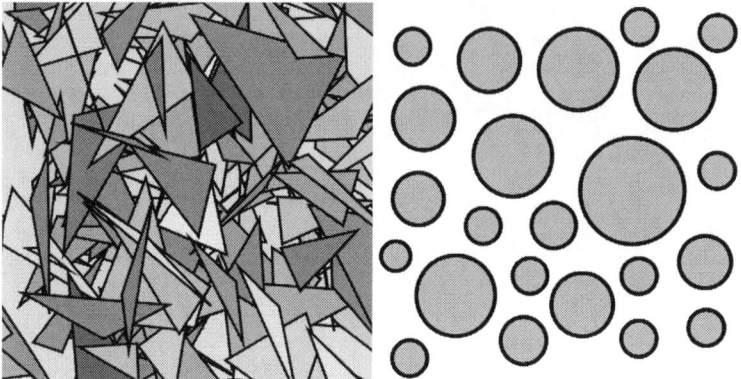

Figure 8.6: Image target with good features (left) and not enough features (right)

6. Once both of them are uploaded and processed, check the database table, and focus on the rating column. You may see that the first one has 5 stars while the second one with circles has just one star.

7. Go into each target by clicking on the name and select the **Show features** option at the bottom of the image target. You will be able to see a number of unique features that the algorithm has identified. In *Chapter 1: Getting Started with Augmented Reality*, we discussed the underlying technology of tracking features instead of a figure. Vuforia uses a similar algorithm, and the database visually shows how each target is seen by the AR SDK. Feature distribution and the star ratings of both are presented in *Figure 8.7*:

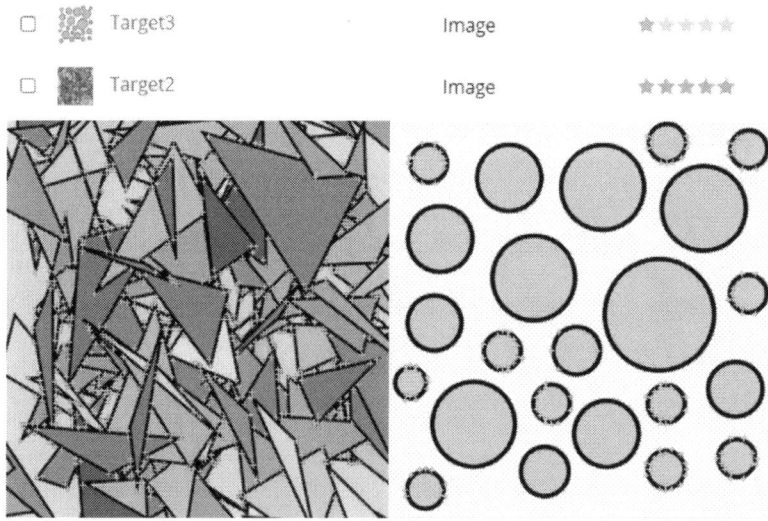

Figure 8.7: Image target feature distribution

Keep in mind that any target with a lower rating will have a hard time being recognized and tracked by Vuforia. Vuforia recommends at least 4 stars for an AR application to track the images seamlessly.

Choosing the best markers/targets

As we saw in the previous section, the rating of the image target depends on the number of trackable features of the image. There are some best practices we need to follow in order to get the best results. Some of them are as follows:

- Pointy corners of the shapes are better features than rounded features of the image. This is purely visible in *Figure 8.7*.

- The features are enhanced more if the contrast of the image is higher, as can be seen in *Figure 8.8:*

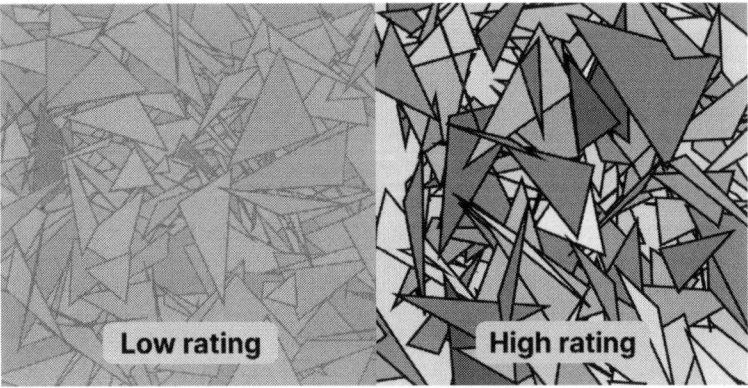

Figure 8.8: Contrast check for image targets

- The features should be distributed throughout the whole image, as shown in *Figure 8.9:*

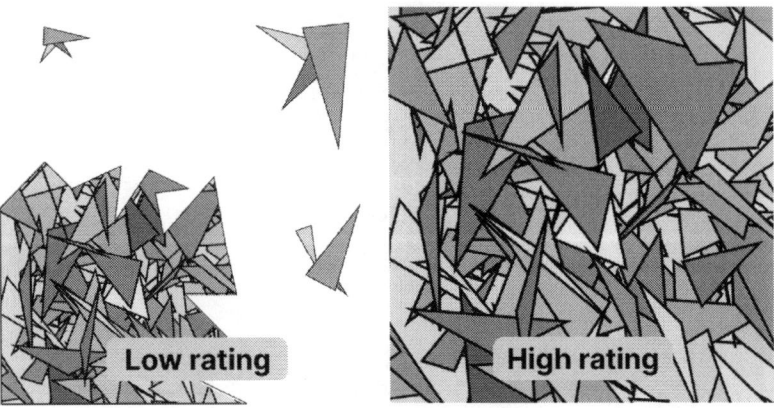

Figure 8.9: Image target feature distribution comparison

- Patterns with similar features are hardly recognizable since the algorithm cannot define the corners of the marker figure. Refer to *Figure 8.10*:

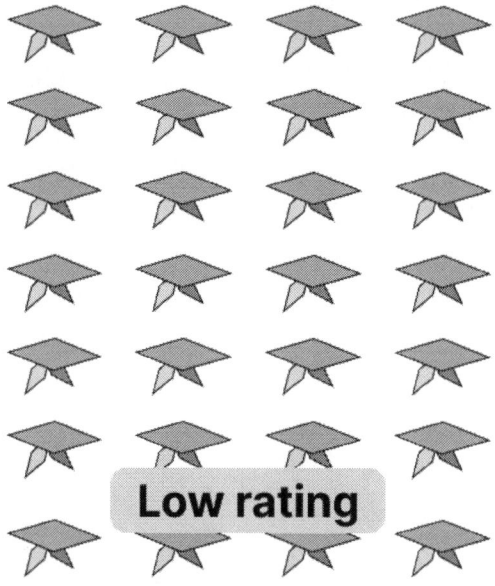

Figure 8.10: Pattern distribution

- Non-rectangular images perform less compared to rectangular images, as can be seen in *Figure 8.11*:

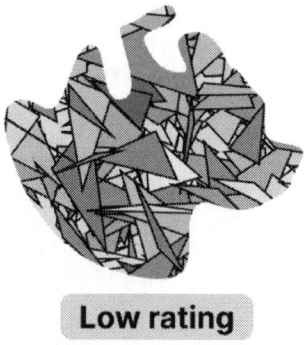

Figure 8.11: Example of a non-rectangular target

Additionally, Vuforia has a descriptive list of all the best practices in the following link: **https://library.vuforia.com/objects/best-practices-designing-and-developing-image-based-targets**

If your application uses only Image targets, you can easily use the asset library of your project instead of the online database library. Although you will not get an insight into how the target would perform, it will be easier to quickly drag and drop the image from the project window to the component. To do that, simply set the **Type** under **Image Target Behaviour** to **From Image** and add the image under **Image** field, as shown in *Figure 8.12*:

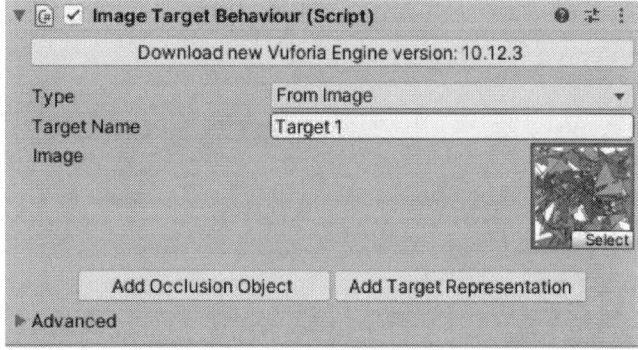

Figure 8.12: Using an image target directly within Unity

Additional features of Image Targets

Imagine that your AR effect requires your 3D models to be hidden under the image. However, just placing the 3D object on top of the image target and moving it under the target will not hide it. This is because the AR effect will only consider the physical target as a reference, and it will not occlude the tracker. Therefore, you will be able to see the object under the target image. This can be resolved by the following methods:

- **Adding an occlusion object:** By clicking on the **Add Occlusion Object** of the **Image Target Behaviour** component, Unity will add an invisible plane on top of the target image and align it. This invisible plane will hide anything that is under that plane. This is done using an occlusion material added to the invisible plane:

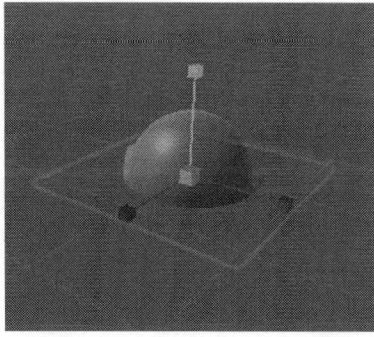

Figure 8.13: Occlusion object to cover the other side of the image target

- **Adding a similar target image**: By clicking on the **Add Target Representation**, Unity will add an image similar to your target image on top of the target. This way, a similar image will be tracking the image target hiding anything underneath.

- **Scan multiple image targets at once**: You may realize that you can add more than one image target, but only one gets scanned at a time. This can be changed by going to **Window | Vuforia Configuration** and changing **Max Simultaneous Tracked Images** from 1 to the number you want.

Note: Higher the number of multiple image targets that is defined to track, higher the processing power it requires to check for image targets. Therefore, use it only when necessary and use the minimum number of targets that your project can scan.

Using cylinder targets

Vuforia SDK can recognize cylinder targets in addition to image targets. Imagine your AR application requires the user to scan a beverage tin can to trigger a 3D animation on top of it. This is comparatively harder to achieve with a flat 2D image used as a target. The cylinder target method in Vuforia matches the curvature of the cylinder-shaped object to match your virtual objects perfectly. *Figure 8.14* is a still image of an AR game known as **Beer invaders** made by `immertia.io` which uses a similar tracking system to detect the beverage can:

Figure 8.14: Sample Cylinder target implementation.
Source: Beer invaders (https://immertia.io/beer-invaders/)

As for the next step, we will use the following sample beverage can in *Figure 8.15* to implement a cylinder scan. Compared to an image target project, this can be troublesome since the images that we upload to Vuforia should exactly match the label of the curved cylinder beverage. The cylinder object we are using in this project has a circumference of 1000 units at the edges. The height of it is 451.85 units with respect to the circumference. The diameter of the circle was taken as 318.31 units. However, these values should be measured and used according to the size of the cylinder shape.

Additionally, you must have the labels around and the sides of the cylinder. Vuforia cylinder tracker can not only scan perfect cylindrical objects, but also cone-shaped objects as well. Therefore, the label dimensions should be added with the correct unit measurements. Refer to *Figure 8.15*:

Figure 8.15: Sample Cylinder target

Source: *"Soda Can" (https://skfb.ly/6WTvu) by Sunich is licensed under Creative Commons Attribution (http://creativecommons.org/licenses/by/4.0/).*

Follow the given steps:

1. Go to the **Target manager** of Vuforia portal and click **Add Target**.
2. Select the **Cylinder** option for the **Type** and add the correct dimensions in units and name the target with a proper name. In Vuforia, the units are in meters, so once imported into Unity, the size can be big. You can add the dimensions

by scaling them uniformly. Refer to *Figure 8.16*. The object will be scaled within Unity once imported:

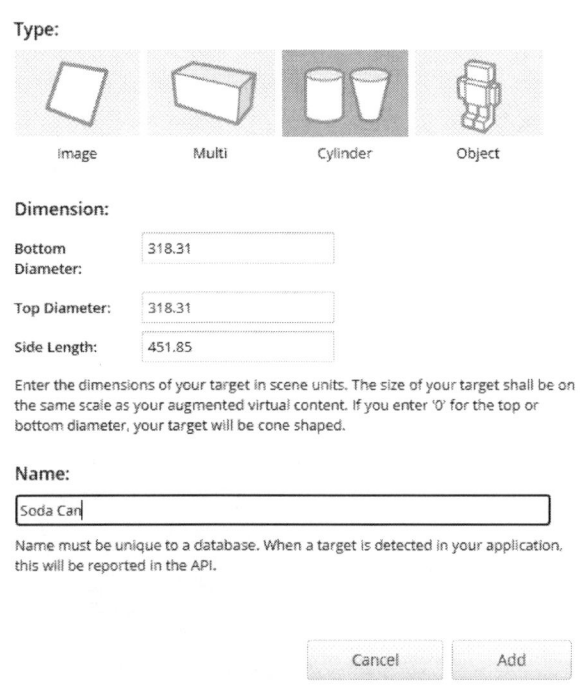

Figure 8.16: Adding a new cylinder target

3. Once added, the list of targets will be populated with a new cylinder target without previews. Click on the name of the marker and open the 3D view of the cylinder target. This is where we upload the side label image and the top and bottom images. Click on each button on the right side of the 3D viewport and add the images. In this case, we added blank grey images to the top and bottom, since our object does not have any textures for them. The final 3D viewport looks as shown in *Figure 8.17*:

Figure 8.17: Cylinder target preview

4. Now, go back to the target manager and download all the targets for Unity.
5. Import the **unitypackage** to Unity and update the Vuforia marker database.
6. Now, along with the AR Camera, add a **Cylinder Target** by going to **Game Object** Menu | **Vuforia Engine** | **Cylinder Target**.
7. If you have imported the database correctly, the cylinder target will be populated and will be added to the scene. If you have multiple targets, you will be able to choose them from the **Cylinder Target Behaviour** component. If you have added high values when creating the target, the size of the target object within Unity will be enormous compared to other objects. It is not recommended to scale a Vuforia target. The best way to scale it down is by expanding the **Advance** section of the cylinder target behavior and changing one value by dividing any number. Other values will change proportionally. *Figure 8.18 (1)* shows how we divided the units by 100 and changed the values to scale down the Cylinder target.
8. Also, as shown in *Figure 8.18 (2)*, we added a simple low poly tree group around the cylinder to appear when tracked. However, the cylinder would not be there when we scan it. Therefore, the trees on the other sides will be visible on top of the actual cylinder target. As explained in the previous section, we can add an occlusion object or a target presentation to occlude the behind of the cylinder object and make it believable when tracked:

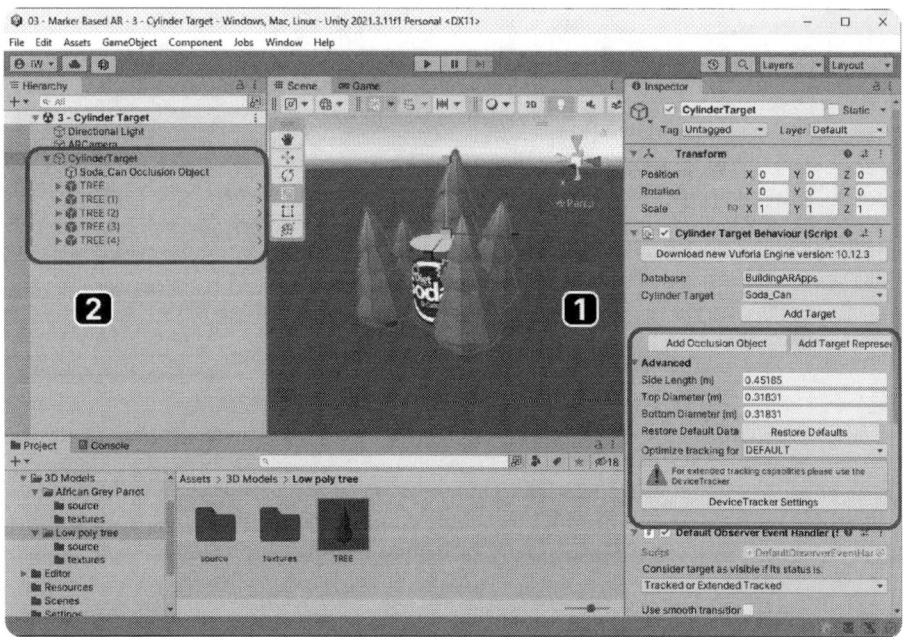

Figure 8.18: Adding AR content to appear around a cylinder target.

Source: *"Low Poly Tree Concept"* (https://skfb.ly/6VosA) by sycoinc is licensed under Creative Commons Attribution (***http://creativecommons.org/licenses/by/4.0/***)

9. Now once you click **Play**, and scan the can with the camera, the trees would appear around the cylinder. Minor adjustments to the scale of the cylinder can be made by changing the scale of the tracking objects and the occlusion object. *Figure 8.19* shows the sample output of the cylinder can being scanned:

Figure 8.19: Demonstration of Cylinder target tracking

Using Multi targets

Multi targets in Vuforia are similar to cylinder targets but allows multiple image targets to work around a single cubic object. A multi target object has width, length, and a height. A multi target can be used to spawn AR content on top of, or around a box shaped object such as a packaging box.

Similar to how cylinder targets are added, the developer must enter the dimensions of the cubic object to create a multi target. In *Figure 8.20*, you can see how to add them to create a new multi target reference:

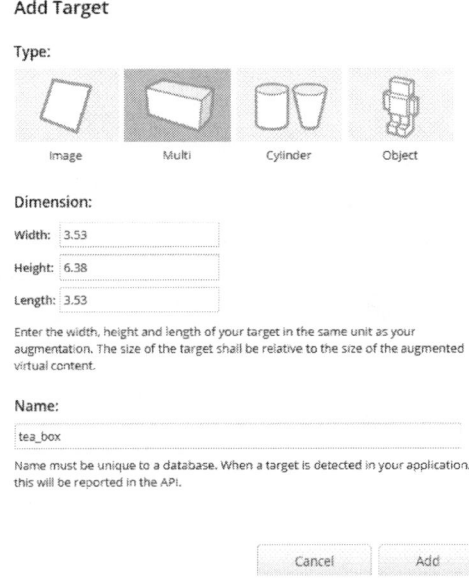

Figure 8.20: Adding a multi target to the database

Similar to how a cylinder target images are uploaded, images for back, front, top, bottom, left and right should be uploaded when you click the created target to upload reference images. In *Figure 8.21*, you can see the rectangular images that we uploaded to the target and the ratios of it. The dimensions of this are given in inches:

Figure 8.21: *Textures of the multi - target in correct dimensions. Source: The artwork is designed by pikisuperstar from Freepik*

Note: The aspect ratio of the images you upload for each side should exactly match the dimension values you added when creating the marker.

Once uploaded, you will be able to see a 3D model of the multi target with the uploaded textures. *Figure 8.22* shows the viewport once all the images are uploaded:

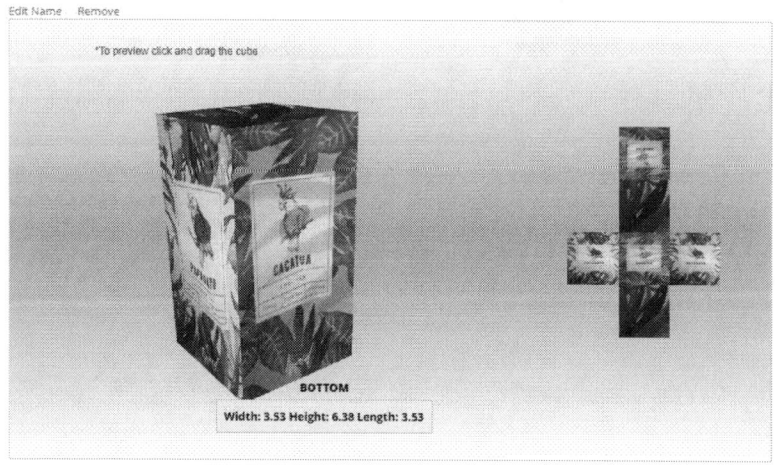

Figure 8.22: *Multi target preview*

Similar to how cylinder targets are imported, download the complete database, and import it back into your project. We are using a different scene to demonstrate multi-target tracking. Once the database is imported, along with the AR Camera, add a **Multi Target** by going to **Game Object** menu | **Vuforia Engine** | **Multi Target**.

You will be able to select the database and the available multi target to get the visual 3D box reference with the texture attached. You can use this object as the base and populate any 3D content to spawn, once scanned in AR.

In *Figure 8.23*, you can see how a 3D model of a parrot is added into the multi target, along with the occlusion object that was added by using **Add occlusion object** within the **Multi Target Behaviour** component:

Figure 8.23: Adding AR content to appear when the target is scanned

Source: "African Grey Parrot" (*https://skfb.ly/6GuRt*) by Gert-Jan van den Boom is licensed under Creative Commons Attribution-ShareAlike (*http://creativecommons.org/licenses/by-sa/4.0/*)

Now click on **Play** and scan the physical box of the same artwork, and you may see the 3D model on top of the box, as shown in *Figure 8.24*:

Figure 8.24: Demonstration of Multi target tracking

Vuforia has a highly intuitive and developer-friendly structure for building an AR app without much coding knowledge. All the different targets perform the same way and use a straightforward approach to show and hide AR content that has been placed in reference to this.

Vuforia supports more types of targets that increase the spectrum of what it can scan in a real physical environment. Some of the extended tracking features are as follows:

- Model target
- Cloud recognition (this will be covered in the next chapter)
- Barcode scanning
- Area targets
- Ground plane
- Device tracking

A complete documentation for Vuforia SDK is provided on the library page: **https://library.vuforia.com/**

In the next section, let us use the **Default Observer Event Handler** to set up trigger events and build a simple AR treasure hunter game.

Development of an AR treasure hunt game

In this section, let us use the knowledge that we gained, by making Image targets to create a simple AR treasure hunter game. This will be a self-paced exploration game and the rules of the game will be as follows:

- The challenge will be to find all the posters placed around the city and reach the final poster. There will be X number of posters and the final poster will provide the treasure.
- The game will provide a hint to find the first poster.
- Scanning a poster will activate a new hint and an AR experience to find the next poster.
- Scanning posters that are not relevant for the hint will not trigger anything.

Although we will be using only 3 posters, you can make any number of them. In our case, the third poster will be the final. *Figure 8.25* shows the flow of the hunt and the posters along with the hints and the augmented content that will be used:

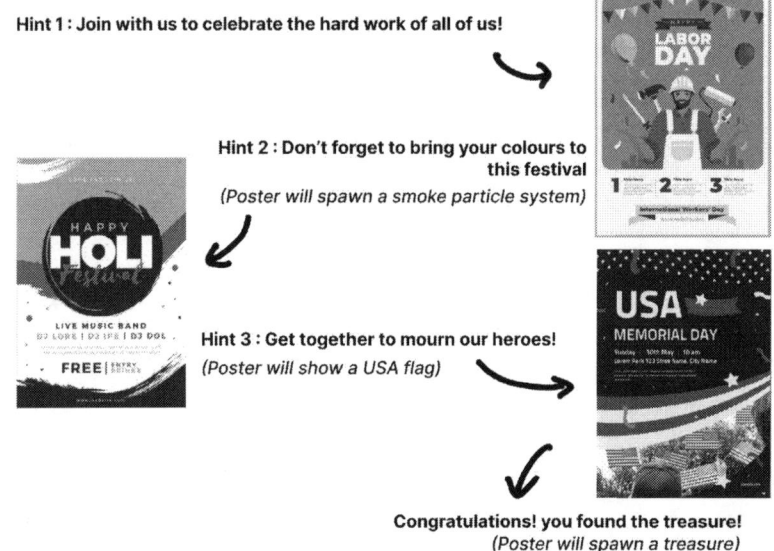

Figure 8.25: Treasure hunt game plan
(**Source**: *Posters designed by Freepik*)

Based on the knowledge we gained in the previous sections, add three images for the posters to Unity and make them Image targets. *Figure 8.26* shows how the assets are added under each image target. We used a particle system within the first poster target and two 3D models inside other posters. Now, all these image targets will activate the content added within them when scanned in play mode. However, we are yet to understand which marker has been tracked and set up functionality around it to make this a game:

Figure 8.26: Image target setup for the treasure hunt

3D models Sources: "Treasure Chest - 3d Game asset (mobile game)" (**https://skfb.ly/6WOHL**) by brainchildpl and "US flag on pole" (**https://skfb.ly/ouOIu**) by ecto is licensed under Creative Commons Attribution (**http://creativecommons.org/licenses/by/4.0/**)

The hints will use a simple canvas text and once you win the treasure hunt, another text box will be activated. Based on the knowledge we got in *Chapter 6: Refreshing in C# concepts with Unity*, add a Screen Space overlay canvas to the hierarchy and add two **TextMeshPro** objects. In *Figure 8.27*, you can see how we configured the canvas:

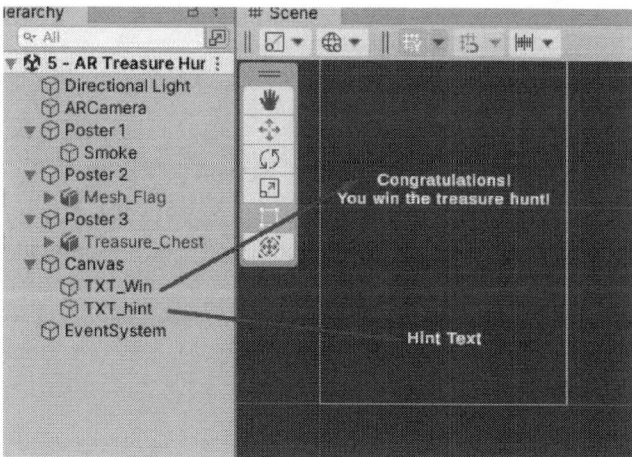

Figure 8.27: Setting up the game canvas

Once you win the treasure, all the posters will show the AR content when scanned, but no hint will be displayed. To manage this, let us create a simple Game Manager:

```
1.  using System.Collections;
2.  using System.Collections.Generic;
3.  using UnityEngine;
4.  using TMPro;
5.
6.  public class GameManager : MonoBehaviour
7.  {
8.
9.      [SerializeField] private TMP_Text TXT_win;
10.     [SerializeField] private TMP_Text TXT_hint;
11.
12.     // The list of all the image targets
13.     [SerializeField] private HintTarget[] targets;
14.
15.     // State management variables
16.     private int state = 0;
17.     private bool isWin = false;
18.
19.     // Singleton pattern to retrieve the game manager by the targets
20.     private static GameManager instance;
21.
22.     private void Awake()
23.     {
24.         if (instance != null && instance != this)
25.         {
26.             Destroy(this);
27.         }
28.         instance = this;
29.     }
30.
31.     // Returns the global instance
```

```
32.     public static GameManager GetInstance()
33.     {
34.         return instance;
35.     }
36.
37.     void Start()
38.     {
39.         //Initialize the state of the game
40.         state = 0;
41.         TXT_win.gameObject.SetActive(false);
42.
43.         //Show the first hint
44.         TXT_hint.text = targets[state].getHint();
    isWin = false;
45.     }
46.
47.     // This method will be called when an image target is tracked
48.     public bool CheckWin(HintTarget target)
49.     {
50.         if(target == targets[state])
51.         {
52.             if(state == targets.Length-1)
53.             {
54.                 //win
55.                 TXT_hint.gameObject.SetActive(false);
56.                 TXT_win.gameObject.SetActive(true);
57.                 isWin = true;
58.             }
59.             else
60.             {
61.                 //correct target, move next
62.                 TXT_hint.text = "Correct! wait for the next hint";
63.
```

```
64.             state++;
65.             //show the hint after 3 seconds
66.             Invoke("ShowHint", 3);
67.         }
68.         return true;
69.     }
70.     else
71.     {
72.         // tracking the wrong target
73.         TXT_hint.text = "Wrong target!";
74.         return false;
75.     }
76. }
77.
78. // Method to show the hint of the current state
79. public void ShowHint()
80. {
81.     TXT_hint.text = targets[state].getHint();
82. }
83.
84. public bool IsWin()
85. {
86.     return isWin;
87. }
88. }
```

Game Manager is a component written on a Singleton pattern for the Image targets to trigger the commands. The game manager mainly tracks the current status of the game. This is done using the **CheckWin()** method. This checks if the target that has been tracked is the same as the reference index of the **targets** array. If the status is not the number of the targets available, it is not a win since there are more targets to scan. Otherwise, it will be the correct target for the hint, which increments the status to move to the next target.

If the status and the target are both not in alignment, it is the wrong target. Therefore, it will show an error message. The **CheckWin()** method is being called by the targets when tracked. If the treasure has not been found, it can only show the content of the correct hint. The return value of the **CheckWin()** method determines the visibility of the AR content within the tracked image.

Now, you may get errors for the **HintTarget** related references. Therefore, let us create the **HintTarget** C# script, as follows:

```
1.  using System.Collections;
2.  using System.Collections.Generic;
3.  using UnityEngine;
4.  using Vuforia;
5.
6.  public class HintTarget : MonoBehaviour
7.  {
8.
9.      [SerializeField] private string hintName;
10.
11.     [SerializeField] private GameObject ARObject;
12.
13.
14.     public string getHint()
15.     {
16.         return hintName;
17.     }
18.
19.     public void OnTargetFound()
20.     {
21.         if (GameManager.GetInstance().IsWin())
22.             return;
23.
24.         ARObject.SetActive(GameManager.GetInstance().CheckWin(this));
25.     }
26.
27.     public void OnTargetLost()
28.     {
```

```
29.          Debug.Log("lost");
30.          GameManager.GetInstance().ShowHint();
31.          ARObject.SetActive(true);
32.      }
33. }
```

The target mainly holds the hint that is to be identified by the player. Game Manager will get the hint and display on the screen. There are two methods added to this script, which are **OnTargetFound()** and **OnTargetLost()**. These two methods are public and will be used by Vuforia to execute when the target has been found and lost. In line 24, the target will check if it is either the correct target or the winning target, and if not, it will hide the AR content by deactivating the game object. Before that, as in line 21, the target will check whether the game has already been beaten. If the game is beaten, it will not check for hints and will not hide the game objects within the target.

Go back to Unity and add the **HintTarget** component to all three Image targets. For each image target, do the following:

1. Add the hint in **Hint Name** parameter. This should be the hint that should describe the same poster.

2. Add the child object as the **AR object**. If you have more than one object, add all of them into a parent empty object and assign that.

3. Now, check the **Default Observer Event Handler** component within the target. For both **On Target Found ()** and **On Target Lost ()** methods, assign the public methods that we created within the **HintTarget** component. Make sure you assign the methods within the same game object.

4. However, when tracking, **OnTargetLost** may not be triggered. This is due to the extended tracking feature of Vuforia keeping the AR content available even if the marker is not in the viewport. To fix it, we need to change the **Consider target as visible if its status is:** option within **Default** object event handler component to **Tracked**.

5. Now, repeat the same for all the posters/image targets. *Figure 8.28* is an example of the component setup for poster 1:

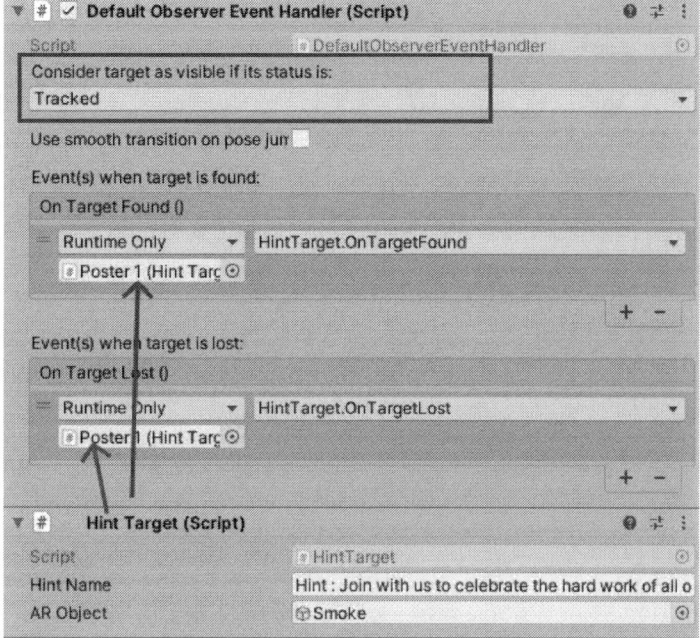

Figure 8.28: Hint target parameter setup

6. Now, create an empty game object and add the **GameManeger** component.

7. Setup all the text box references and the targets. Make sure that you add all the targets to the **Targets** parameter based on the correct flow. *Figure 8.29* shows how the parameters are set up.

8. In this section, the main intention was to get an introduction to the target found and lost events. We manually added the methods to the events provided by Vuforia. This is a simple task for just 3 targets, but it can be overwhelming if there are more targets. Therefore, we can remove the methods from the events (remove the added **OnTargetFound** and **Lost** methods) and assign them within the **start** method. This can be done by adding the following to the **start** method of **HintTarget** script. Make sure to add **using Vuforia;** at the top of the script:

```
1.    private void Start()
2.    {
3.        DefaultObserverEventHandler eventHander = GetComponent<DefaultObserverEventHandler>();
4.        eventHander.OnTargetFound.AddListener(OnTargetFound);
5.        eventHander.OnTargetLost.AddListener(OnTargetLost);
6.    }
```

9. Click play to try it on your editor or build and run on your mobile device to test the flow of the game. What we built was a basic implementation of marker-based AR. We will look into polishing techniques and other enhancements in another chapter, in order to enhance the quality of the AR experience.

Conclusion

In this chapter, we practically implemented multiple marker-based AR exercises using Vuforia SDK. Unity and AR can be treated as two separate entities in the same room. You can use all the unity-based functionalities considering the tracked AR target as a local environment space. In the next chapter, let us check how to build dynamic AR applications with Vuforia that do not require importing image targets into unity project.

Key points

- Vuforia SDK uses a license key to check the validity of the use of their tool.
- Vuforia Image targets get processed by the database manager from Vuforia cloud.
- Image targets must have certain details and should adhere to best practices in order to be scanned by the SDK properly. This is known as *trackability rating*.
- If you upload images to Vuforia database, you will be able to see how the target would perform in play mode.
- You can also add Image targets locally within the project without using the database method. This is done in **Image Target Behaviour** by changing the target mode to **From Image**, instead of **From Database**.
- To test cylinder targets and multi-targets, you must have a physical object with proper printed surfaces.
- Vuforia targets emit events when the targets are tracked and untracked. These events can be used to add interactivity to your applications that trigger marker scans.

Question

1. Increase the number of targets in your own project and add more interactions and puzzle elements to the treasure hunt game. Use different targets, such as multi-targets and cylinder targets.

CHAPTER 9
Developing Marker-based Dynamic AR Apps

Introduction

Now that we have a basic overview of how Vuforia works within Unity, we are capable of developing any Unity based application logic that can run within a local space around a trained marker (image target, cylinder targets and so on). However, building enhanced AR applications effectively requires additional knowledge on how data can be manipulated and transferred across platforms.

In this chapter, we will be building two AR projects while learning concepts on data processing and retrieval. One project will be an AR machine inspection tool that uses only one AR Image target but with a method to identify each marker using an encoded method called **VuMarks**. Using the encoded data, we will retrieve more data using an **Application Programming Interface** (**API**) and convert that raw data to usable methods within Unity. For the second project, we will be building an AR billboard app that does not rely on Image targets we import into Unity. We will be using Vuforia Cloud Targets to dynamically update the image target and retrieve the content accordingly.

Structure

In this chapter, we will discuss the following topics:

- Machine inspection tool

- Unity serialization and deserialization
- Creating a simple mock API
- Using UnityWebRequest to request data based on input
- Vuforia VuMark introduction
- Designing a VuMark using Adobe Illustrator
- Connecting the marker recognition with networking to request dynamic data and displaying them in **Augmented Reality (AR)**
- Dynamic AR billboard
  - Setting up the AR poster project
  - Implementing Vuforia Cloud targets
  - Creating Asset Bundles in Unity
  - Uploading the asset bundles in the cloud
  - Updating the meta files to update AR experience
  - Downloading content and displaying in AR

Objectives

After completing this chapter, you will be able to design and develop AR applications that uses distributed systems to load data dynamically and visualize them in a 3D AR space. You will also be able to develop marker based dynamic AR apps, that do not require users to update the app every time a new experience has been created. You will be able to use cloud storages to store your data and load them to your AR application during run-time.

Machine inspection tool

Imagine you are supposed to build an AR based machine inspection tool to retrieve current data of each machine, just by pointing an AR camera or a wearable at it. Moreover, the requirement is to do it using marker-based tracking and has over 50 machines to attach a marker (image) that must be scanned. If you keep the data retrieval process for each machine aside and decide to use the traditional way of using image targets to build the application, you must first design 50 different image targets for each machine.

Additionally, two image targets cannot create similar features since the AR algorithm may misidentify the target if both look similar. Even if you have 50 different image targets, you must add all of them to the database and setup every image target within unity manually. In addition to that, the application will not be scalable to cater new machines that will require the AR inspection.

In order to overcome this challenge, Vuforia has introduced a new marker-based detection system known as VuMark. This allows anyone to encode data into an image marker and load that data decoded into the application using their SDK. Keeping the same image marker aesthetics, a portion of the image target can be modified to encode any data.

The project we will be building will use VuMark as the detection system and use data retrieval methods to dynamically load data from a remote system. The following in *Figure 9.1* is an overview of the flow of the machine inspection tool:

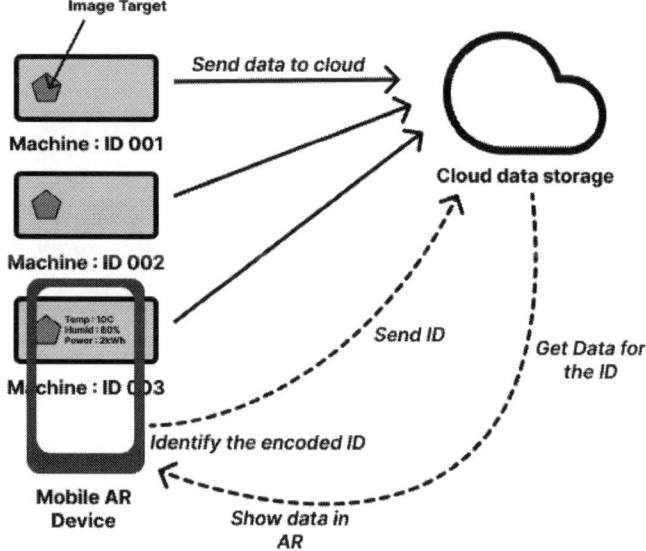

Figure 9.1: *Flow of the machine inspection AR app*

As per *Figure 9.1*, there are three machines with the same image target pasted on the surface of each. Occasionally, the machines are sending sensory data to a cloud storage. A cloud storage can be a database, or a raw storage based in a remote location and the machines will be using a connected network (internet) to send data along with its unique ID through an **Application Programming Interface (API)**.

The VuMark system can encode the machine IDs inside the target images without hindering the aesthetics of the marker. Now, the AR application will be able to decode the IDs when scanned using the Vuforia SDK. We will be using the decoded ID to filter and request the same machine data from the cloud storage, and the data will be shown over the machine with other 3D elements, over the VuMark image target.

This way, the AR developer can use a single image target and dynamically show different data on different machines. The display of AR content can also be customized based on the data that will be retrieved from the cloud.

As you can realize, apart from AR development, this application requires the knowledge for the following reasons:

- **Request data from an external source dynamically:** Each machine has its own ID. Therefore, data request should be different for each machine.
- **Retrieve data from the external source dynamically:** Data from each machine can be dynamic and raw.
- **Convert data into a format that can be visualized:** Convert raw data to usable data format, such as variables (string, int, float and so on).
- Visualize data in AR, within the image target.

Unity serialization and deserialization

Before requesting data from an external source, we must identify the structure of a data format, and how the structure can be helpful for us in terms of splitting it into individual information. There are different ways how we can present data in a structured format. There are many data structures that have been used over the world, but **Extensible Markup Language** (**XML**) and **JavaScript Object Notation** (**JSON**) are two of the mostly used data structures that can represent data in a textual format. However, a text string is not data. The text data structure should be converted into a format that can be saved within an object format. This conversion is known as data serialization. Converting an object into a textual format is called data deserialization. Text data can be converted into bits that can be transmitted through any data transmission method, such as the Internet. Therefore, data serialization and deserialization are processes that many software use, in order to exchange data. Unity directly supports JSON serialization with its API. JSON is a lightweight data structure that is built on two structures:

- **A collection of key-value pairs:** A key can be the name of a variable and the value is the value of the variable. The value can be anything such as a number, an integer, a string, a Boolean or even another JSON.
- A list of values, which is an array, list, or a sequence of objects.

The following is a simple JSON that represents basic data of a machine:

```
1. {
2.   "machine_id": 1,
3.   "name": "Xtract ABC 123",
4.   "make": "CAT",
5.   "version": 1.3
6. }
```

Notice how the JSON is wrapped by curly brackets (**{** and **}**). Within the JSON object, there are 4 variables: the Machine ID, name, make, and the machine version. See how each variable type is presented, based on the type of the variable. An extended version of the data structure can be seen as follows:

```
1.  {
2.      "machine_id": 1,
3.      "name": "Xtract ABC 123",
4.      "make": "CAT",
5.      "version": 1.3,
6.      "is_running": true,
7.      "location": {
8.         "building": "A",
9.         "isle": "X5",
10.        "section": 10
11.     },
12.     "current_data": [{
13.        "id": 1001,
14.        "name": "temperature",
15.        "unit": "C",
16.        "value": 66.45
17.     },
18.     {
19.        "id": 1002,
20.        "name": "humidity",
21.        "unit": "%",
22.        "value": 78
23.     },
24.     {
25.        "id": 1003,
26.        "name": "Units processed",
27.        "unit": "unit/min",
28.        "value": 3.4
29.     }
```

30.]
31. }

The preceding JSON includes strings, integers, floats, Booleans, another JSON, as well as a list of JSONs. You can visit **https://www.json.org/** to learn more about JSON. In Unity, we use C# to create scripts which are by default inherited from the **MonoBehaviour** class. The components we add using a **MonoBehaviour** class are the instances of that class. We can use C# classes to create instances of any object that is defined by the script. Instances can hold actual variables. Serialization converts the text data into defined C# instances, which can be used in data visualization. The following C# script called **MachineData.cs** is a serializable class that can be used to serialize the data of the first JSON:

1. [System.Serializable]
2. public class MachineData
3.
4. {
5.   public int machine_id;
6.   public string name;
7.   public string make;
8.   public float version;
9. }

If you compare the JSON object, the key names are similar to the variables of the serializable class. Unity needs to know that is a serializable class by adding **[System.Serializable]**.

For the extended user data, we can see three data types including the parent object, which is **MachineData**, **Location** and **CurrentData**. Here, **CurrentData** objects are placed in an array. To cater to this, we need to create two more classes to define the objects that can be generated. In C#, you can add multiple classes within one script as long as they are not for Unity components. The standard is to create separate files to increase maintainability. However, for this example, let us add two more classes and modify the **MachineData.cs** script as follows:

1. [System.Serializable]
2. public class MachineData
3. {
4.   public int machine_id;
5.   public string name;
6.   public string make;

```
7.      public float version;
8.      public bool is_running;
9.      public Location location;
10.     public SensorData[] current_data;
11. }
12.
13. [System.Serializable]
14. public class Location
15. {
16.     public string building;
17.     public string isle;
18.     public int section;
19. }
20.
21. [System.Serializable]
22. public class SensorData
23. {
24.     public int id;
25.     public string name;
26.     public string unit;
27.     public float value;
28. }
29.
```

As you can see, all the classes are noted as serializable and the machine data class has two new data types, which are defined as **SensorData** and **Location**. If you convert the complete JSON into one serialized object, there will be one instance that contains one **Location** instance and three **SensorData** instances.

In order to test the conversion within Unity, we need to load the JSON as a string. We can store a file and load it in run time using **StreamingAssets** in Unity. Create a new folder in the **Assets** folder and name it **StreamingAssets**.

Now open the folder and add a new text file and rename it to **data.json**. This extension is optional to read the file but it is better for maintainability. Now, open the text file and add the previous extended JSON string as the text and save the file.

Create a new C# script called **DataSerializationTest.cs** and add the following:

```
1.  using System.IO;
2.  using UnityEngine;
3.  
4.  public class DataSerializationTest : MonoBehaviour
5.  {
6.      void Start()
7.      {
8.          string json = File.ReadAllText(Application.streamingAssetsPath + "/data.json");
9.  
10.         MachineData machineData = JsonUtility.FromJson<MachineData>(json);
11. 
12.         Debug.Log(machineData.name);
13.         Debug.Log(machineData.location.building);
14.         Debug.Log(machineData.current_data.Length);
15.         Debug.Log(machineData.current_data[0].name);
16.     }
17. }
```

Add this to an empty game object and run the scene. The script will print:

```
Xtract ABC 123

A

3

temperature
```

We were using **System.IO** to read the text file from the streaming assets path as a string. The text string is converted to an object by using the **JsonUtility**, which is a feature provided within **UnityEngine**.

We can iterate through the whole instance and pick each individual value and use it to represent data within Unity. We will be mostly using data serialization in our machine inspection project. If we need to convert an object into the JSON format, we need to deserialize the object. A sample test script for data deserialization is as follows:

```csharp
1.  using UnityEngine;
2.
3.  public class DataDeserializationTest : MonoBehaviour
4.  {
5.      void Start()
6.      {
7.          MachineData machineData = new MachineData();
8.          Location location1 = new Location();
9.          SensorData temperatureData = new SensorData();
10.
11.         temperatureData.id = 1;
12.         temperatureData.name = "temperature";
13.         temperatureData.unit = "F";
14.         temperatureData.value = 456.3f;
15.
16.         location1.building = "b1";
17.         location1.section = 1;
18.         location1.isle = "A";
19.
20.         machineData.machine_id = 1;
21.         machineData.is_running = false;
22.         machineData.name = "Machine 1";
23.         machineData.make = "AXG";
24.
25.         machineData.location = location1;
26.         machineData.current_data = new SensorData[1];
27.         machineData.current_data[0] = temperatureData;
28.
29.         string json = JsonUtility.ToJson(machineData);
30.         Debug.Log(json);
31.     }
32. }
```

Notice how an individual object is created and added to the parent machine data object array. When you run this, the console will display the following JSON. The variables with no values in the objects have taken default values, as shown:

{"machine_id":1,"name":"Machine 1","make":"AXG","version":0.0,"is_running":false,"location":{"building":"b1","isle":"A","section":1},"current_data":[{"id":1,"name":"temperature","unit":"F","value":456.29998779296877}]}

Creating a simple mock API

In our previous example, we used a JSON file stored within the application to serialize data. However, the data must be retrieved from a remote service. A method to request and retrieve data from another source is known as an API. **Representational State Transfer (REST API)** is one of the popular and widely used network-based APIs. You can read more about REST API from the following link:

https://www.redhat.com/en/topics/api/what-is-a-rest-api

In order to test the data retrieval process with Unity, we are going to build a simple virtual remote server (computer) within our own computer. This is usually known as the `localhost`. We are going to achieve this by using a simple software known as **Mockoon**. Visit the following link and download and install the mockoon application: **https://mockoon.com/**

You may see a sample project setup in the app when you open it for the first time. In this scenario, we are going to add one datapoint to retrieve information about a machine.

In Mockoon, go to **File** and select new environment. Save it in any location with a name you prefer. In our case, we chose **Machines**. As shown in *Figure 9.2*, add the path `machines/1` as in *(1)* and copy the complete JSON we used before, into the Inline section *(2)*. Once done, click on the **Play** button to start the server.

Now, open any web browser window and type `localhost:<port>/machines/1` into the address bar. Here `<port>` means the number you see under **Machines** in mockoon right next to `0.0.0.0`:

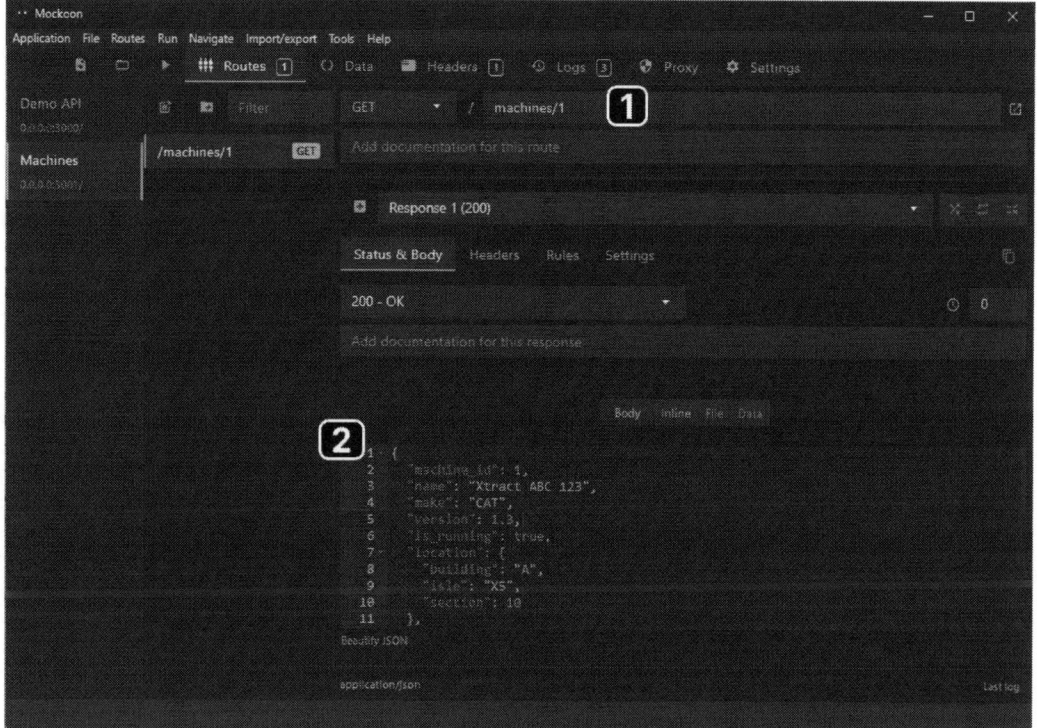

Figure 9.2: Mockoon basic GET request configuration

Now, create more paths that resemble the following pattern with different data:

localhost:<port>/machines/<machine_id>

This gives us an opportunity to request mock data for different machines based on the machine id. Now, let us see how to get this data into Unity.

Using UnityWebRequest to request data based on input

Unity Web Request is a library provided by Unity that lies within Unity Networking features to send and receive data through HTTP protocol. It uses **DownloadHandler** and **UploadHandler** to send REST API requests such as **Get**, **Post**, **Put** and **Delete**. In our previous subsection, we created a mock **API endpoint** (**API path**) that returns a **GET** response. In this subsection, let us use Unity web request to send a **GET** request and retrieve data into Unity as a string. We can then use the knowledge gained previously, to convert it into an object.

Create a new C# script and call it **DataConnector.cs** and add the following:

```
1.  using System.Collections;
2.  using UnityEngine;
3.  using UnityEngine.Networking;
4.  
5.  public class DataConnector : MonoBehaviour
6.  {
7.      void Start()
8.      {
9.          StartCoroutine(RequestData());
10.     }
11. 
12.     IEnumerator RequestData()
13.     {
14.         UnityWebRequest getMachineDataRequest = UnityWebRequest.Get("http://localhost:3001/machines/1");
15.         yield return getMachineDataRequest.SendWebRequest();
16.         DownloadHandler hander = getMachineDataRequest.downloadHandler;
17.         Debug.Log(hander.text);
18.     }
19. }
```

In the preceding example, the link should be the one you have created with Mockoon. Make sure you have it running before you test this script.

As you can see, the request is added into an **IEnumerator** instead of a method, and has called it as a coroutine. This is because an API request is not real time and will take time to process. Therefore, we need to wait until it returns a response. If this works without any issues, you will be able to see the JSON getting printed in the console.

Now we understood the structure of a text-based data structures, how to retrieve them from a remote service using **GET** REST API methods, and how to convert it to an object that is usable within Unity. The idea of this application is to request data dynamically, based on an AR scan. Different machine data can be requested changing the **machine_id** of the path. This machine ID can be encoded into an AR marker, which can be retrieved using Vuforia VuMarks.

Now, let us understand what VuMark is, how we can create a VuMark and how to retrieve data encoded within a VuMark.

Vuforia VuMark introduction

VuMark is similar to a QR Code or a bar code but with added customized designs. A VuMark can serve as a barcode as well as a logo of a trademark or a company.

Compared to a normal image target, VuMark is a vector image in the SVG format that has light and dark components in the middle to encode a value. A sample VuMark image can be seen as in *Figure 9.3*:

Figure 9.3: A VuMark

A VuMark consists of multiple sections listed as follows:

- **Border**: A dark border that surrounds a VuMark.
- **Contour**: The line where clear space inside the border meets the surrounding border. Vuforia mainly uses the contour for the initial marker recognition.
- **Clear space**: It is the clear space under the VuMark.
- **Code elements**: These are the dark and light elements that are placed on top of each other to represent two states. The number of elements within a VuMark depends on the length of the encoded data. When designing, it is better to optimize your encoded data to have less elements in your design.
- **Background**: It is the area inside the code elements, or outside the VuMark that does not involve any tracking purpose. This can be a logo or any design element.

Designing a VuMark using Adobe Illustrator

Augmented Reality is the designer's as well as the developer's job. Therefore, getting used to a design tool comes in handy when you are building AR applications. In order to design a VuMark, Vuforia has created a designer tool that works only with Adobe Illustrator. You can download a free trial version of Adobe Illustrator by visiting **https://www.adobe.com** and signing up for a Creative Cloud account.

You also need to download the VuMark Designer tool by visiting the following link:

https://developer.vuforia.com/downloads/tool

Now, extract the ZIP file you downloaded as the VuMark Designer tool and copy the three JSX files within the VuMark folder into the following folders:

- **MacOS**: **/Applications/Adobe Illustrator CC folder/Presets/en_US/Scripts** (Right click the Illustrator Icon and select **Show Package Contents** to go in to the **application-content** folder).

- **Windows:** **<Illustrator Installation path>\Presets\en_US\Scripts**

Now, open Adobe Illustrator and, go to **File | Scripts | VuMark-Setup**.

This will give you the window shown in *Figure 9.4*, where you can set up your template. In here, name your design and choose the type of the encoded values in your VuMark. The number of elements you require for each type is different. At the bottom of the window, you can see the amount of encoding elements required within the design. In our example, we have chosen **Numeric** to hold the ID of the machines, and as the maximum value, added 10. This VuMark now requires us to create 28 encoding dark and light elements for our VuMark.

Refer to *Figure 9.4*:

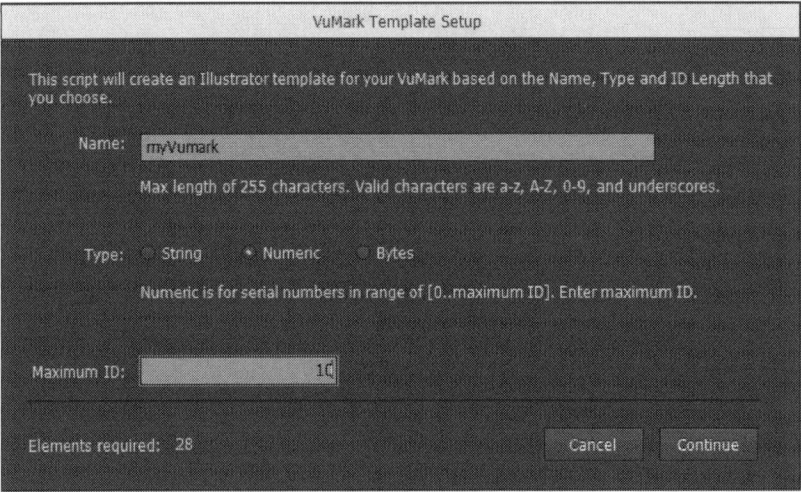

Figure 9.4: VuMark Setup Dialog

Design step 1

Select the **VuMark-ClearSpace** layer and draw a rectangle that should include your VuMark Logo. Make sure the background color of this is white and does not have a stroke. *Figure 9.5* shows a sample clear space layer.

> **Note: The stroke (border) of the VuMark target is added for showcase only. You can change the colors of background and borders by the top panel.**

Refer to *Figure 9.5*:

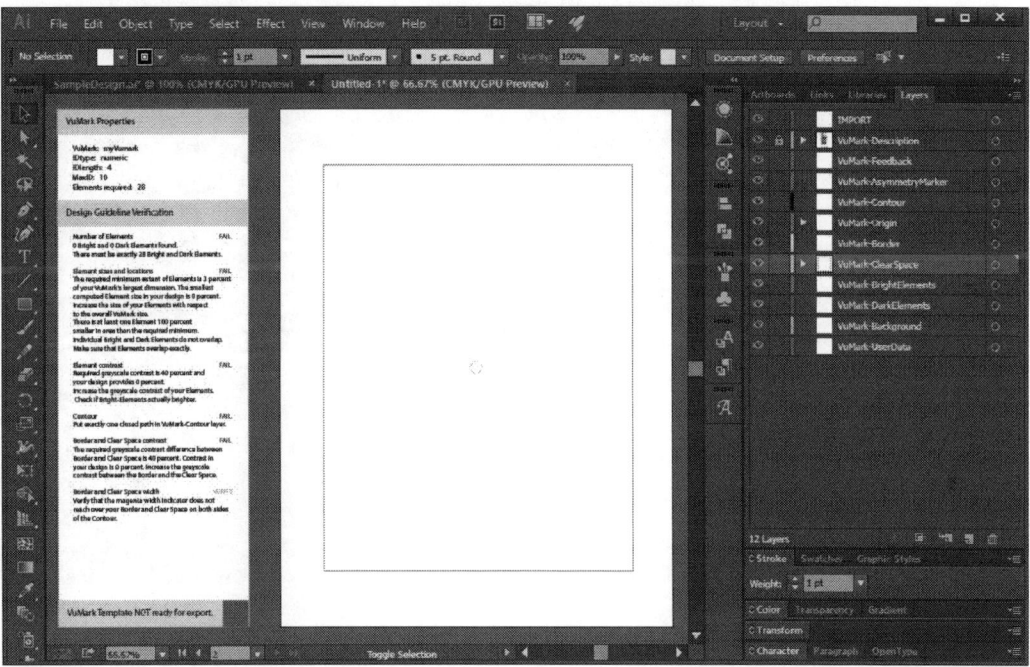

Figure 9.5: VuMark Clear space

Design step 2

Select the **VuMark-Border** layer and add the shape of your logo. This should be a darker element and the contrast between the clear space and the border should be more than at least 40%. You can test this by choosing **File | Scripts | VuMark-Verify**. The VuMark properties section next to your design will update with status whether your design is passed or failed. *Figure 9.6* shows how my design border is passed:

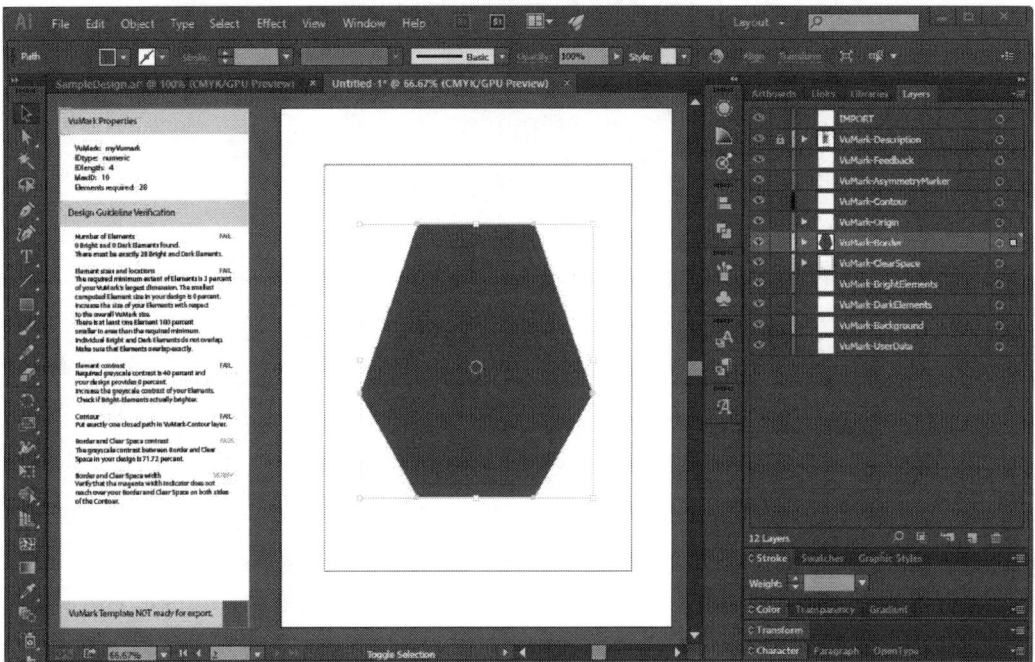

Figure 9.6: VuMark Border

Design step 3

Select the **VuMark-Contour** layer and add a border (only the stroke) that goes around the border shape we added before. In our case, we copied the same object, changed the background color to transparent and set the stroke color to black only. Now, verify the design. This will update some of the other layers of the design adding more magenta-colored elements. A designer should not overlap the magenta elements since these elements are important for Vuforia to track the marker. *Figure*

9.7 shows how the contour of my design is verified. Check the digital assets for the color images:

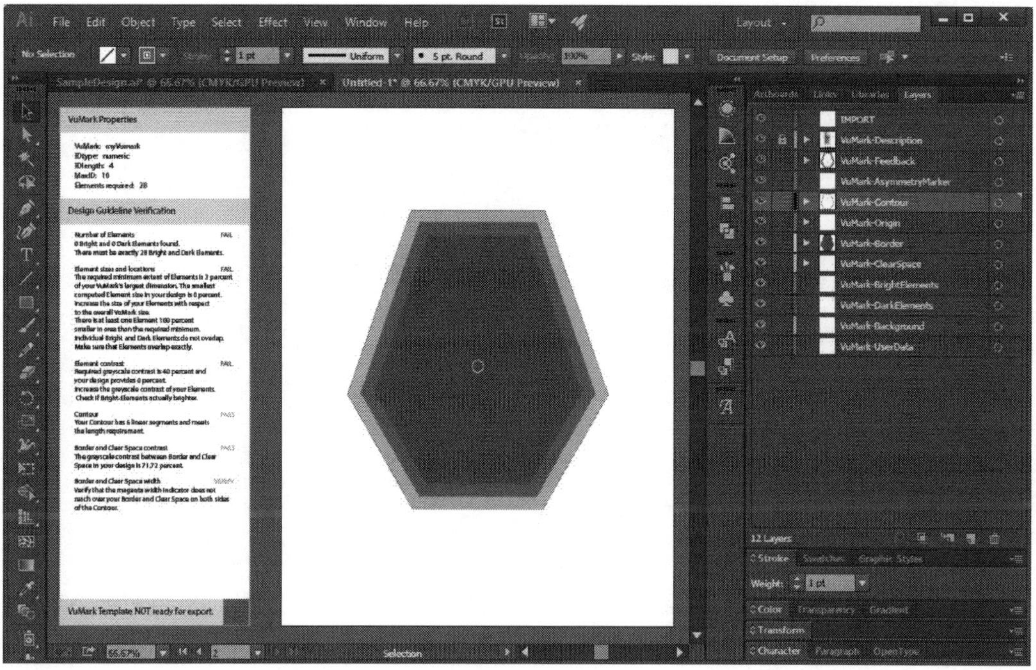

Figure 9.7: VuMark Contour

Design step 4

This is the most important step of the design: adding the coded elements. In your left side **Properties** section, the **Elements Required** number must be the number of elements that you need in your design. A single code element has a dark element and a bright element. These two sub-elements should be placed exactly on top of each other. Select both **VuMark-DarkElements** and **VuMark-BrightElements** layers, and move them above the contour. If you can isolate only these two layers, that would be great. Now select the dark elements layer and add a single small element which is in a dark color.

We made the color black since it is easier to distinguish. Now copy the element and paste the same in place (**Edit | Paste** in place). Move the copy into the bright elements layer and change the color to a light one. We chose white in our design. *Figure 9.8* shows how we added one code element with dark and bright sub-elements:

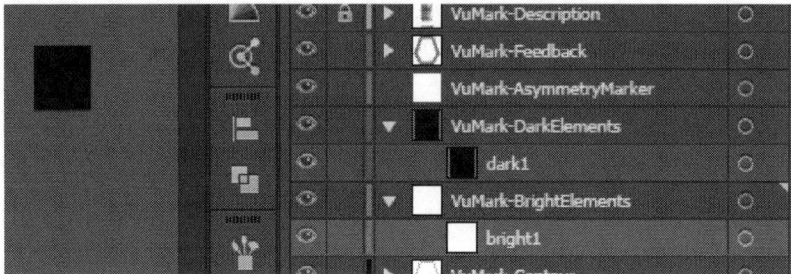

Figure 9.8: Bright and dark single element

Design step 5

Now copy dark and bright elements within the contours to fill up the required elements. Always make sure that your bright and dark elements are on top of each other in two different layers as the previous step. Now click and verify. Make changes as required by the tool. Once this step is done, you can export the design. However, you can still add more design elements in the **VuMark-Background**. You can move the layer above the border as well. Verify again to check any issues. *Figure 9.9* shows the final design once verified:

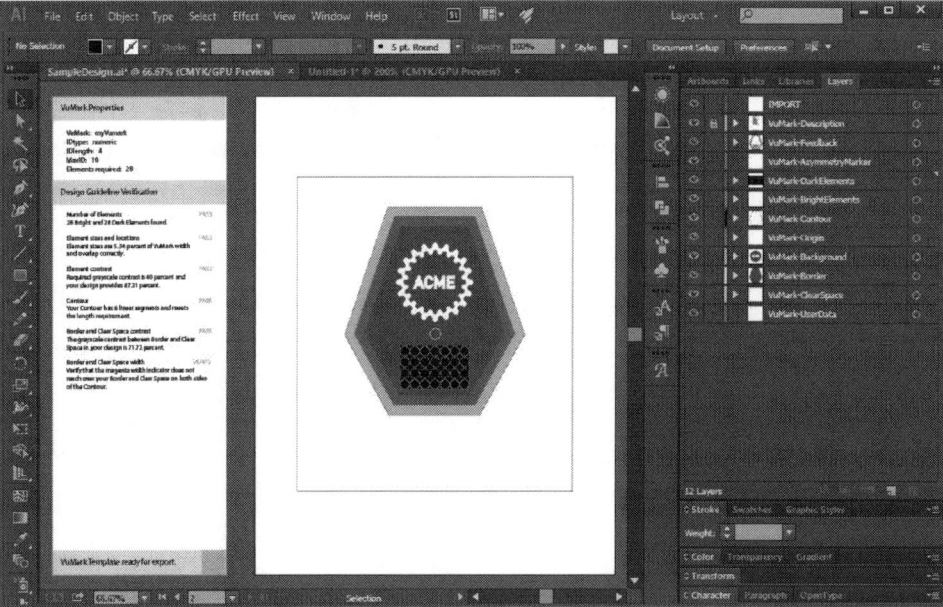

Figure 9.9: Final VuMark verified design

Now, go to **File** | **Scripts** | **VuMark-Export**. This will create an SVG file in a location you prefer. This is the file that you need to upload to Vuforia target manager.

You can learn more about VuMark design considerations from the following link:

https://library.vuforia.com/vumarks/vumark-design-guide

Now, follow the given steps:

1. Go to Vuforia developer portal and make a new VuMark database.
2. Add a new target and upload the SVG file generated from Illustrator.
3. Download the complete database for **UnityEngine** and import it into your project.
4. Similar to previous Vuforia target setups, add a VuMark object into your scene hierarchy by going to **GameObject** | **Vuforia** | **VuMark**. *Figure 9.10* shows how the VuMark target is placed in the scene. This can be considered as an image target with an added encoded data element:

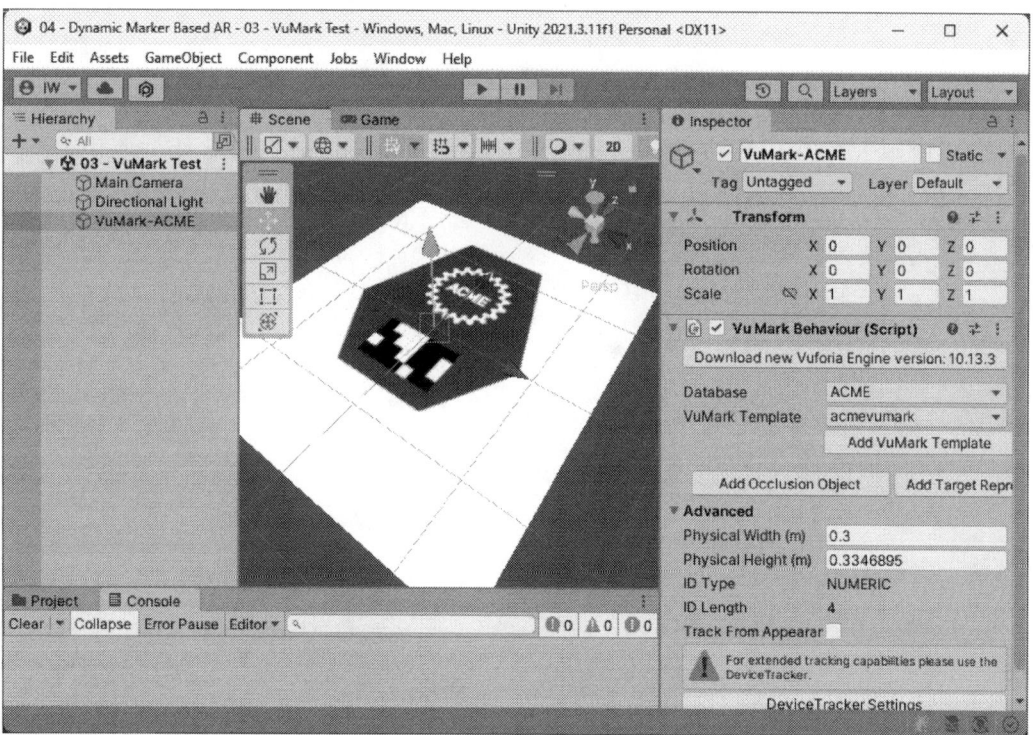

***Figure 9.10:** VrMark added into Unity with Vuforia SDK*

Connecting the marker recognition with networking to request dynamic data and displaying them in AR

Based on the flow discussed in *Figure 9.1*, we know how to access mock data, encode that data into a VuMark and also the principles of retrieving data from the remote location and deserialize it to a comfortable format. In this section, we will learn how to decode the VuMark data and display relevant data based on the decoded data.

Downloading VuMark targets

In order to test this, we need to download targets that have different encoded data. If we recall, we made our VuMark hold numbers from 1 to 10. Therefore, when downloading an encoded VuMark to test, we need to add the encoded data. Follow these steps:

1. Go to Vuforia target manager and open the VuMark database you added before.

2. Click on the **Generate VuMark** link next to your uploaded VuMark.

Here, you need to add the encoded value to download the image, as shown in *Figure 9.11*. You can also choose the Graphic format you want the image target to be. This target can be printed and pasted on a machine for testing:

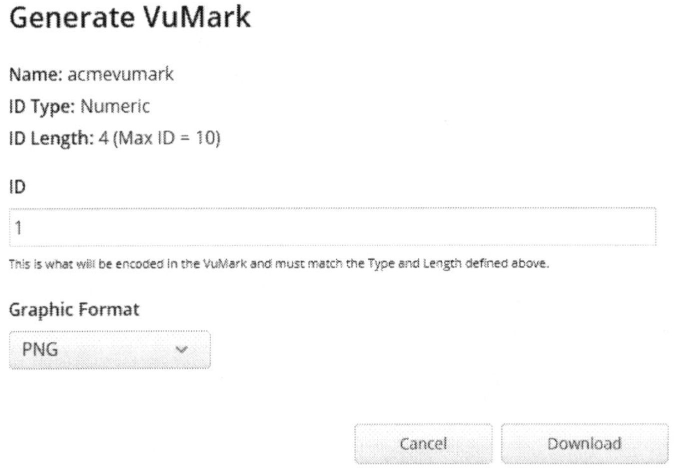

Generate VuMark

Name: acmevumark
ID Type: Numeric
ID Length: 4 (Max ID = 10)

ID

```
1
```
This is what will be encoded in the VuMark and must match the Type and Length defined above.

Graphic Format

PNG

[Cancel] [Download]

Figure 9.11: Add the number as the ID to encode

In our case, we will download 3 image targets that encoded 1, 2 and 3 numbers respectively, as shown in *Figure 9.12*:

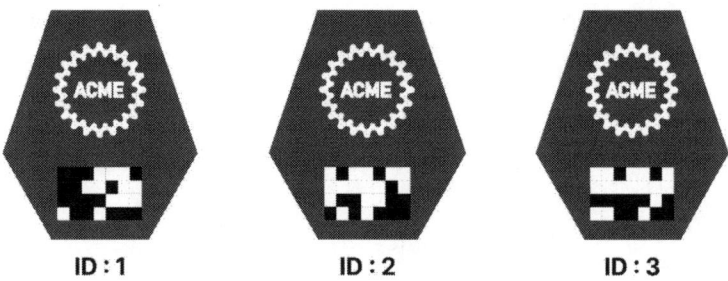

Figure 9.12: VuMark targets with IDs 1, 2, 3

Decoding VuMark data

In this section, let us decode the data and log in the console. Create a new C# script and name it **VuMarkDataRetriever.cs** and add the following:

```
1.  using UnityEngine;
2.  using Vuforia;
3.
4.  public class VuMarkDataRetriever : MonoBehaviour
5.  {
6.      private VuMarkBehaviour vuMarkBehaviour;
7.      private DefaultObserverEventHandler vuObserver;
8.      private string data = "";
9.      private VuMarkInstanceId instance;
10.
11.     void Start()
12.     {
13.         vuMarkBehaviour= GetComponent<VuMarkBehaviour>();
14.         vuObserver = GetComponent<DefaultObserverEventHandler>();
15.
16.         if(vuObserver!= null)
17.             vuObserver.OnTargetFound.AddListener(OnTargetFound);
18.     }
19.
20.     public void OnTargetFound()
21.     {
```

```
22.          if(vuMarkBehaviour)
23.          {
24.              instance = vuMarkBehaviour.InstanceId;
25.              switch (instance.DataType)
26.              {
27.                  case InstanceIdType.STRING:
28.                      data = instance.StringValue;
29.                      break;
30.                  case InstanceIdType.NUMERIC:
31.                      data = instance.NumericValue.ToString();
32.                      break;
33.                  case InstanceIdType.BYTE:
34.                          data = System.Text.Encoding.Default.GetString(instance.Buffer) ;
35.                      break;
36.                  default:
37.                      data = "";
38.                      break;
39.              }
40.          }
41.
42.          Debug.Log(data);
43.      }
44.
45.      public string GetData()
46.      {
47.          return data;
48.      }
49. }
```

This is an intermediate, yet a simple script to call **VuMark Behaviour** and retrieve the **InstanceID** of the target we scan.

In line 13 and 14, we get references to **VuMarkBehaviour** and **DefaultObserver EventHandler** components, which are both included default components of a VuMark object.

In line 16 and 17, we check if there is a valid observer component. If the component is available, we add the public method **OnTargetFound** as a listener to the **OnTargetFound** event in the observer. Now, every time Vuforia identifies a new image, this method will be executed. Now, let us look at the **OnTargetFound** method.

VuMarkBehaviour only provides the ID of the instance. This does not mean it is the data encoded within the image. Therefore, we need to retrieve the data from the instance. In line 24, we create a temporary instance and reference it to the instance retrieved by the **VuMarkBehaviour**. Using a switch case, we check the **Type** of the encoded data. In VuMark, encoded data can be a number, a string, or a byte array, as we learned earlier. This script can identify different types and convert the data into a string and store in the **data** private variable. If no identifiable type is retrieved, data value will be defaulted to an empty string.

We also have another **Get** method to return what is saved in the data variable.

Now, add the script to the VuMark target **gameobject** alongside other components, as shown in *Figure 9.13 (1)*. Click on the **Play** button and show different target images of the same logo to the camera. As presented in *Figure 9.13 (2)*, you can see different ID data is captured and logged in the console:

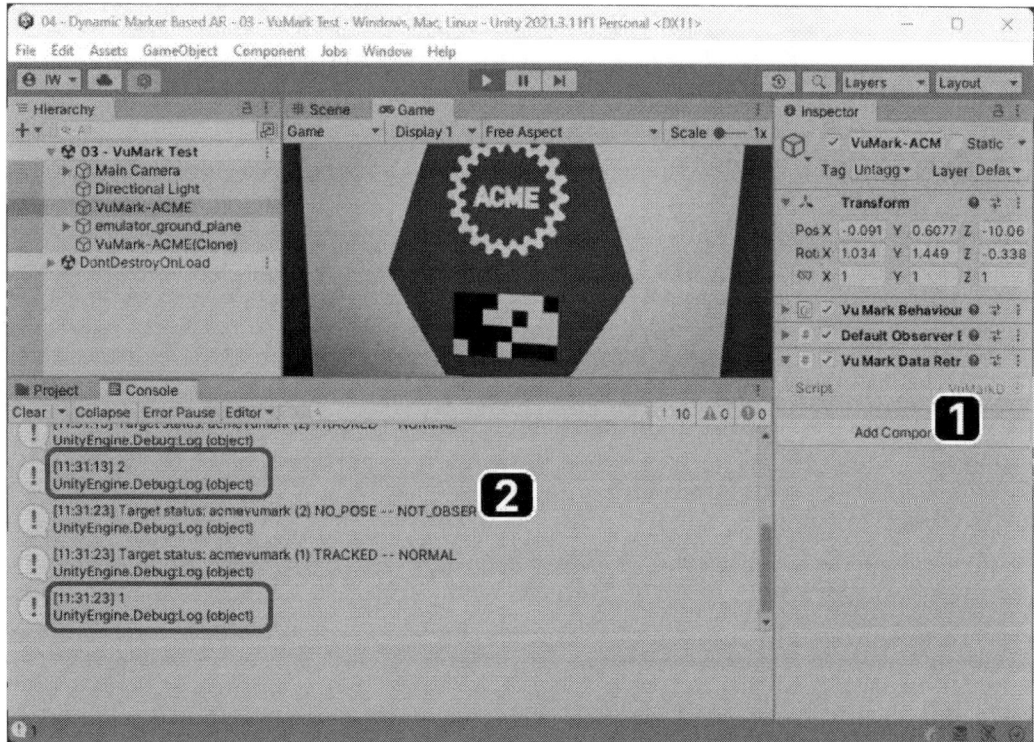

Figure 9.13: Running VuMark and get decode preview

Using decoded values to retrieve data from the remote server through API

Now that we can decode the ID within the image target, it is the time to retrieve data relevant to the ID and show them in AR. First of all, let us look at the structure of a JSON that we made earlier. It has basic information about the machine, the location information, and an array of sensor data which consists of the name, unit, and the value. Creating a data structure like this helps transmit data effectively as well as it is scalable. If a new machine is added with different kinds of sensory data, adding one to the sensor data array is flexible.

The following *Figure 9.14* is a simple sketch to define how to display sensory data in AR around the marker. Here, there are static data types which are machine information and dynamic types which are sensor data:

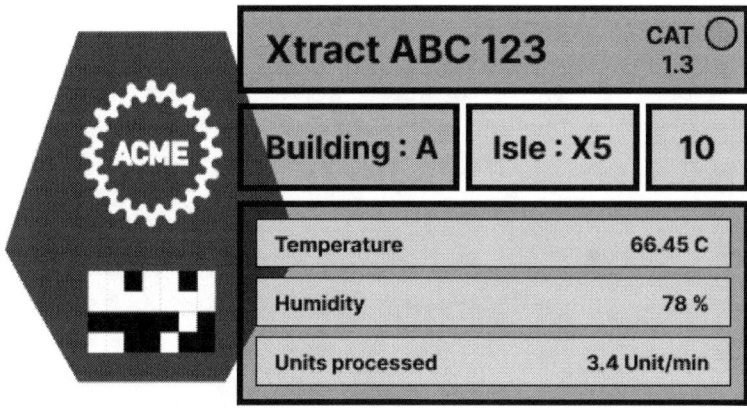

Figure 9.14: AR Information display sketch

All the data that is sent across the previous JSON has been added to the AR information display sketch. In Unity, this can be represented by a world space canvas placed inside the VuMark Game object.

Create an empty world space canvas inside the VuMark game object and add the panels and `TextMeshPro` UI objects as shown in *Figure 9.15 (1)*. The required assets for the canvas can be found within this chapter's GitHub repository:

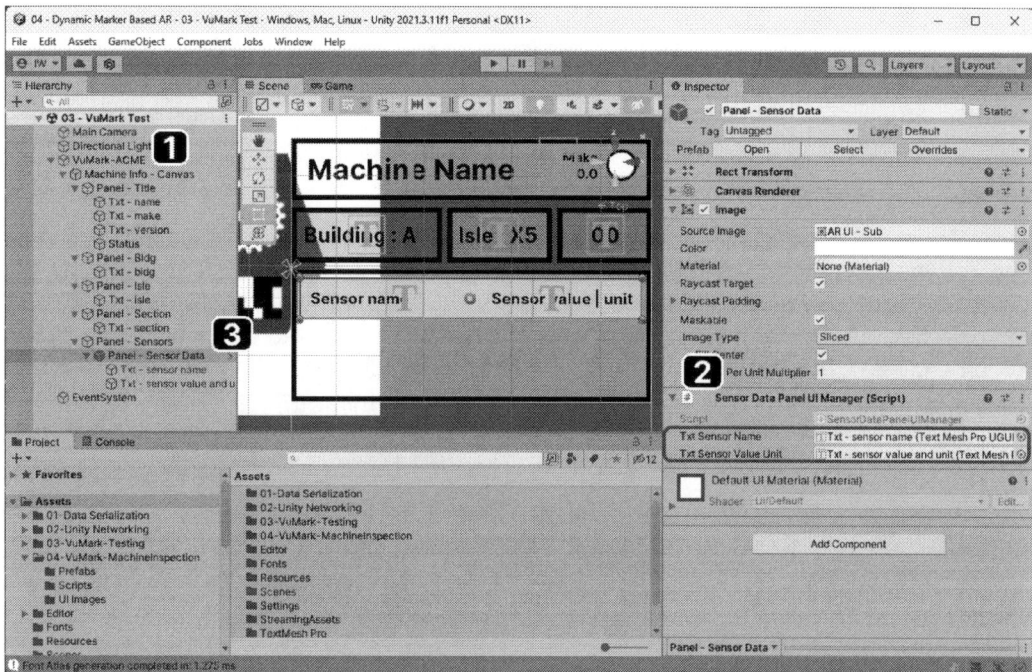

Figure 9.15: Setting up the AR canvas within VuMark

The world space canvas added inside the VuMark contains Images as panels, and **TextMeshPro** UI objects as placeholders to fill with machine data. The amount of sensor data differs from machine to machine. Therefore, those panels must be instantiated at run time. In order to cater this, we create a simple script called **SensorDataPanelUIManager.cs**. This script will refer to the 2 text objects within a sensor data panel and open a public method to set the values of the text boxes. We then attach the text objects to the properties as shown in *Figure 9.15 (2)* and convert the sensor data panel to a prefab, as shown in *Figure 9.15 (3)*. The code for **SensorDataPanel** is as follows:

```
1. using TMPro;
2. using UnityEngine;
3.
4. public class SensorDataPanelUIManager : MonoBehaviour
5. {
6.     [SerializeField] private TMP_Text txtSensorName;
7.     [SerializeField] private TMP_Text txtSensorValueUnit;
8.
9.     public void SetData(string sensorName, string valueUnit)
```

```
10.    {
11.         txtSensorName.text = sensorName;
12.         txtSensorValueUnit.text = valueUnit;
13.    }
14. }
```

Select the UI panel that we will be populating sensor data add a **VerticalLayout Group** component. This component will automatically arrange the populated sensor data prefabs vertically. Set the padding and spacing as needed. Also, set the **Child Alignment** as **Upper Center** and untick **Height** from **Child Force Expand**. Now remove the prefab from the main canvas panel. This will be instantiated when we retrieve data.

Similarly, let us create a script for the complete canvas data visualization. Create another script called **MachineDataUIManager.cs** and add the following:

```
1. using TMPro;
2. using UnityEngine;
3. using UnityEngine.UI;
4.
5. public class MachineDataUIManager : MonoBehaviour
6. {
7.     [Header("Text Boxes")]
8.     [SerializeField] private TMP_Text txt_MachineName;
9.     [SerializeField] private TMP_Text txt_MachineMake;
10.    [SerializeField] private TMP_Text txt_MachineVersion;
11.    [SerializeField] private TMP_Text txt_Building;
12.    [SerializeField] private TMP_Text txt_Isle;
13.    [SerializeField] private TMP_Text txt_Section;
14.
15.    [Header("Machine Status")]
16.    [SerializeField] private Image imgMachineStatus;
17.    [SerializeField] private Color turnedOnColor;
18.    [SerializeField] private Color turnedOffColor;
19.
20.    [Header("Machine Sensor data")]
```

```
21.     [SerializeField] private Transform sensorDataPanel;
22.     [SerializeField] private GameObject sensorDataPanelPrefab;
23.
24.     public void SetMachineData(MachineData machineData)
25.     {
26.         txt_MachineName.SetText(machineData.name);
27.         txt_MachineMake.SetText(machineData.make);
28.         txt_MachineVersion.SetText(machineData.version.ToString());
29.         txt_Building.SetText("Building : "+machineData.location.building);
30.         txt_Isle.SetText("Isle : "+machineData.location.isle);
31.         txt_Section.SetText("Section : "+machineData.location.section.ToString());
32.
33.         //Set machine status
34.         imgMachineStatus.color = machineData.is_running ? turnedOnColor : turnedOffColor;
35.
36.         //Set machine sensor data
37.         foreach (SensorData item in machineData.current_data)
38.         {
39.             //Create a new sensor data element
40.             SensorDataPanelUIManager dataElement =
41.                 Instantiate(sensorDataPanelPrefab, sensorDataPanel)
42.                 .GetComponent<SensorDataPanelUIManager>();
43.
44.             dataElement.SetData(
45.                 item.name,
46.                 string.Concat(item.value.ToString(), " ", item.unit));
47.         }
48.     }
49.
50.     public void OnClearData()
```

```
51.     {
52.         txt_MachineName.SetText("");
53.         txt_MachineMake.SetText("");
54.         txt_MachineVersion.SetText("");
55.         txt_Building.SetText("");
56.         txt_Isle.SetText("");
57.         txt_Section.SetText("");
58.
59.         imgMachineStatus.color = Color.white;
60.
61.         foreach (Transform item in sensorDataPanel)
62.         {
63.             Destroy(item.gameObject);
64.         }
65.     }
66. }
```

In this script, we get references to all the text fields inside the canvas element, the rounded image to display the machine status, a transform reference to populate the sensor data of the machine dynamically, and the previously made prefab to instantiate within the sensor data display panel at the bottom.

In line 24, the **SetMachineData** method will get a **MachineData** as a parameter input. The variable values within the parameter value will be distributed among the text fields and populate other content within the canvas.

In line 34, the color of the Image used to visualize the machine status will be either **turnedOnColor** or **turnedOffColor**, based on the value.

In line 37, a **foreach** loop will iterate through the **current_data** array of **SensorData** object type, and instantiate new prefab instances. It will also refer the **SensorDataPanelUIManager** component of the prefab and execute the **SetData** method we created in the previous script.

There is also a method called **OnClearData()** which will be called when the marker is moved away from the camera. This will clear all the data, and destroy the sensor data instances created, if there are any. Now add the script to the main function and attach all the reference objects. *Figure 9.16* shows how each **GameObject** is referenced in the component:

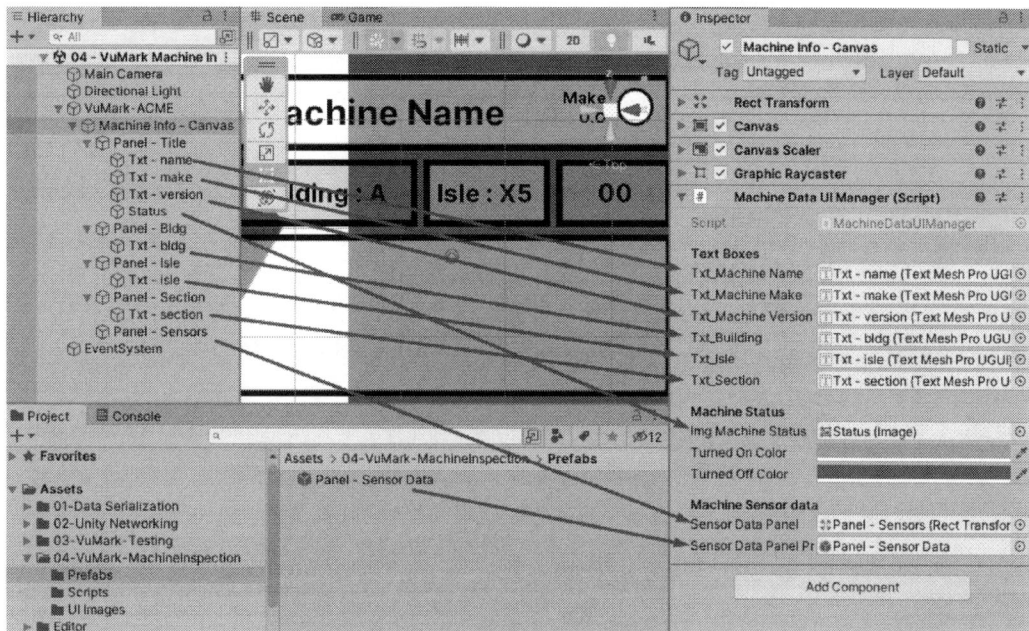

Figure 9.16: Machine data UI manager

Now, it is the time for us to request data from the local server based on the machine ID. 1. Open the **VuMarkDataRetrieved** script again and add the following to the top:

using UnityEngine.Events;

1. Add this secondary class before the **Monobehaviour** class. Here, we are making a custom **UnityEvent** that takes a string as a parameter, as shown below:

    [System.Serializable]

    public class StringEvent : UnityEvent<string>

    {}

2. Create a public **StringEvent** variable within the **Monobehaviour**:

    public UnityEvent OnDataReceived;

3. Instead of logging data, replace the **Debug.Log** line with the following:

    OnDataReceived?.Invoke(data);

    Now we have a Unity Event that can be invoked whenever VuMark data is received and the machine ID is passed to the listeners.

4. Now, create a new C# Script called **MachineDataRequester** and add that to the VuMark alongside the **VuMarkDataRetriever** component.

The script should be as follows:

```
1.  using System.Collections;
2.  using UnityEngine;
3.  using UnityEngine.Networking;
4.
5.  public class MachineDataRequester : MonoBehaviour
6.  {
7.      [SerializeField] private MachineDataUIManager machineDataUI;
8.      private void Start()
9.      {
10.         GetComponent<VuMarkDataRetriever>().OnDataReceived.AddListener(RequestMachineData);
11.         GetComponent<DefaultObserverEventHandler>().OnTargetLost.AddListener(machineDataUI.OnClearData);
12.     }
13.
14.     private void RequestMachineData(string machineID)
15.     {
16.         StartCoroutine(RequestData(machineID));
17.     }
18.
19.     IEnumerator RequestData(string machineID)
20.     {
21.         UnityWebRequest getMachineDataRequest =
22.             UnityWebRequest.Get("http://localhost:3001/machines/" + machineID);
23.
24.         yield return getMachineDataRequest.SendWebRequest();
25.         DownloadHandler handler = getMachineDataRequest.downloadHandler;
26.
```

```
27.         MachineData machineData = JsonUtility.FromJson<MachineData>(handler.text);
28.
29.         machineDataUI.SetMachineData(machineData);
30.
31.     }
32. }
```

As we did before, this script has a data requester that requests data from the remote server. In the above script, we register the **RequestMachineData** method to the **OnDataReceived** method that we created before, and also the **OnClearData** method to the **OnTargetLost** method of **DefaultObserverEventHandler** by Vuforia:

"localhost:<port>/machines/<machine_id>"

As the above link, the machine ID is the dynamic section that changes based on the VuMark ID. In line 22, we used the machine ID that is invoked from the previous class to change the link for every data request. If the data is available, line 27 will set up the response into a C# object and pass the data to the **SetMachineData** method from the referenced **machineDataUI** component. This component must be assigned to the Unity interface before testing. Make sure that Mockoon app is running along with the mock API with the correct path and click play. The following *Figure 9.17* shows how the attached VuMark sticker shows mock data in AR with proper colors and text data within the UI panel.

> Note: The scripts added to the project require refactoring to handle different kinds of unexpected data inputs. Read Unity's documentations on UnityWebRequest and JsonUtility classes to learn more about the properties and functions of them.

Refer to the following *Figure 9.17:*

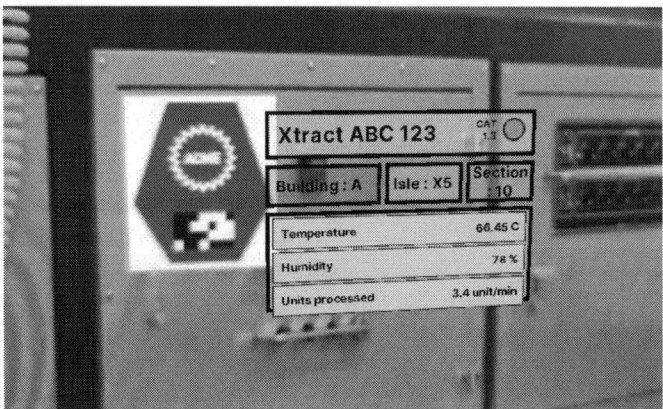

Figure 9.17: Dynamic AR app with VuMark displaying data on a machine

> **Note:** Downloading VuMarks one by one from the developer console can be an overwhelming process. Vuforia has a VuMark generation Web API that can generate VuMark instances using a POST REST API call. This API can be used in a recurring manner to generate and download many instances within a short period of of time.

Go to the following link to learn more about the API:

https://library.vuforia.com/web-api/vumark-generation-web-api

Dynamic AR billboard

Imagine you are supposed to build an AR application that requires marker-based recognitions without app updates. As an example, we can consider a billboard that changes over time and an AR app that dynamically supports the content in the billboard which shows related AR content. In a standard way, new markers must be added into the project and the app must be updated with additional content.

In this section of this chapter, we are going to build an AR app that does not require app updates, but one that can recognize new markers via Vuforia Cloud Targets and download content from an external source using Unity Asset Bundles. The following *Figure 9.18* shows the flow of how Vuforia Cloud targets can be integrated with Unity Asset Bundles:

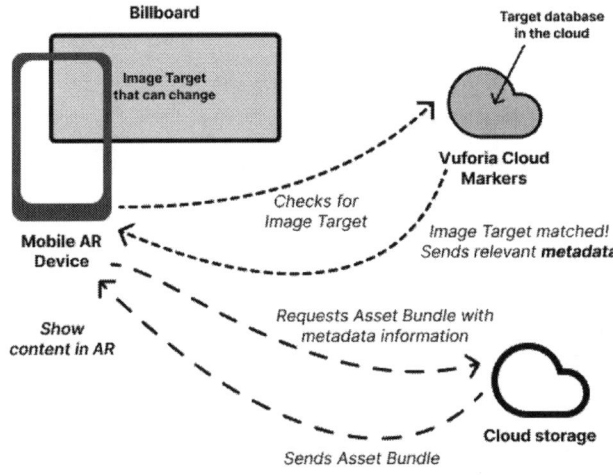

Figure 9.18: Flow of the dynamic billboard AR app

Setting up the AR poster project

For this project, we will be using two AR markers that are not added to the app but uploaded separately to Vuforia Cloud. Before that, we need to set up the project and the scene with Vuforia Cloud targets.

Go to Vuforia developer console and create a new Target database. This time, choose **Cloud** as the database type and choose the license key we created in the beginning. For Cloud detection, the license key is important since it determines our cloud detection usage allocated for the license plan.

Inside the database, click on the **Database Access Keys** tab and check for **Client Access Keys**. These keys are required to be added into your project as these keys are used by the app we make, to check for image targets in the cloud.

In Unity, open a new scene and add the following two Game objects from the hierarchy: **GameObject | Vuforia Engine | Cloud Recognition | Cloud Recognition & Cloud Image Target.**

Select the **Cloud Recognition** game object, copy the **Access Key** and the **Secret Key** from the developer portal we checked before, into the required properties in the **Cloud Reco Behaviour** component.

Now, let us upload some markers to the database in the developer dashboard. Here, you are supposed to upload not only the **Image Target**, but also another text file known as the `metadata` file. As shown in *Figure 9.18*, the metadata text will be sent to your app when the image target is recognized. This way, you can easily identify the image target you tracked and any additional data such as:

- An updatable link to a video that can be played on the target image.
- Dynamic data that can be changed time to time.
- Links to assets (3D models, sounds, images and so on) that can be downloaded and placed on the image target.

This metadata text file can contain a JSON with anything you prefer, to retrieve once the target is recognized. For the sample project, we will be using the following billboard designs with the respective JSON as metadata as in *Figure 9.19*:

Figure 9.19: Cloud Image targets and meta data example

Go to the target database and upload both the images along with the metadata text files. Both the images and text files are given with this book. Once uploaded, you can go in and double check the if target rating is good, and the metadata is uploaded correctly.

Implementing Vuforia Cloud targets

For cloud recognition, we must use the Cloud reco behavior and register for its events to manage different statuses of the target detection, since this is a network-based scenario which leads to many errors that occur during the process. When the cloud reco behavior is enabled, it starts scanning immediately, which costs one **reco** from the license. Scanning the same image target multiple times, without disabling the component will lead to wasting **reco** session given to us by Vuforia. Therefore, we must use it carefully.

Create a new C# script, name it **CloudTargetDataReciever.cs** and add the following:

1. `using UnityEngine;`
2. `using UnityEngine.Events;`
3. `using Vuforia;`
4.
5. `[System.Serializable]`
6. `public class CloudTargetSearchResultEvent : UnityEvent<string>{}`
7.
8. `public class CloudTargetDataRetriever : MonoBehaviour`
9. `{`
10. `    [SerializeField] private ImageTargetBehaviour imageTarget;`
11. `    public CloudTargetSearchResultEvent OnMetaDataReceived;`
12. `    CloudRecoBehaviour cloudRecoBehaviour;`
13. `    bool isScanning = false;`
14. `    string targetMetaData = "";`
15.
16. `    void Awake(){`
17. `        cloudRecoBehaviour = GetComponent<CloudRecoBehaviour>();`
18. `        cloudRecoBehaviour.RegisterOnInitializedEventHandler(OnInitialized);`
19. `        cloudRecoBehaviour.`

```
         RegisterOnInitErrorEventHandler(OnInitError);
20.      cloudRecoBehaviour.
RegisterOnUpdateErrorEventHandler(OnUpdateError);
21.      cloudRecoBehaviour.
RegisterOnStateChangedEventHandler(OnStateChanged);
22.      cloudRecoBehaviour.
RegisterOnNewSearchResultEventHandler(OnNewSearchResult);
23.      }
24.
25.      private void Start(){
26.          cloudRecoBehaviour.enabled = false;
27.      }
28.
29.      void OnDestroy(){
30.          cloudRecoBehaviour.
UnregisterOnInitializedEventHandler(OnInitialized);
31.          cloudRecoBehaviour.
UnregisterOnInitErrorEventHandler(OnInitError);
32.          cloudRecoBehaviour.
UnregisterOnUpdateErrorEventHandler(OnUpdateError);
33.          cloudRecoBehaviour.
UnregisterOnStateChangedEventHandler(OnStateChanged);
34.          cloudRecoBehaviour.
UnregisterOnNewSearchResultEventHandler(OnNewSearchResult);
35.      }
36.
37.      public void OnNewSearchResult(CloudRecoBehaviour.
CloudRecoSearchResult newSearchResult)
38.      {
39.          targetMetaData = newSearchResult.MetaData;
40.          Debug.Log(targetMetaData);
41.
42.          OnMetaDataReceived?.Invoke(targetMetaData);
43.
44.          if(imageTarget){
```

```
45.             cloudRecoBehaviour.EnableObservers(newSearchResult,
imageTarget.gameObject);
46.         }
47.
48.         cloudRecoBehaviour.enabled = false;
49.     }
50.
51.     public void OnStateChanged(bool scanning){
52.         isScanning= scanning;
53.         if(scanning){
54.             //Clear previously scanned targets
55.             targetMetaData = "";
56.
57.         }
58.     }
59.
60.     public void OnInitialized(CloudRecoBehaviour behaviour)
61.     { Debug.Log("Cloud recognition initialized : " + behaviour.name); }
62.
63.     public void OnInitError(CloudRecoBehaviour.InitError initError)
64.     { Debug.Log("Cloud recognition initializion error : " + initError.ToString()); }
65.
66.     public void OnUpdateError(CloudRecoBehaviour.QueryError queryError)
67.     { Debug.Log("Cloud recognition update error : " + queryError.ToString()); }
68.
69.     public void StartScanning(){
70.         cloudRecoBehaviour.enabled = true;
71.         isScanning= true;
72.         targetMetaData = "";
73.     }
```

```
74.
75.     public bool ScanStatus(){
76.         return isScanning;
77.     }
78. }
```

In this code, we have a reference to the cloud reco behavior component (line 12) which gets initialized in the **Awake** method. Once getting initialized, the **Awake** method registers the following events with methods within the class.

- **On initialized event:** This gets called, once the cloud recognition is initialized and working properly.
- **On init error event:** This gets called if the initialization has an error, such as network issues, license issues and so on.
- **On update error event:** This gets called if there is an error in the recognition update.
- **On state changed event:** This gets called every time there is a state change in the scanning.
- **On new search result event:** This is the main event we need, which gets called once it recognizes an image target from the cloud. We can use this to retrieve the metadata associated with the tracked target.

In the code, we created 5 methods that are registered to all the 5 events with necessary parameters. For the first 3 events mentioned above, only a log will be made in the console. **OnStateChanged** method will clear data if preparing for a new scan.

OnNewSearchResult method has a **CloudRecoSearchResult** parameter which contains the image target information with the metadata.

In this method, we set a string with the metadata (line 39) and pass it to a custom Unity event. In line 5, we have the inherited unity event which takes a string parameter and in line 11, a public variable instance of the same custom event object (**CloudTargetSearchResultEvent**) is made so that our other components can listen to this event. In line 42, we invoke this event passing the metadata to any actions that are listening to the event.

In line 45, we enable the observers by referring the cloud image target. This will enable the visuals of any game object we attached inside the **Cloud Image Target** object we added in the Unity Scene. This image target is dynamic and enabling the observers will register the latest scanned image to this target. Simply said, if we add a cube inside the image target, the cube will be visible only when we call this, and it will also be the same cube for all the markers we upload to the cloud database.

In line 48, we disable the cloud reco behavior since we already have the scanned image cached until we require scanning a new image target. This also saves us from spending additional recos from the license.

In the Start method, we disable the reco behavior. Therefore, we can manually initiate scanning by calling the **StartScanning** method we have in line 69.

In order to maintain any memory leaks, we unregister all the events we registered when we unload this scene. This is done in line 29 within the **OnDestroy** method.

Go back to Unity, and add this component onto **Cloud Recognition** game object, next to the cloud reco behavior component. Drag and drop the **Image Target** from the scene onto the **ImageTarget** variable. Add a **UI** button to Start scanning and attach the **Start Scanning** method to the button. Hide the button when tapped on it using **SetActive** method and show it again when meta data is received.

You can also add a cube inside the image target and scale it down to match the placeholder image **Cloud Reco**. We added this within another empty game object as seen in *Figure 9.20*. You can also see how the keys and the cloud image target is added on to the properties:

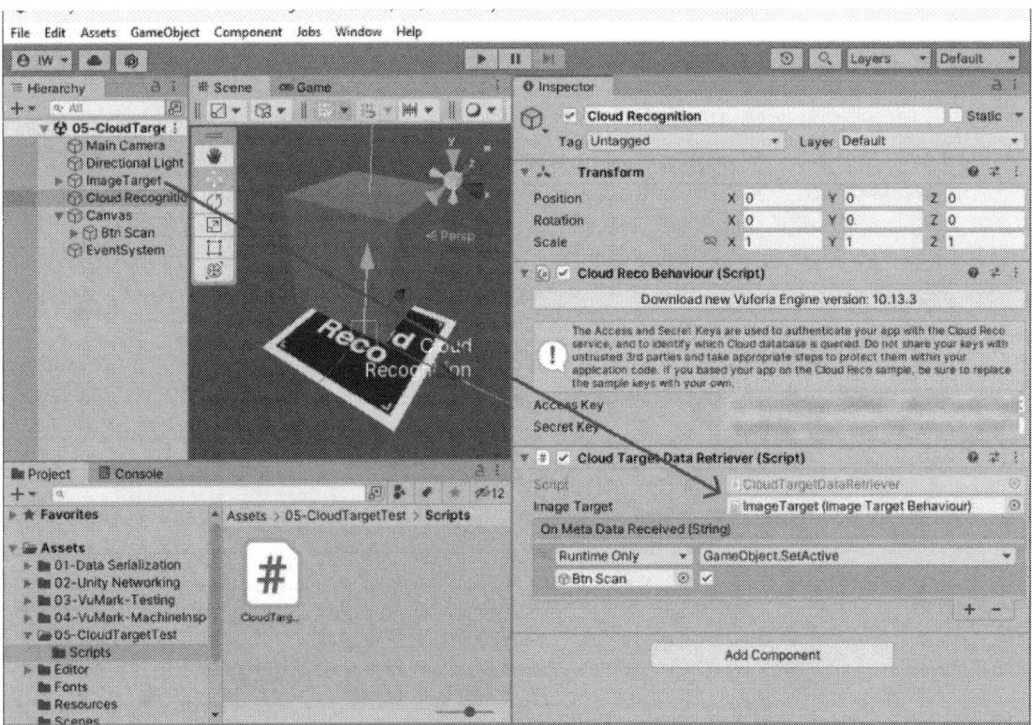

Figure 9.20: Setting up the scene for cloud target recognition

Now click on the **Play** button, show the camera to a poster, and press the **Scan** button and observe how the meta data JSON is displayed in the log and the appearance of the cube on the marker.

Creating asset bundles in Unity

Now that cloud target works perfectly, we have a new problem to solve. It only shows a cube for all the targets. Our plan is to build an app that does not need app updates to show content. Now that we are halfway through, we need a way to download and show 3D content on the AR marker based on the poster we scan. This can be done easily by using asset bundles.

Asset bundles are a feature in Unity that allows us to package and manage assets and scripts for our Unity projects. An asset bundle is essentially a collection of assets that are stored in a single file and can be loaded and unloaded dynamically at runtime. This allows you to easily manage and distribute assets, as well as optimize your game's loading times by only loading the assets that are required at any given moment.

With asset bundles, we can package assets such as models, textures, audio clips, and animations into a single file, and then load them into our app at runtime. This makes it easy to manage and update the content of our app without an app update. We can upload these asset bundles in cloud storage and load them to our app externally.

We are going to build two Asset bundles to download for both the billboards. In our project here, both of the cloud targets are 5 meters in width. In a new Scene, we added a Quad, placed it rotated on the origin plane and scaled it to match our image target size and placed it as a size reference.

Now, add an empty game object and name it **billboard-1**. Position it on the origin and add any 3D model inside of it with reference to the quad and convert the parent to a prefab. Repeat the same for **billboard-2** as well. In our project, we are using an iPhone and a 3D pizza for both the billboards.

Installing asset bundle browser

To install the asset bundle browser, follow the given steps:

1. Go to the **Package manager**, and click the **plus** button to the top left and choose **Add package by name**. Then type **com.unity.assetbundlebrowser** and press **Add**. This will install the asset bundle generator.

2. Now open the asset bundle explorer from the Window menu.

3. In the **Configure** tab, right click on the new window, and click **Add new bundle**. This will create a new bundle and you can add assets to this bundle. In this

project, we are going to build a bundle per image target. Therefore, we will need two bundles that are named `billboard-1` and `billboard-2`.

4. From the **Prefabs** folder, drag each prefab and drop on top of the asset bundle name we created in the Asset Bundle Browser window. In *Figure 9.21*, you can see how two prefabs are added in to the browser window, along with the previews of the prefabs we created. You can see that all the dependent files are included in the package along with the prefab:

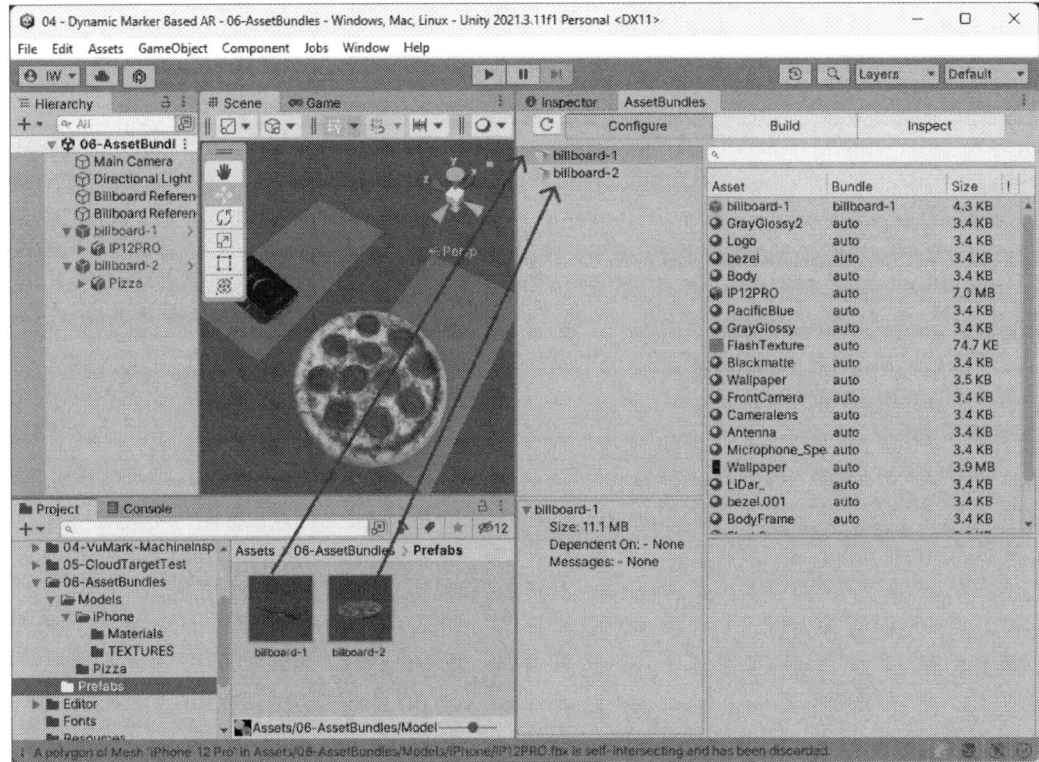

Figure 9.21: Creating asset bundles with prefabs.

3D Models used for this project: "iPhone 12 Pro" (**https://skfb.ly/6WoUB**) by DatSketch , "Pizza" (**https://skfb.ly/6DGT6**) by Jeremy E. Grayson which are licensed under Creative Commons Attribution

Now go to **Build** tab, provide a Build target and an output path, and click **Build**. Please note that Asset Bundles are platform specific. If you are building for iOS and Android, we need to make two bundles for both the platforms. Also, choosing different build targets will convert the complete project to that platform. It is always better to use a different Unity project to build asset bundles. In our example, we will be demonstrating on the Windows machine, and therefore we will go ahead with the Standalone Windows as our build target. Once the asset bundles are built, go to the output path and check if both bundles are available.

Now, we can upload these asset bundles and load them on to the targets when scanned.

Uploading the asset bundles in the cloud

There are many options in terms of uploading data to a cloud server, such as:

- Google Cloud Storage (Buckets)
- Amazon S3
- Azure Storage
- DropBox

Out of these options, Drop Box is free and easier to setup a public folder to host all our asset bundles. To use Drop Box, follow these steps:

1. Go to **https://www.dropbox.com/** and create a new account.
2. Once the free account is set up, create a new folder in your files and share it publicly by choosing **Anyone with this link can view**.
3. Go in to your new folder and upload both the asset bundles. Adding other generated files are not necessary.
4. Now we need to copy the public links of the bundles and update the meta files for Unity to download them in run time. Right click each bundle in drop box and **Copy Link**.
5. In drop box share links, there is a URL parameter at the end which is **dl=0**. Change it to **dl=1** to get direct access to the file. One of our sample links are as follows:

    https://www.dropbox.com/s/xxxxxxxxxx/billboard-1?dl=1

Updating the meta files to update AR experience

In order to download an asset bundle and display in AR, we need to know the URL of the bundle and the name of the asset. In our example, we made two bundles and added two prefabs named **billboard-1** and **billboard-2**. We are going to update our meta files with the respective names and the asset bundle link and other information. The following are the two updated metafiles:

1. {
2.   "message" : "Flash Sale!",

3. "link" : "https://www.dropbox.com/s/xxxxxx/billboard-1?dl=1",
4. "name" : "billboard-1"
5. }

1. {
2. "message" : "Italian Pizza",
3. "link" : "https://www.dropbox.com/s/xxxxxx/billboard-2?dl=1",
4. "name" : "billboard-2"
5. }

> Note: The links in the JSONs are modified and will not work if you copy and paste them.

Go to the Vuforia cloud database we created earlier. Open each image target, delete the meta file, and upload the new one. Test in Unity for both the targets before moving further.

Downloading content and displaying in AR

Delete the cube we added inside the image target. Create a new script called **BillboardData.cs** and add the following:

1. [System.Serializable]
2. public class BillboardData
3. {
4.   public string message;
5.   public string name;
6.   public string link;
7. }

We will be using the preceding script to deserialize the JSON to an object. Create a new script called **BillboardContentLoader.cs** and add the following:

1. using System.Collections;
2. using UnityEngine;
3. using UnityEngine.Networking;
4.
5. public class BillboardContentLoader : MonoBehaviour
6. {

```
7.      [SerializeField] private Transform contentHolder;
8.
9.      public void ExecuteMetaData(string metadata)
10.     {
11.         BillboardData data = JsonUtility.FromJson<BillboardData>(metadata);
12.         Debug.Log(data.message);
13.
14.         StartCoroutine(DownloadAssetBundle(data.link, data.name));
15.     }
16.
17.     IEnumerator DownloadAssetBundle(string url, string assetBundleName)
18.     {
19.         UnityWebRequest assetBundleRequest = UnityWebRequestAssetBundle.GetAssetBundle(url);
20.
21.         yield return assetBundleRequest.SendWebRequest();
22.
23.         if (assetBundleRequest.result == UnityWebRequest.Result.ConnectionError
24.             || assetBundleRequest.result == UnityWebRequest.Result.ProtocolError
25.             || assetBundleRequest.result == UnityWebRequest.Result.DataProcessingError)
26.         {
27.             Debug.LogError("Error downloading asset bundle: " + assetBundleRequest.error);
28.         }
29.
30.         //Log the download progress
31.         while (!assetBundleRequest.isDone)
32.         {
33.             Debug.Log("Download progress: " + (assetBundleRequest.downloadProgress * 100f).ToString("0.0") + "%");
        yield return null;
```

```
34.         }
35.
36.         //Load the asset bundle
37.         AssetBundle bundle = DownloadHandlerAssetBundle.GetContent(assetBundleRequest);
38.         GameObject asset = bundle.LoadAsset<GameObject>(assetBundleName);
39.         Instantiate(asset, contentHolder);
40.     }
41. }
```

In this example, we have a public method which has a string parameter that generates an object by deserializing the JSON. Once data is collected, a web request is initiated to download the asset from the cloud storage.

We use **UnityWebRequestAssetBundle** to download the asset bundle and once the process is complete, the **DownloadHandlerAssetBundle** class is used to get the asset bundle content loaded in to the app storage. Once downloaded, the **LoadAsset** method in the **AssetBundle** class is used to find the prefab we included in the bundle by name. The identified prefab is then instantiated and placed into a transform reference known as **contentHolder**. This will be the empty game object inside the cloud Image target in out scene.

Add the script to any game object and assign the **ExecuteMetaData(string)** method as a listener to the **OnMetaDataReceived** custom event we created in our cloud target data retriever component. Additionally, assign the transform of the game object inside our image target to the content holder to load content inside the AR marker, as shown in *Figure 9.22*:

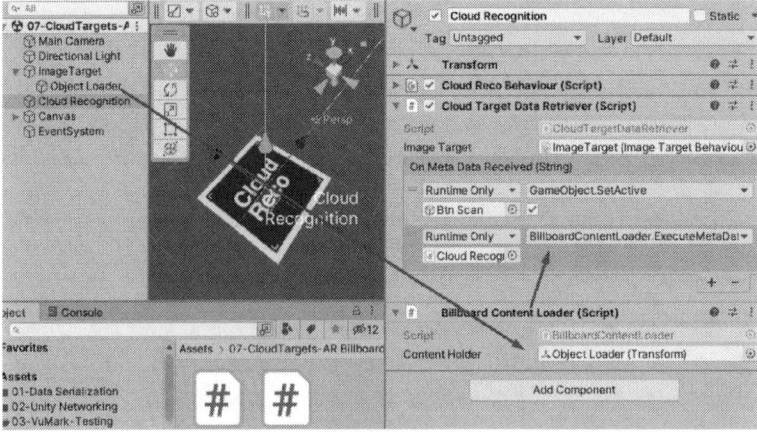

Figure 9.22: Asset loading configuration for cloud targets

Click **Play** and click the **Scan** button added before, to see how it downloads and shows the object on the target. Now we can publish the app and dynamically update new markers, metadata, and asset bundles to build a Dynamic AR app that does not require app updates.

Conclusion

In this chapter, we covered the basics of building a dynamic AR app, and the supporting content to achieve that by building two projects. We discussed JSONs as data holders and how serialization and deserialization can be made within Unity, along with `UnityWebRequest` to download text data as well as asset bundles. We understood the high-level architectures of each project and how data is transferred across platforms to build applications by connecting them together. However, both of the projects were far from being production ready. They need polishing, proper error handling and additional user interfaces integration to make them useful.

From this chapter, we end discussing the possibilities with Vuforia. However, Vuforia has more integrations such as Area targets, Barcode readers, Model targets and ground planes, which are out of the scope of this book. You can reach Vuforia documentation to get a wider knowledge on all the components we discussed in the previous chapter as well as the current one.

In the next chapter, we will be talking about ARCore and ARKit with ARFoundation to build marker less applications.

Key points

- JSON is a method used to store data in textual structured format.
- JSON can be serialized into objects and vice versa.
- VuMark is an image target system by Vuforia to encode data into an image.
- `UnityWebRequest` class is used in Unity to retrieve and send data through REST API.
- Vuforia cloud markers can be used to retrieve marker information without storing them in the app.
- Asset bundles are a way of bundling assets and loading them in runtime.

Questions

Use the concepts and knowledge about building dynamic apps acquired from this chapter and develop a simple AR based weather application.

- Allow the user to scan pictures of different cities and locations.
- Based on the locations, use an API to request real-time weather information.
- Use 3D models, animations and text to present weather information nicely on the scanned picture in AR.

Join our book's Discord space

Join the book's Discord Workspace for Latest updates, Offers, Tech happenings around the world, New Release and Sessions with the Authors:

https://discord.bpbonline.com

Chapter 10
Marker-less AR Apps with AR Kit and AR Core

Introduction

The fundamental behind **Augmented Reality (AR)** is placing objects in front of the camera input plane to mimic the positioning of a 3D model in the actual world. We learned this in *Chapter 2: Visualizing AR Environment and Components*; *Chapter 8: Building Marker-based AR Apps with Vuforia,* and *Chapter 9: Developing Marker-based Dynamic AR Apps*, as we used Vuforia to build marker-based AR applications that provide a local space to hold 3D models.

In this chapter, we are going to use Unity's AR Foundation, a package that uses Apple AR Kit and Android AR Core to build markerless AR applications with Unity. As mentioned in *Chapter 2: Visualizing AR Environment and Components*, tracking a plane, a face, or a body will provide a reference point in the 3D space that can be used as a local space to manipulate 3D objects. We will learn how to import and configure AR foundation with Unity, build simple AR projects, and learn how to interact with 3D objects using ray casting.

Structure

In this chapter, we will discuss the following topics:

- Setting up AR Foundation (iOS/Android)

- Setting up a marker-less tracking scene
  - Simulating the scene in the editor
- Plane detection and tracking – building an AR object viewer (object placement and manipulation)
  - Placing an object in the AR space
  - Move object on touch if the object is placed already.
  - Scaling the object with two touches.
  - Rotating the object with a single touch and drag
- Face tracking – creating an AR face filter with AR Foundation
  - Default face tracking setup
  - Adding custom objects around a face
  - Adding face interactions
- Device tracking – building an AR shooter.
- Additional components of AR Foundation

Objectives

After completion of this chapter, you will be able to use AR Foundation to build markerless AR applications that can spawn 3D content without pre-defined markers. You will be able to place objects on a scanned location, a face, or just around any physical environment and use different input interactions to manipulate content in AR.

Setting up AR Foundation

At the time of writing this book, Unity 2022.3 is the LTS version and, by default, supports AR Foundation version 5.0.6. However, if you are using an older version of Unity and see a different older version other than 5.0.6, you can manually install the package using it is updated version number. AR Foundation uses AR Kit and AR Core, which require the app to be tested only on the device and not through the Unity editor. AR Foundation version 5 includes a new tool to visualize an AR environment without the need to build and run on an actual device.

You can check the latest available AR Foundation package by visiting this link:

https://docs.unity3d.com/Packages/com.unity.xr.arfoundation@5.0/manual/index.html

To set up AR Foundation, follow these steps:

1. In a new project, open the package manager by going to **Window** menu | **Package Manager**.
2. If you are using the latest version of Unity (2022.3) and do see AR Foundation version 5.x, click **Install** in the package manager and skip to step 6.
3. Click the plus **+** button at the top left corner and choose **Add package by name**.
4. In the name text box, type `com.unity.xr.arfoundation`.
5. In the version text box, type **5.0.6** and click **Add**.
6. AR Foundation works only if AR Kit and AR Core are available within the project. Therefore, make sure you install either of them alongside AR Foundation. If you see a different version of AR Kit and AR Core in the package manager, install the **same** version as AR Foundation using the same method above.
   a. If you are building for Apple iOS, use `com.unity.xr.arkit` with version **5.0.6**.
   b. If you are building for Android, use `com.unity.xr.arcore` with version **5.0.6**.
7. Additionally, Unity requires **XR Plug-in Management** to be installed alongside the above packages in order to maintain the platform support and plugins for XR.
8. Now, go to **Edit** | **Project Settings**, and select **XR Plugin Management**.
9. To your right side, there are tabs that show your installed platforms. Each tab lists available plug-in providers that we must activate to enable XR support from Unity, as shown in *Figure 10.1:*
   a. For Apple, click the **iOS** tab and tick **AR Kit**.
   b. For Android, click the **Android** tab (with the robot icon) and tick **AR Core**.

Refer to *Figure 10.1*:

Figure 10.1: XR Plugin Management for iOS and Android

If you are using **Universal Render Pipeline** in your project, you must have a URP Asset and a renderer asset that contains your graphics settings. To render the camera background, you need to add a setting to your URP renderer asset. Without this option, your background will be rendered black.

Find the URP renderer asset in your Assets folder. If you are using the URP template offered by Unity, this asset is placed inside **Settings** folder of your assets.

Click the renderer asset, and from your inspector window, click on **Add Renderer Feature**. From the dropdown, choose **AR Background renderer Feature**.

Setting up a marker-less tracking scene

When it comes to marker-less tracking with AR Foundation, it can be either device tracking, plane tracking, or facial or body tracking now. The best way to test is through plane tracking, which is used to identify planes around a scan area.

Follow these steps:

1. In a new scene, remove the Main Camera. We will be using a different setup provided by Unity.

2. From your **GameObject** menu (right-click the hierarchy or click **GameObject** menu), choose **XR | XR Origin (Mobile AR)**. This will create an empty game object with a camera in it inside another empty game object known as **Camera Offset**.

3. XR Origin is your starting origin point of the AR world. By default, the starting point of your AR session will be the position of the AR origin. The Camera offset within your XR origin will move the camera based on a given offset. When you move your device, your Main camera will move, keeping the XR origin in its place. This enables device tracking in an AR session that allows you to place any 3D model in the global space and visualize them in AR moving around your device.

4. From the XR menu, add **AR Session**. The components in this game object control the life cycle of an AR session. Without an AR session, the camera will not load, and an AR session will never occur. You should always have only one AR session available in your Scene.

Now we have a basic marker-less tracking scene. But we have not specified allowed targets. For this example, let us create a simple plane detection scene. Follow these steps:

1. Select the XR Origin and add the **AR Plane Manager** component. This component tracks the planes in an AR scene and generates planes by referring a **Plane Prefab** object.

2. From the **XR menu** add **AR Default Plane**. This is a GameObject with an AR plane component and an AR Plane mesh visualizer component. This will act as a 3D model placed on planes detected by the AR plane manager.

3. Drag and drop the **AR Default plane** onto the **Plane prefab** parameter on the **AR Plane manager** added before.

4. If you are using URP, the default material added into the **AR Default plane** may not render correctly. You can create a new material and swap it with the **DebugPlane** material in Mesh renderer component of the AR Default Plane. For better visualizations, change the material shader to URP/unlit, set the Surface type to **Transparent**, and change the color with an Alpha around 20%.

5. If you build and run this application on your Apple or Android device, scanning the environment will show 2D polygons on top of your

surroundings, as shown in *Figure 10.2*. This indicates the app and the plugins are working as expected:

Figure 10.2: *AR Plane visualization*

Simulating the scene in the editor

If you are building an app using AR Foundation, building and running iteratively on your device can be tiresome. With AR Foundation 5.0, there is a way to simulate an AR environment.

To set it up with your project, follow these steps:

1. Go to **Edit** | **Project Settings** and select **XR Plugin Management**.

2. Under the first tab (Windows, Mac, and Linux), tick **XR Simulation**.

3. Go to **Window** | **XR** | **AR Foundation** | **XR Environment**. This will provide you with another window similar to a scene widow. This scene populates a sample environment to test your application. You can make your own environment here or use a sample environment provided by Unity.

4. To install sample environments, click the **XR Environment** floating dropdown at the top of the window and choose **Install Sample Environments**. This will import a package with a set of sample environments into your project. This may require you to choose environments and add what you require. You can import all if you prefer.

5. Once the package is imported, you will be able to select an environment from the same drop-down as before.

6. Click on the **Play** button and notice how your chosen environment is now visible within your Game view. You can use W, A, S, D keys while holding your mouse right-click to look around, as shown in *Figure 10.3*:

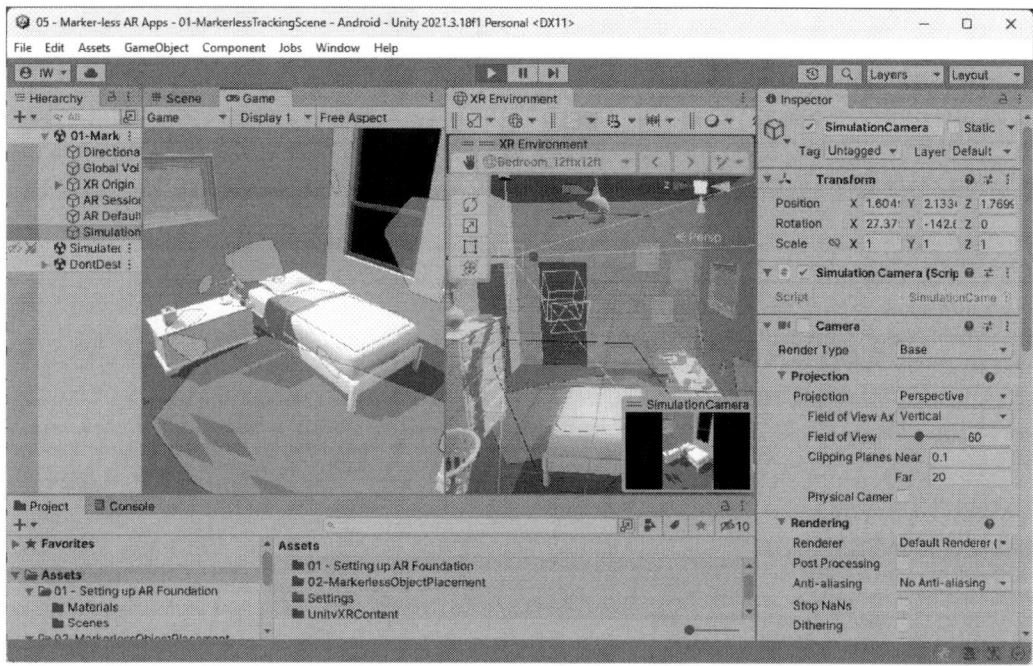

Figure 10.3: Simulation of AR plane detection

Plane detection and tracking: building an AR object viewer

One of the major use cases of markerless tracking is to place a virtual object in a physical space and visualize it by moving, rotating, and scaling it. In this section of the chapter, let us learn how to use ray casting and build a simple object viewer.

Placing the object on a scanned plane

Now that we have instantiated planes in the AR world, we must place a 3D model on any of those planes. There are multiple ways of performing an object placement. One of the easiest ways is to get a position from a screen tap. Let us call this **TapToPlace**.

Create a new C# script and name it **ObjectPlacementManager.cs**. Add the following:

1. using System.Collections;
2. using System.Collections.Generic;
3. using UnityEngine;
4. using UnityEngine.XR.ARFoundation;

```csharp
5.  using UnityEngine.XR.ARSubsystems;
6.
7.  public class ObjectPlacementManager : MonoBehaviour
8.  {
9.      [SerializeField] private GameObject placementPrefab;
10.     [SerializeField] private ARRaycastManager raycastManager;
11.
12.     private List<ARRaycastHit> hitList = new List<ARRaycastHit>();
13.     private GameObject lastPlacedObject;
14.
15.     void Update()
16.     {
17.         TapToPlace();
18.     }
19.
20.     private void TapToPlace()
21.     {
22.         if (placementPrefab != null)
23.         {
24.             if (Input.touchCount == 1 && Input.GetTouch(0).phase.Equals(TouchPhase.Began))
25.             {
26.                 PlaceObject(Input.GetTouch(0).position);
27.             }
28.         }
29.     }
30.
31.     void PlaceObject(Vector2 screenPosition)
32.     {
33.         // If there is an object placed already
34.         if (lastPlacedObject != null)
35.             return;
36.
```

```
37.         if (raycastManager.Raycast(
38.                 screenPosition,
39.                 hitList))
40.         {
41.             lastPlacedObject = Instantiate(
42.                 placementPrefab,
43.                 hitList[0].pose.position,
44.                 Quaternion.identity);
45.         }
46.     }
47. }
```

Here, we have a reference to a component known as **ARRaycastManager**. This component can cast a ray specifically for AR trackers such as the planes we added before. In line 31, we call the **Raycast** method using the **ARRaycastManager**, which returns a **true** if it hits an object. We cast the ray from the touch position. As there can be many hits that the ray would hit, the method uses an existing List of **ARRaycastHit** and populates it with the positions that the ray hits in the 3D world.

We check if there has been an object placed already, and if not, we place a new object and assign it to a temporary **Game** object known as **lastPlacedObject**.

Move object on touch if the object is placed already

When we place an object, we have a reference to the object we placed. If there is only one touch point and that touch is being moved, we are going to move the object along the plane. To achieve this, we are going to modify the previous code.

Add the following method to your **ObjectPlacementManager.cs** script:

```
1.  void MoveObject()
2.  {
3.      if (Input.touchCount == 1 && Input.GetTouch(0).phase.Equals(TouchPhase.Moved))
4.      {
5.          if (raycastManager.Raycast(
6.              Input.GetTouch(0).position,
7.              hitList))
```

```
8.              {
9.                      lastPlacedObject.transform.position = hitList[0].pose.position;
10.             }
11.        }
12.
13.    }
```

Now, in your **Update** method, add this after **TapToPlace();**:

```
1. if(lastPlacedObject != null) {
2.      MoveObject();
3. }
```

Here, if there is an object placed already, the **MoveObject** method would check for a single touch and change the position of the object to wherever the ray cast hits the plane.

If you want to test this on your editor, note that **Input.GetTouch** or any touch-related methods and variables would not work directly. The easiest way is to use **Unity Remote 5**, with which you can cast your game window to an Android device and grab touch input from the screen. You can get more information on Unity remote through the following link:

https://docs.unity3d.com/Manual/UnityRemote5.html

Build and run this and see how you can move the object once placed on a plane and change its position.

Scaling the object with two touches

Scaling the object while moving can be tricky. Here, we use a single touch to move the object. If we have more than one touch on the screen, we can check for two touches and use a pinch move of two fingers to scale the object, as shown in *Figure 10.4:*

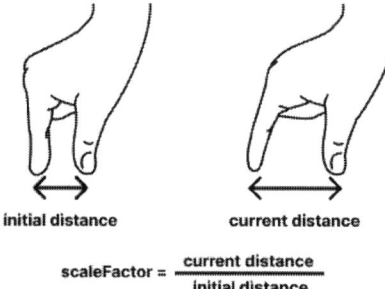

Figure 10.4: *Getting finger distance to calculate a scale factor*

As presented in *Figure 10.4*, when we get two touches, we can store the initial distance of the two touches and, every other time, store the distance of two fingers in another variable. This provides a scale factor with respect to the initial distance. We can use this factor to scale the object placed. The scale of the object should also be with respect to its scale at the time we capture the initial distance. In our script, add the following variables at the top:

```
1.    //Scale
2.    private float initialFingerDistance = 0;
3.    private Vector3 initialScale = Vector3.one;
4.    private float currentFingerDistance = 0;
5.    private float scaleFactor;
```

Now, create a new method called **ScaleObject()** and add the following:

```
1.    void ScaleObject()
2.    {
3.        if (Input.touchCount == 2)
4.        {
5.            if (Input.GetTouch(0).phase.Equals(TouchPhase.Began))
6.            {
7.                initialFingerDistance = Vector2.Distance(Input.GetTouch(0).position, Input.GetTouch(1).position);
8.                Debug.Log(initialFingerDistance.ToString());
9.                initialScale = lastPlacedObject.transform.localScale;
10.           }
11.           else
12.           {
```

13.   currentFingerDistance = Vector2.Distance(Input.GetTouch(0).position, Input.GetTouch(1).position);

14.   scaleFactor = Mathf.Clamp(currentFingerDistance / initialFingerDistance, 0.01f, 10f);

15.   lastPlacedObject.transform.localScale = initialScale * scaleFactor;

16.   }

17.   }

18. }

As explained above, we capture the initial distance as well as the local scale of the object and then multiply it with the scale factor we calculate when we move our fingers. In order for this to work, add the following in your update method after **MoveObject()** method inside the conditional statement:

ScaleObject();

Rotating the object with a single touch and drag

Now, rotating the object can be tricky with a single touch since we use the same gesture to move the object. There must be a way to distinguish between a touch for the movement and a touch for the rotation. Different AR apps use it in different ways. In this example, let us use the following scenario to identify a touch to rotate or move:

- If there is no object, place the new object for any touch on the screen.
- If there is an object and the touch point is at the bottom of the screen, rotate the object based on the horizontal movement of the finger.
- Otherwise, move the object for all the touches that are not from the bottom of the screen.

To check if the touch point is at the bottom of the screen, we can do a proportional check. Unity's touch positions are calculated from the bottom. Therefore, the y-axis is closer to 0 when the touch point is at the bottom. Add the following method to the script:

1. bool IsTouchingScreenBottom(float threshold)
2. {
3.   if (Input.touchCount == 1)
4.   {
5.   return (Input.GetTouch(0).position.y / Screen.height)

```
                < threshold;
6.          }
7.
8.          return false;
9.      }
```

This method takes in a threshold value (between 0 and 1) and returns true if the touch position proportion with respect to the height of the screen is less than the threshold value.

We can use the same principle we used in scaling the object to rotate it. Here, we get the first touch position and the current touch position and convert the difference of the **x** values of the two touch points to a rotation value. Add the following method to the script:

```
1.      void RotateObject()
2.      {
3.          if (Input.touchCount == 1)
4.          {
5.              if(Input.GetTouch(0).phase.Equals(TouchPhase.Began))
6.              {
7.                  initialFingerPos = Input.GetTouch(0).position.x;
8.                  initialRotation = lastPlacedObject.transform.localRotation;
9.              }
10.             else
11.             {
12.                 currentFingerPos = Input.GetTouch(0).position.x;
13.                 lastPlacedObject.transform.rotation = initialRotation * Quaternion.Euler(0, initialFingerPos - currentFingerPos , 0);
14.             }
15.         }
16.     }
```

In this method, we grab the initial x position and the rotation of the object when we touch the screen. When we move our finger, we capture the current x position using **Quaternion.Euler**, we add the rotation to the initial rotation of the object around the y-axis. Here we use (**initialFingerPos – currentFingerPos**), which gives an opposite value to the direction you want the object to rotate. Rotating clockwise requires the angle to be reduced. Hence, the finger movement should be towards left.

Now, to get this to work, modify the complete update method as follows:

```
1.    void Update()
2.    {
3.        TapToPlace();
4.
5.        if(lastPlacedObject != null) {
6.            if (IsTouchingScreenBottom(0.15f))
7.            {
8.                RotateObject();
9.            }
10.           else
11.           {
12.               MoveObject();
13.               ScaleObject();
14.           }
15.       }
16.   }
```

Here, we have given 0.15f as the threshold to check for the object rotation, which provides a 15% screen space at the bottom to rotate the object. As shown in *Figure 10.5*, build and run to test the object manipulation using finger gestures:

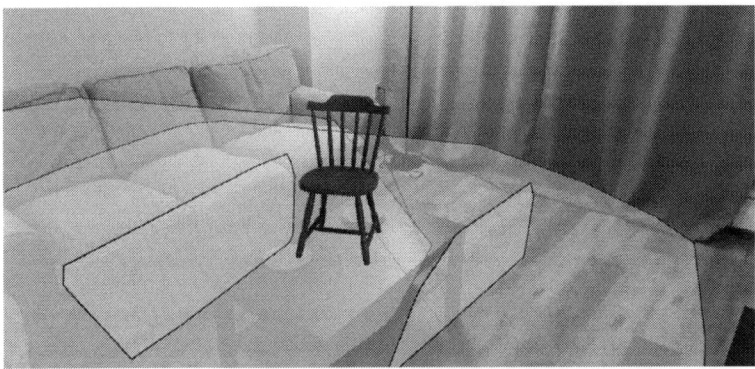

Figure 10.5: AR Object Placement and manipulation

The prefab that visualizes the planes can be distracting and make the project unpolished. You can disable the **AR Plane Mesh Visualizer** component in the AR default plane object to remove the visualization. Also, add a simple shadow plane object at the bottom of the placement prefab to make it look realistic with the environment around. You can do that by adding a simple shadow image attached to a quad.

Face tracking – Creating an AR face filter with AR Foundation

AR Kit and AR Core support face recognition and tracking. In this section of the chapter, let us use the face-tracking components of the AR foundation package to create a face filter. Follow the given steps:

1. Create a new scene and remove the **Main Camera**. Add the following Game Objects

    a. XR | AR Session

    b. XR | XR Origin (Mobile AR)

2. Now, select the **Main Camera** inside **XR Origin | Camera Offset**. Change the **Facing Direction** under **AR Camera Manager** component to **User** instead of World. AR Foundation only supports face tracking with the front camera of the device.

3. For iOS devices, Face tracking only works with devices that support face ID. Therefore, face tracking would not work for iPhone SE or any iPad without a face ID feature. Since we are using AR Foundation 5.0, Face tracking feature is integrated into AR Kit unity package. Any earlier versions would require another package to be installed to support face tracking (**com.unity.xr.arkit-face-tracking**)

Default face tracking setup

To setup a default face tracking setup, follow the given steps:

1. Select the XR Origin and add **AR Face Manager** component. Similar to what we did with the Plane manager, add the game object **XR | AR Default Face**.

2. Create a new material and change the material under Mesh render component of the AR default face. We can also add a texture to this material.

3. Convert the AR Default face to a prefab by dragging and dropping it into the project window.

4. Now, use this prefab as the **Face Prefab** under **AR Face Manager** component we added before.

5. Unfortunately, face tracking cannot be tested directly from the editor. Build and run the scene in your device and see how it generates the face, as shown in *Figure 10.6*:

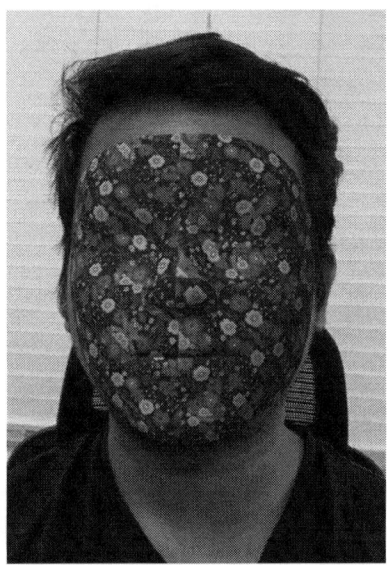

Figure 10.6: AR Default face with a custom material

Adding custom objects around a face

What the default face prefab provides us is a mesh that wraps around the face of us. By default, there is no way to simulate the face prefab within the editor. We can add a sample face object within the AR Face prefab and use it as a reference to place other objects.

Google AR Core SDK open-source project has provided a sample face 3D model to be used when making face applications. The same asset is provided within the asset package of this book. (`Canonical_Face_Mesh.fbx`)

To add custom objects around a face, follow these steps:

1. Create a new **AR Default Face** object and disable **AR Face Mesh Visualizer** component.

2. Drag and drop the face mesh 3D model inside the default face object and reset its position and rotation to zero while keeping the scale to 1.

3. Now you can use this face mesh as a reference and add any 3D model around your face. The assets contain a 3D model of a Sunglass that can be placed inside the face object, as shown in *Figure 10.7*.

4. Now, convert this to a prefab and assign it to the Face Prefab reference like before. Building and running the scene would provide an output as in *Figure 10.7 (2)*:

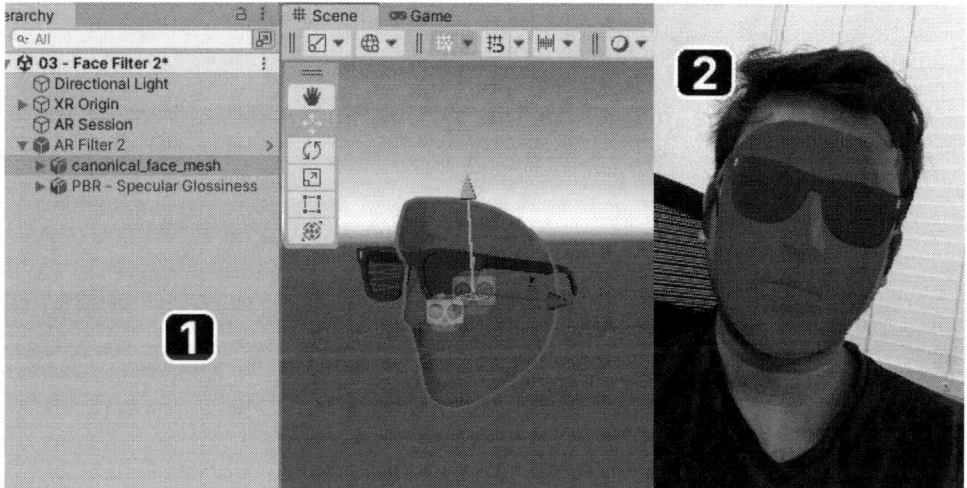

Figure 10.7: Visualizing a custom AR Face object

Now, we need to hide the face mesh we added so that only the sunglass will be visible. We can do that by just deleting the face mesh. However, if we do that, the temple sides of the sunglass will be visible when we turn our face. The 3D model is just an illusion that is placed in front of our face image. Therefore, we need to mimic a 3D face within the app to hide the sunglass but not our face, as shown in *Figure 10.7 (2)*. This is known as **occlusion**, and it is similar to the occlusion object we added for image targets in *Chapter 8, Building Marker-based AR Apps with Vuforia*. Follow these steps:

1. Create a new material and change the shader to **VR / SpatialMapping / Occlusion**.

2. Now change the material of the face mesh object to this. It may look distorted within the editor, but when you build and run it on your device, it will look

as shown in *Figure 10.8*. Remember to update the prefab every time you make a change on the face prefab:

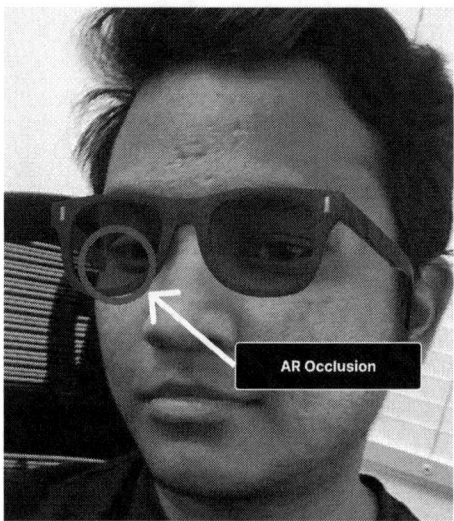

Figure 10.8: AR Filter with occlusion

Adding face interactions

Just like we used ray casting to place objects on a plane, we can use touch interactions to identify a face mesh and place objects. AR Foundation does not support ray casts against face meshes. Therefore, we have to use Unity's physics ray cast method to identify touch points on our tracked faces. To add face interactions, follow these steps:

1. Create a new Layer in Unity by clicking the **Layers** dropdown at the top right corner of Unity. Name the Layer **Face**.

2. Create a duplicate of the previous face prefab. Change the layer of the parent game object only to **Face**.

3. Enable the AR Mesh visualizer, and use the occlusion material we created earlier for the AR mesh.

4. Deactivate or remove the face mesh 3D model we added before.

5. Apply the changes we did to the prefab by clicking **Overrides** in the inspector window. Remove the prefab from the scene.

6. Now, create a new prefab to place on the face when we tap it. In the **assets** folder, you may find a 3D model of a flower. We will be using this as a prefab to instantiate on the face with touch input.

Create a new C# script called **FaceEffectPlacementManager.cs** and add the following:

1. using System.Collections;
2. using System.Collections.Generic;
3. using UnityEngine;
4. using UnityEngine.XR.ARFoundation;
5.
6. public class FaceEffectPlacementManager: MonoBehaviour {
7.   [SerializeField] private GameObject placementPrefab;
8.   [SerializeField] private Camera cam;
9.   [SerializeField] private LayerMask faceMask;
10.
11.   private Transform placementParent;
12.   private RaycastHit rayCastHit;
13.
14.   GameObject tempPlacementObject;
15.
16.   void FindPlacementParent() {
17.   placementParent = FindObjectOfType < ARFace > ().transform;
18.   Logger.Log(placementParent.position.ToString());
19.   }
20.
21.   void Update() {
22.   if (Input.touchCount >= 0) {
23.   if (Physics.Raycast(cam.ScreenPointToRay(Input.GetTouch(0).position), out rayCastHit, 10 f, faceMask.value)) {
24.   Logger.Log("Hit success! " + rayCastHit.point);
25.   FindPlacementParent();
26.
27.   if (placementParent != null) {
28.   tempPlacementObject = Instantiate(placementPrefab, placementParent);
29.   tempPlacementObject.transform.position = rayCastHit.

```
             point;
30.                    tempPlacementObject.transform.up = rayCastHit.normal;
31.              }
32.          }
33.      }
34.  }
35. }
```

Here, we need to identify the face object in runtime. We create a reference as **placementParent** and during a touch event, we find and save the object using **FindObjectOfType** method. A layer mask is used to identify touches against only the face. Once the object is instantiated within, the parent, the position is set on the touch point of the face and rotated perpendicular to the face.

To cast a ray directly from the screen touch point, we need to use the camera as a reference, which allows us to use **ScreenPointToRay()** method in camera component.

Add the component to a game object within the scene and assign the placement game object (flower), the Main Camera (**XR Origin | Camera Offset | Main Camera**), and set the Layer mask to Face.

Additionally, make sure to add the new Face Prefab (with the layer **Face**) to the AR Face Manager component.

Now build and run the application. Once the face is detected and the face prefab is available, tap on the face and populate flowers, as shown in *Figure 10.9*. Please note that when you move away from the camera, the face prefab will be destroyed, and you will lose all the objects you placed during run-time:

***Figure 10.9**: Placing objects on the face using Ray Casts*

Device tracking: building an AR shooter

Compared to plane and face tracking, device tracking does not require additional managers. Every AR application built with AR Foundation contains device tracking by default. When an AR session starts with the camera, the XR origin creates a virtual origin point in the 3D space that makes the camera rotate and move with respect to the movement of your device. We can use device tracking for various applications such as GPS (location) based AR navigation, spatial games, 360 video-based AR applications and so on. In this section, let us use device tracking to build a simple game.

This will be a simple shooting game that the players shoot objects coming toward them.

There will be enemies that spawn around the player regardless of the position and move toward the player. A button on the screen would cast a ray toward the enemies coming at the player that destroys the enemy while adding a point to the total score.

Create a new scene in Unity and add the XR Origin (Mobile AR) and AR Session. Believe it or not, the device tracking setup is now complete!

To try how device tracking works, add some 3D models around the origin point of your scene and see how it runs when you click play. Make sure the objects are placed alongside your origin since your device position at the start is going to be the origin point in the physical space. To demonstrate an example, *Figure 10.10* shows a simple setup of planets and how you see it in the app, as follows:

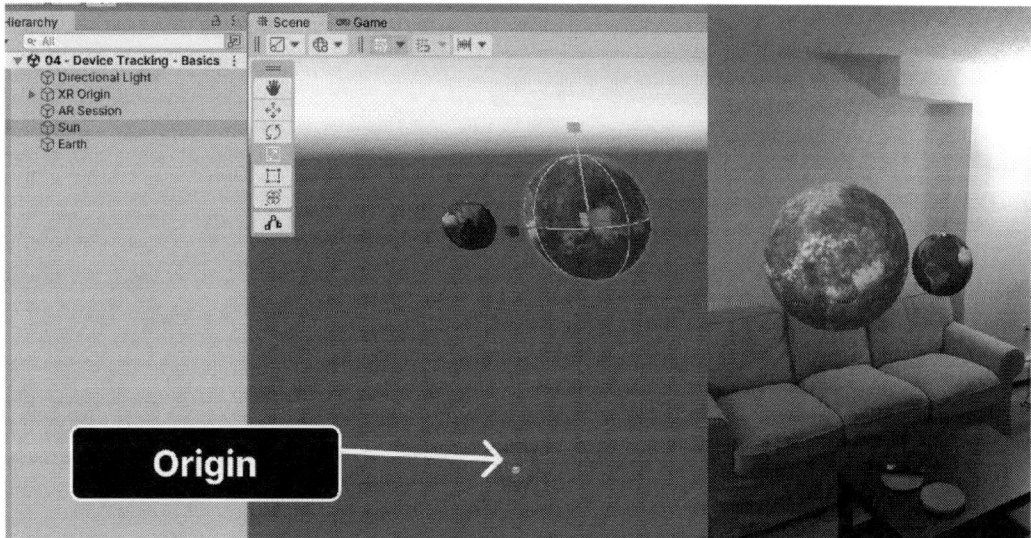

Figure 10.10: Device Tracking example

Setting up the enemy

Remove the planet objects from the scene and add any 3D model that represents an enemy. For this example, we will use a **Space Invader** enemy 3d model from **sketchfab** (*Space Invader* (**https://skfb.ly/QoTL**) by *ZentoZekto*).

Create a new C# script called **Enemy.cs** and add the following:

```
1.  using System.Collections;
2.  using System.Collections.Generic;
3.  using UnityEngine;
4.
5.  public class Enemy: MonoBehaviour {
6.     public float speed = 100;
7.
8.     private Transform player;
9.     private GameManager manager;
10.
11.
12.    public void SetPlayer(Transform _player, GameManager _manager) {
13.       //Setting the target for the enemy
14.       player = _player;
15.       manager = _manager;
16.    }
17.
18.    void Update() {
19.    // Check if the player is available, if, moves the enemy towards the player
20.       if (player != null) {
21.          transform.LookAt(player);
22.          transform.position = Vector3.MoveTowards(transform.position, player.position, speed * Time.deltaTime);
23.       }
24.    }
25.
26.    private void OnCollisionEnter(Collision collision) {
```

```
27.     if (collision.transform.CompareTag("player")) {
28.        manager.GetDamage();
29.        Debug.Log("DIE!");
30.        Destroy(gameObject);
31.     }
32.  }
33. }
```

Based on the preceding code, as soon as the enemy object is placed in the scene, it will move toward the player at a given speed (**Vector3.MoveTowards**) while rotating itself toward the player (**transform.LookAt**). Using **OnCollisionEnter** and checking the player tag damages the player using a **GetDamage()** method from a game manager. Moreover, the enemy game object gets destroyed after the collision.

Setting up the Game Manager

Since we do not have a Game Manager yet, this code will give errors. Let us create a new C# script called **GameManager.cs** and add the following:

```
1.  using System.Collections;
2.  using System.Collections.Generic;
3.  using UnityEngine;
4.
5.  public class GameManager: MonoBehaviour {
6.
7.     public BoxCollider spawnBoundBox;
8.     public GameObject enemyPrefab;
9.     public Transform shootPoint;
10.    public Transform player;
11.
12.    private int Score;
13.    private int Health;
14.    private bool isRunning;
15.
16.    RaycastHit hit;
17.
```

```
18.    // Start is called before the first frame update
19.    void Start() {
20.       isRunning = false;
21.    }
22.
23.    public void StartGame() {
24.       Score = 0;
25.       Health = 10;
26.       isRunning = true;
27.       StartCoroutine(spawnEnemy());
28.    }
29.
30.    IEnumerator spawnEnemy() {
31.       while (isRunning) {
32.          // Get a random position using the bounds of the box collider
33.          var randomPosition = new Vector3(Random.Range(spawnBoundBox.bounds.min.x, spawnBoundBox.bounds.max.x),
34.                Random.Range(spawnBoundBox.bounds.min.y, spawnBoundBox.bounds.max.y),
35.                Random.Range(spawnBoundBox.bounds.min.z, spawnBoundBox.bounds.max.z));
36.
37.          // Spawn a new enemy
38.          GameObject enemy = Instantiate(enemyPrefab, randomPosition, Quaternion.identity);
39.          enemy.GetComponent<Enemy>().SetPlayer(player, this);
40.
41.          // Wait for some time before spawning again
42.          yield return new WaitForSeconds(2.0 f);
43.       }
44.    }
45.
46.    public void ShootLasers() {
47.       if (Physics.Raycast(shootPoint.position, shootPoint.forward,
```

```
           out hit)) {
48.            if (hit.collider.CompareTag("enemy")) {
49.                Score++;
50.
51.                //Destroy the enemy
52.                Destroy(hit.collider.gameObject);
53.            }
54.        }
55.    }
56.
57.    public void GetDamage() {
58.        Health--;
59.        if (Health <= 0) {
60.            //Game Over
61.            isRunning = false;
62.            StopAllCoroutines();
63.        }
64.    }
65. }
```

The Game Manager has a public method **StartGame()**, that resets all the values and starts a coroutine called **spawnEnemy()**.

The IEnumerator **spawnEnemy()** runs until the Boolean **isRunning** becomes false (at game over). It uses a box collider to generate a random position in a box area and spawn the enemy prefab inside of it. After spawning each enemy, Game Manager sets the current player transform (referred from a variable) as well as the Game Manager itself to call **GetDamage()** method.

The **GetDamage()** method reduces the health of the player and if it reaches zero, the game stops and the coroutine will end.

There is a **ShootLasers()** method that takes a **shootpoint** (camera position) and casts a ray in the forward direction. This method destroys objects after filtering for enemies using the tagged **enemy**.

Go back to Unity and add the Enemy object to the enemy 3D model. Add a box collider and a rigid body to the object. Additionally, add a new tag called **enemy** and assign it to the model. Choose a smaller value for the speed in the Enemy component from the inspector window (around 3) and convert this to a prefab. You can now remove the prefab from the scene.

Select the **Main Camera** inside the XR Origin and add a cube inside it. Rename the cube to **Spawner** and move it along the z-axis around 10 units.

Disable the **Mesh renderer** component of the box and enable **Is Trigger** tick box inside Box Collider component. You can scale the box towards its local x direction to expand the enemy spawn region.

Now, add a sphere inside the main camera and attach a rigid body component to it. Change the tag of the sphere to **player**. Disable **Is Kinematic** and **Use Gravity** of the rigid body component and disable the mesh renderer of this as well.

Now, add the Game Manager script to an empty game object and assign the following variables:

- `spawnBoundBox`: The Box inside the main camera.
- `enemyPrefab`: Enemy prefab we created with the Enemy script earlier.
- `shootPoint`: Main Camera transform.
- `Player`: Main Camera.

Now, add two buttons in a canvas and label them as **Start** and **Shoot**. Assign the following methods to the **OnClick** event under the button component of the **Start** button:

- **Start** Button | `GameObject` | `SetActive()` | Untick (false)
- `GameManager` | `GameManager` | `StartGame()`
- **Shoot** Button | `GameObject` | `SetActive()` | Tick (true)

Refer to the following *Figure 10.11*:

Figure 10.11: Start button methods

This will deactivate the **start** button, activate the **shoot** button, and start the game.

Assign the following method to **OnClick** event under the button component of **Shoot** button.

- `Game Manager | GameManager | ShootLaser()`

Refer to the following *Figure 10.12*:

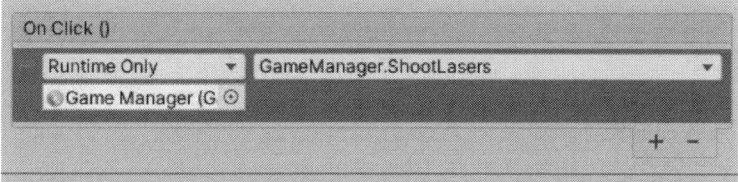

Figure 10.12: Shoot button method

Now, deactivate the **Shoot** button from the scene, and build and run to test the game. The following *Figure 10.13* is an enhanced version of the same game that uses text objects to show the score and the health. The project files are provided with the book:

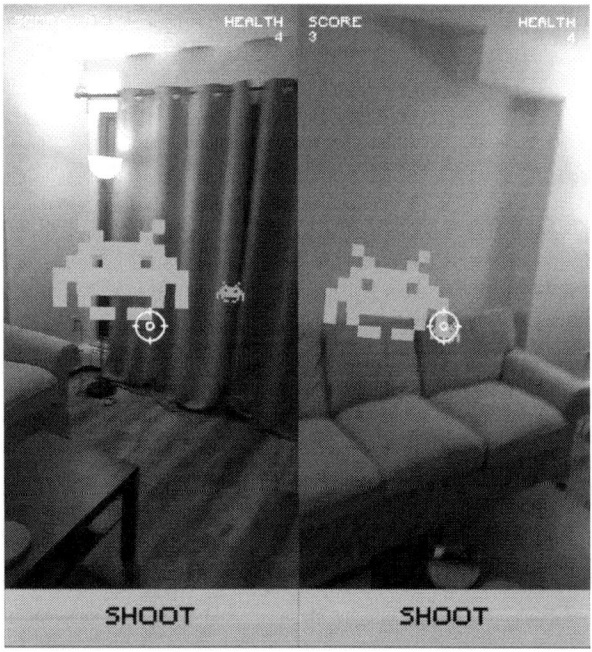

Figure 10.13: AR Shooter game with UI

Additional components of AR Foundation

AR Foundation is powerful since it uses both AR Kit and AR Core and provides a unique codebase to build applications for both iOS and Android. Following are some of the components that are provided by the AR Foundation to build different AR projects.

AR human body manager

This only works with iOS devices with an A12 chip or above running iOS 13. A human body manager can track a human body from the back camera of an iOS device. This can be used to create AR avatars, filters that use body tracking, and body gestures in your applications.

Point clouds

AR Point Cloud Manager uses prefabs with an AR Point Cloud component attached to generate a point cloud based on the objects it tracks in your environment. A point cloud can be used to understand granular-level details of the points in your space. If you are developing a measurement application, getting point cloud data increases the accuracy of your measurements since you can capture the distances between each point.

Anchors

Anchors are specially tracked points in your space. You can spawn an AR Anchor using the AR Anchor manager. An anchor is a specially tracked point in space. Anchors can be used for navigation-based AR applications since they can track a given point more accurately. Anchors are resource intensive; therefore, it is recommended to use as few anchors in your application as possible.

Image tracking

You can use AR Foundation to track markers as well. Unlike Vuforia, this does not provide you with a cloud database to configure. Moreover, the AR Tracked Image Manager component uses a library of images (AR Reference Image library) and one prefab that instantiates during runtime. This is similar to how face objects are placed once a face is tracked.

Conclusion

In this chapter, we learned how to use AR Foundation to create markerless AR applications. As we learned in *Chapter 2: Visualizing AR Environment and Components*, all the AR toolkits provide us with a local space that moves along with a tracked point in space. It can be a pre-trained tracked marker or an anchor that was identified during run time. In this chapter, we made three different applications that use such a local space. However, once the marker was identified, the rest of the application did not require any AR development knowledge. What follows is your ability to manipulate the Game objects in the local space in a meaningful way; it could either be a game or any other interactive application.

In our next chapter, let us move to another popular AR SDK, which allows us to build world-scale AR applications.

Key points

- AR Kit is used to build AR applications for Apple devices (iPhone, iPad).
- AR Core is used to build AR applications for Android devices.
- Both AR Kit and AR Core run on specific devices only with hardware capabilities. Older devices may not work.
- AR Foundation is a Unity package that uses both AR Kit and AR Core, and it allows developers to use just one code base to build applications that run on both types of devices.
- AR Foundation supports plane tracking, face detection and tracking, body tracking (iOS only), point cloud tracking, anchoring, Image tracking, and meshing.
- AR Foundation has **Manager** components that enable tracking of different trackers.
- XR Origin (Mobile AR) is the physical world starting point of your app, which matches the position of XR Origin.
- AR Session component manages the lifecycle of the AR tracking session.

Question

1. Using the knowledge about AR Foundation obtained reading this chapter, build an AR game that allows players to build Lego like structures using simple blocks. Use raycasts to place blocks on touched surfaces and different touch gestures to rotate and change colors of them.

Join our book's Discord space

Join the book's Discord Workspace for Latest updates, Offers, Tech happenings around the world, New Release and Sessions with the Authors:

https://discord.bpbonline.com

CHAPTER 11
World Scale AR App with Niantic Lightship

Introduction

In the previous chapters, we used Vuforia and AR Foundation to build marker-based and markerless AR applications. Vuforia's marker-based tracking is highly optimized to run on many Android and iOS devices. AR Foundation only runs on devices that support AR Kit and AR Core. Niantic Lightship is another AR SDK that allows markerless AR tracking. Apart from the basic plane detection, it has many features such as AR meshing (generates virtual boundaries on physical obstacles), occlusion, visual positioning system, semantic segmentation as well as an integrated multiplayer capability system. Niantic lightship runs on many Android and iOS devices and does not require any hardware capability, such as for AR Core and AR Kit.

Niantic Lightship targets mainly world-based scans. Their mesh recognition system allows detecting large-scale environments and generating virtual meshes that allow users to interact with the physical boundaries of the environment.

Structure

In this chapter, we will discuss the following topics:

- Setting up Niantic Lightship with Unity

- - o Downloading required tools and assets
  - o Setting up a simple plane tracking scene
- Object placement in AR
  - o Object occlusion
- Environment meshing
  - o Setting up the Scene to mesh the environment boundaries
  - o Creating a simple physics simulation in AR
- Introduction to Niantic lightship VPS
  - o Scanning the environment for VPS
  - o The flow of VPS scan recognition
  - o Adding anchors using the VPS authoring tool
  - o Updating anchor prefabs with proper visual elements
  - o Using Niantic API to restore anchor data
  - o Using Niantic VPS for scalable AR aplcaitons.

Objectives

After completion of this chapter, you will be able to learn the fundamentals of Niantic lightship, object placement, and detecting and tracking large-scale environments. You will also improve the realism of AR content by integrating occlusion and meshing.

You will learn additional C# scripting methods used in Niantic lightship and subscribe to different events and perform actions based on subscribed events.

Setting up Niantic Lightship with Unity

Similar to Vuforia SDK, Niantic Lightship (ARDK) uses a license to authenticate the usage of the SDK. This license also is used to request world data for your application and also to establish multi-user connections across the network.

Niantic Lightship SDK is known as *Lightship ARDK,* and it can be downloaded by creating an account through the following link:

https://lightship.dev/

After creating the account, log in to the dashboard.

Downloading required tools and assets

In your dashboard, click **Downloads** under the resources section.

For the examples explained in this book, we need to download the following:

- Lightship ARDK (v2.5.x at the time of writing this edition of the book. If you see version 3.x or latest, there have been some API changes that are noted in this chapter in addition to details of version 2.x)
- ARDK example scenes
- ARDK mock environments

All of these packages will be downloaded in `unitypackage` format. Now, we can create a new Unity project and import all the downloaded packages. For this project, we will be using standard graphics pipeline (3D) for the base graphics pipeline as some of the assets within ARDK are not compatible with **Universal Render Pipeline** (**URP**).

Adding a new license key and authenticating an application

Go back to Lightship dashboard and click on the **Projects** tab. The moment you click on the **Create new project** button at the top, it will generate a new project with an **API Key**, as shown in *Figure 11.1*. You can now edit the name of the project and copy the API key:

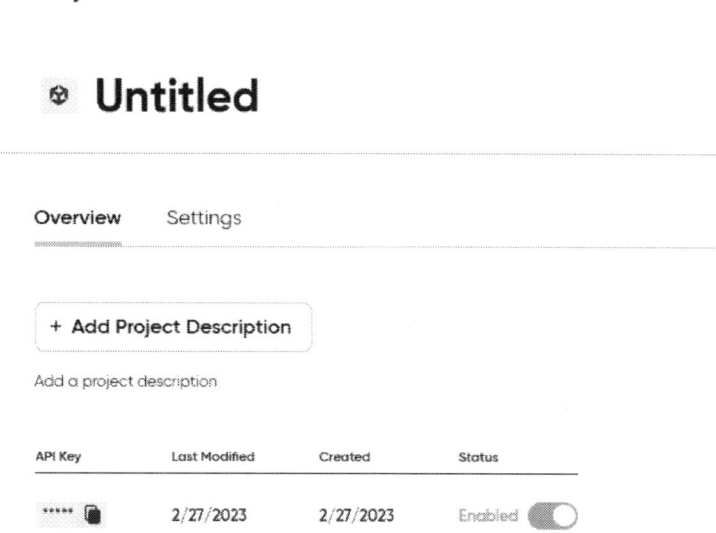

Figure 11.1: Creating a new API Key in ARDK

Once you have copied the license key, head over to the Unity project with all the ARDK assets imported. The method of adding the license key for ARDK is different. In your project, create a new **Resources** folder. Inside the **Resources** folder, add a new folder named **ARDK**.

Now, inside the ARDK folder, right-click and select **Create | ARDK | ArdkAuthConfig**.

This will create a unity asset with the name **ArdkAuthConfig**, as shown in *Figure 11.2*. You should now rename this:

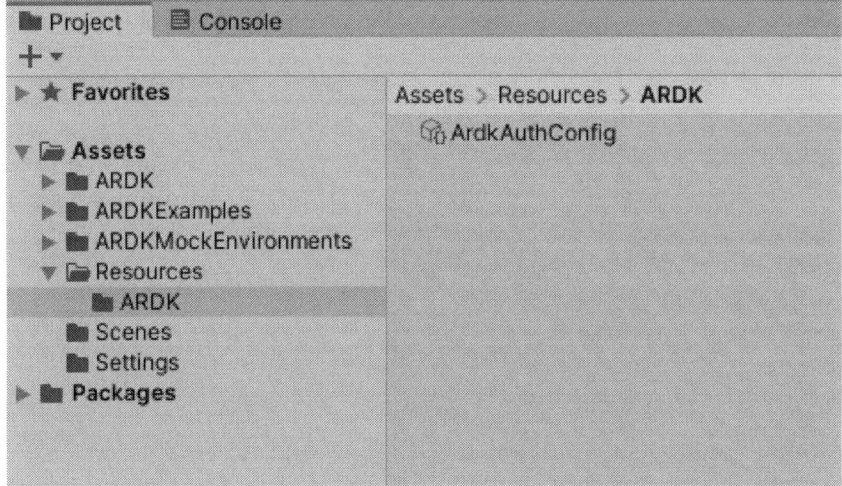

Figure 11.2: ARDK authentication setup

Then select the asset, and in the inspector window, paste your API Key inside **API Key** parameter input.

> Note: If you are using Lightship version 3.0 or up, you do not have to create the ArdkAuthConfig file. You can open lightship settings by selecting Lightship menu > Settings and pasting the API key in the inspector window into the appropriate field.

Setting up a simple plane tracking scene

Now the basic installation and authentication setup is complete. Niantic Lightship comes with in-built tools and examples to test the AR application without iteratively building on an Android or iOS device, similar to AR Foundation sample environments.

To setup a sample environment, follow these steps:

1. Go to the **Lightship** menu and click **ARDK | Virtual Studio**.

2. Make sure you have installed all three packages we downloaded before to enable the new **Lightship** menu in your menu bar.

3. Once the virtual studio is open, select the **Mock** tab. Here, you will be able to see different AR Mock Scenes with a drop-down.

4. From the drop-down, select **Living Room**.

Setting up the camera

> **Note: If you are using ARDK version 3.0 or up, you must install AR Foundation version 5.0+ and relevant OS SDK (AR kit or AR Core), as the latest versions of ARDK have handed over the AR session capabilities to AR Foundation. You must also install XR plugin management package from the package manager. Once done, skip to point 7.**

Now, in an empty scene, select the **Main Camera**, and perform the following:

1. In the **Camera** component, change the **Clear Flags** to **Solid Color**.

2. Change the color of the camera to **black**.

3. Add the following components to Main Camera:
    a. AR Camera Position Helper
    b. AR Rendering Manager

4. Make sure that the same Main camera is referenced as **Main Camera** for both of the components.

5. Now, create an empty game object in the scene and add the following components. You can also rename the game object to `AR Session` and reset its transform to tidy up the scene.
    a. **AR Session Manager**: This will also add a **Capability Checker** component to the same game object, as shown in *Figure 11.3*.
    b. If you are building for an Android device, add **Android Permission Requester** component.

6. In the **Android permission requester** component, click the **Plus** button under **Permissions** and select **Camera** from the dropdown.

7. If you are using ARDK version 3.0 or up, use the XR Origin and AR session provided by AR Foundation to set up the basic camera rig. Go back to *Chapter 10, Marker-less AR apps with AR Kit and AR Core*, if you would like to review the installation process. Now, our basic AR session setup is complete.

8. To enable plane tracking, add **AR Plane Manager** component to the same game object. (*ARDK Version 3: Add this to "Camera Offset" in the XROrigin*) Similar to AR Foundation, Niantic too can detect horizontal and vertical planes. Click the **Detected Plane Types** dropdown and choose **Horizontal** and **Vertical**.

Refer to *Figure 11.3*:

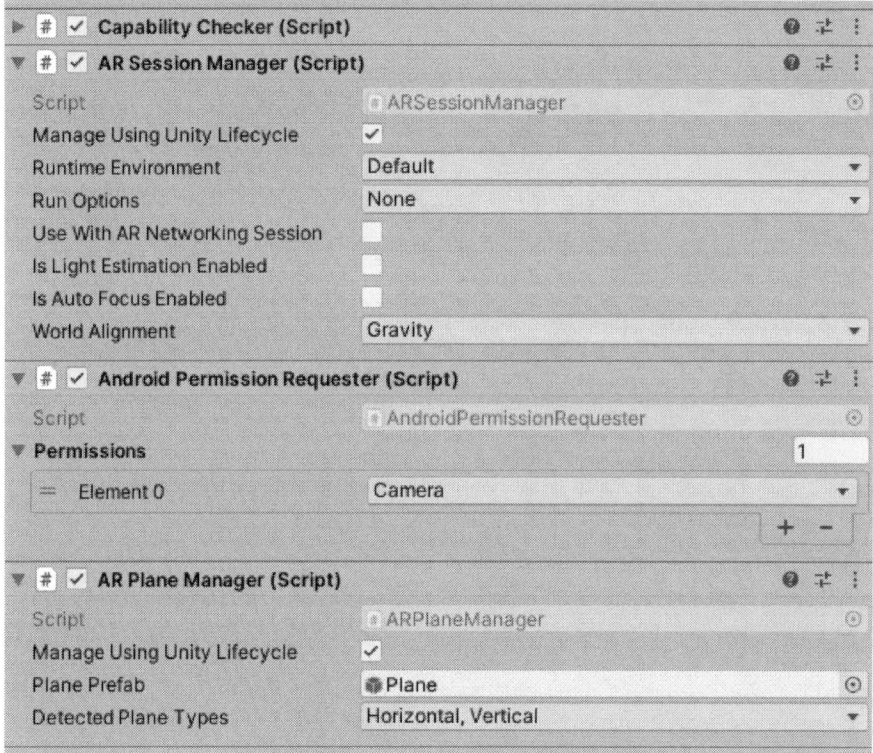

Figure 11.3: Setting up the AR Session object

9. In order to visualize the planes that are tracked, we can add a **Plane Prefab**. Niantic has already provided a sample prefab to add here. Go to **ARDK | Extensions | Planefinding** and choose **PlanePrefab** prefab as the plane prefab of the AR Plane Manager, as shown in *Figure 11.3*.

10. Now, click the **Play** button and notice how the sample scene appears, as shown in *Figure 11.4*. You can hold your right click and move around using W, A, S, D keys of your keyboard to identify horizontal and vertical planes. You can also build and run the application and scan your environment to view scanned planes. Refer to *Figure 11.4*:

Figure 11.4: ARDK Mock scene with plane detection

Object placement in AR

In Lightship ARDK, many of the interactions are using C# Actions, which allows developers to create methods and subscribe to different actions (events). It contains several classes and interfaces; we will be using in order to use the current AR session that is running and subscribe to its current frame to identify touch hits. Lightship ARDK also has its in-build Input manager that can track both touch and mouse clicks with a single call. This can be a little complicated, but let us look at the following script and understand the algorithm:

```
1.  using UnityEngine;
2.
3.  using Niantic.ARDK.Utilities.Input.Legacy;
4.
5.  using Niantic.ARDK.AR;
6.  using Niantic.ARDK.Utilities;
7.  using Niantic.ARDK.AR.ARSessionEventArgs;
8.  using Niantic.ARDK.AR.HitTest;
9.
10. public class ARPlacement : MonoBehaviour
11. {
12.     [SerializeField] private GameObject placementObject;
13.     [SerializeField] private Camera cam;
14.
```

```
15.     Touch touch;
16.     IARSession session;
17.
18.     void Start()
19.     {
20.         ARSessionFactory.SessionInitialized += OnSessionInitialized;
21.     }
22.
23.     private void OnSessionInitialized(AnyARSessionInitializedArgs args)
24.     {
25.         ARSessionFactory.SessionInitialized -= OnSessionInitialized;
26.         session = args.Session;
27.     }
28.
29.
30.     void Update()
31.     {
32.         if (PlatformAgnosticInput.touchCount <= 0)
33.         {
34.             return;
35.         }
36.
37.         touch = PlatformAgnosticInput.GetTouch(0);
38.         if (touch.phase == TouchPhase.Began)
39.         {
40.             TouchBegan(touch);
41.         }
42.     }
43.
44.     void TouchBegan(Touch touch)
45.     {
46.         // check a valid frame
```

```
47.         var currentFrame = session.CurrentFrame;
48.
49.         if (currentFrame == null) return;
50.
51.         if (cam == null) return;
52.
53.         var hit = currentFrame.HitTest(cam.pixelWidth, cam.pixelHeight, touch.position, ARHitTestResultType.ExistingPlaneUsingExtent | ARHitTestResultType.EstimatedHorizontalPlane);
54.
55.         if (hit.Count == 0) return;
56.
57.         // Move the object to the position
58.         placementObject.transform.position = hit[0].WorldTransform.ToPosition();
59.
60.         // lookat
61.         placementObject.transform.LookAt(new Vector3(
62.             currentFrame.Camera.Transform.GetPosition().x,
63.             placementObject.transform.position.y,
64.             currentFrame.Camera.Transform.GetPosition().z
65.         ));
66.
67.     }
68. }
```

In this code, we subscribe a method **OnSessionInitialized(AnyARSessionInitialized args)** to the **SessionInitialized** action of ARDKs **ARSessionFactory**. In simple terms, when the SDK initializes the session, it passes data and executes the **OnSessionInitialized** method we have added in the preceding script.

If you check the **OnSessionInitialized** method, you can see that we have immediately unsubscribed from the action (line 25) and taken the session from the argument data that was passed by the AR session factory. We need this session to access frame information from the screen later on.

We are using a static class called **PlatformAgnosticInput** which works on both mobile and the editor (touch and mouse clicks) and checks for touches. If we have more than one touch, we grab the position of the first touch and call a method **TouchBegan**. This is the method we will be casting a ray to get the hit position to instantiate an object.

In **TouchBegan** method, which runs in the update loop, checks the **CurrentFrame** of the session at the time of the touch to get frame information.

If we have valid frame information, we use the method **HitTest** which is an integrated method of the **CurrentFrame** object, with Camera information (**pixelWidth** and **pixelHeight**), **touchPosition,** and hit plane information. This method returns an array of hits, which allows us to choose the first element of the array and obtain its world position by calling **WorldTransform.ToPosition()** method.

We already added a simple snippet to make the object rotate towards the camera when changing the position. As you can see, this code does not instantiate an object for the first time. It uses an existing object in the space. Now, let us head back to Unity to arrange the component.

Add the **ARPlacement** component to the game object you have the AR session attached with. Reference the **MainCamera** to the **Cam** variable.

For the **Placement Object** variable, we need to have a model in the scene. ARDK examples contain an object we can use for testing purposes (**Assets** | **ADRK Examples** | **Common** | **Prefabs** | **Yeti**).

Drag and drop the object to the scene and set its position to (1000,1000,1000). This is to make the object not visible when you open the camera for the first time.

Now, assign it as the **Placement Object**.

Now, click play and touch on a tracked floor and notice how the object gets placed in the scene. You can try the same using building the app on your mobile device.

Object occlusion

Lightship ARDK has a very powerful AI-based mesh recognition system without the use of additional sensors. This system can generate occluding meshes in run time and render them before the object, so the objects can be seen behind physical obstacles.

To enable occlusion for the above project, follow these steps:

1. Select the **Main Camera** (AR Camera) and attach the **AR Depth Manager** component.

2. If you want to optimize the occlusion for an object already on the scene, you can add **AR Depth Interpolation Adaptor** component to the main camera and add the **renderer** component of the `Yeti` object. This is optional, but it overrides the **Interpolation Preference** value you have in your **AR Depth Manager** component.

3. If you are using ARDK version 3.0, use `AROcclusionManager` component from AR Foundation to the XR Origin component. Also, add `OcclusionContentProvider` component in place of **AR Depth Interpolation Adaptor.**

The following *Figure 11.5* shows how the object placement works with and without the AR Depth Manager:

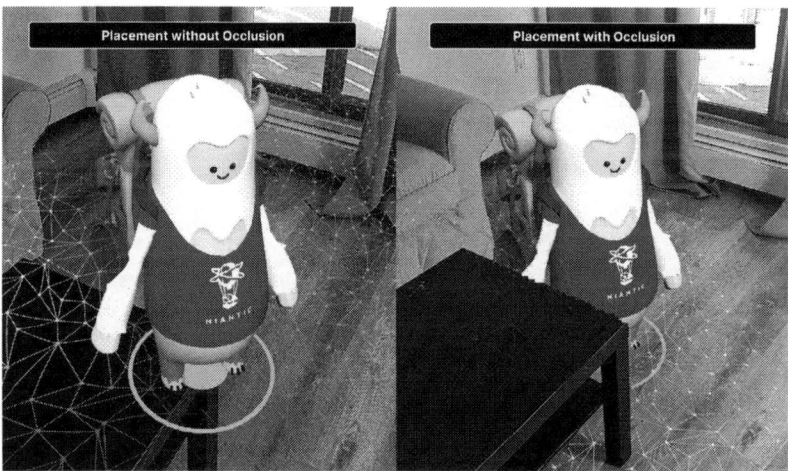

Figure 11.5: Difference of using the AR Depth Manager/ AR Occlusion Manager

Environment meshing

Niantic ARDK comes with in-built functionality to mesh the world obstacles without the need for a dedicated sensor such as the lidar sensor. AR Depth manager component is used to enable and track the mesh spaces, but currently, it does not have any physical properties included. As for the first exercise, we will add a mesh visualizer and see how the mesh is being recognized.

Setting up the scene to mesh the environment boundaries

Create a new basic Niantic AR scene setup without the **AR Plane Manager**. However, make sure that your Main camera has the **AR Depth Manager** component attached.

Follow these steps:

1. Open **Assets | Extensions | Meshing** and find the **ARMesh** prefab in the folder.

2. Drag and drop the prefab into the scene.

3. Click the prefab and notice the **ARMeshManager** component added to it. This component uses the AR Depth manager information and the namespace **Niantic.ARDK.AR.Mesh** to generate a mesh in runtime.

4. Unfortunately, meshing cannot be tested in the editor. Therefore, we will build and run and scan the environment. Notice how it scans and draws a mesh on the environment as shown in *Figure 11.6*:

Figure 11.6: Visualizing the AR Mesh (Check the color image for better clarity)

Creating a simple physics simulation in AR

The basic AR mesh prefab does not offer collisions, and the simulation is not realistic with the visualization. In this exercise, we will create a simple ball throw with touch input to create and throw objects in the environment, making them collide with the physical objects in the environment.

Creating an object to throw

Follow these steps:

1. Create a new sphere and make the scale of the object (0.3,0.3,0.3).

2. Add a material to the sphere and rename it as **Ball**.

3. Select the ball and add a **Rigidbody** component.
4. We are also going to create a *physic material*. In your assets folder, right-click inside a folder and select **Create | Physic Material**.
5. Rename the material as **Rubber** and select it. Set the **Dynamic friction** to **0.2**, **Static friction** to **0.3**, and **Bounciness** to **0.8**. Keep other dropdowns **Average**. We use physical materials to provide collision effects, such as friction and bounciness, to make a realistic simulation.
6. Now add the physic material asset created as the `Material` of the `Sphere Collider` of the ball object.
7. Drag and drop the ball into the project window folder to convert it to a prefab.

Throwing the ball at runtime

Create a new C# script called **ThrowObject.cs** and add the following. This script simply uses touch input, instantiates a prefab instance and applies a force towards the forward direction of the camera, and destroys it after a given time:

```
1.  using UnityEngine;
2.  using Niantic.ARDK.Utilities.Input.Legacy;
3.
4.  public class ThrowObject: MonoBehaviour {
5.      public GameObject throwObjectPrefab;
6.      public float throwForce;
7.      public Camera cam;
8.      public float timeToDestroy = 10;
9.
10.     Touch touch;
11.     Vector3 throwPosition;
12.     GameObject throwObject;
13.
14.     void Update() {
15.         if (PlatformAgnosticInput.touchCount <= 0) return;
16.         if (cam == null || throwObjectPrefab == null) return;
17.
18.         touch = PlatformAgnosticInput.GetTouch(0);
```

19.

20.   if (touch.phase == TouchPhase.Began) {

21.   throwPosition = cam.transform.position + cam.transform.forward;

22.

23.   throwObject = Instantiate(throwObjectPrefab, throwPosition, Quaternion.identity);

24.

25.   throwObject.GetComponent < Rigidbody > ().AddForce(cam.transform.forward * throwForce);

26.

27.   Destroy(throwObject, timeToDestroy);

28.   }

29. }

30. }

Go back to Unity and add the script to any game object (prefer the one with the AR session).

Add the Ball prefab as the **Throw Object Prefab**. Drag the Main Camera into the **Cam** property. You can add any values to the **Throw Force** and **Time to Destroy**. With typical scales, 200 and 10, respectively, would be good values.

Now, select the **AR Mesh** prefab in your scene. Within the **ARMeshManager** component, click **Use Invisible Material** to replace the AR visualization with invisible material.

For the **Mesh Prefab**, add the prefab **MeshColliderChunk** from **Assets | ARDK | Extensions | Meshing** folder. If you select the prefab, you can see that it has a mesh collider as well as a mesh renderer. This Mesh collider will be used to calculate physics boundaries of the mesh it generates, allowing us to interact with physics integrated objects in the scene.

Build and run the scene. Scan the environment and keep tapping on the screen to see how it throws balls from the screen towards the physical space and how they bounce off and interact with your physical obstacles in the environment, as shown in *Figure 11.7*:

Figure 11.7: AR Meshing with collisions

Introduction to Niantic lightship VPS

Niantic ARDK contains the ability to identify and track and identify world scale environments. This can be an indoor location that is private to the developer, such as a private venue, or a public place, such as a city attraction or an exterior of a building. This allows developers to build AR applications that work on certain geolocations and track waypoints very accurately. Some of the use cases of world-scale AR applications are:

- Location-based AR games, such as Niantic's very own Pokémon GO, Jurassic Park AR game, and Minecraft worlds.
- AR wayfinding applications; an example use case would be a theme park guide app to guide people towards certain parts of the theme park.
- AR Billboards are placed in the exteriors of buildings for marketing activations.
- Large-scale training simulations in AR.

People around the world contribute to scanning the places in the world and submitting that data to Niantic's VPS cloud. This allows anyone to create AR applications that involve tracking world places. You can do that by using an app called *Niantic Wayfarer*.

Niantic Wayfarer partners with people around the world to add content to the Niantic **Geospatial** library. You can check the current map of all the scanned places around the world by visiting the **Geospatial Browser** section of the lightship developer console.

Individual developers can also scan their own environments and upload them to the cloud but make them private. This allows developers to build private environment-based AR applications limited to their private scans.

In this section, we will scan a private space and use lightship VPS to localize that space to spawn a custom 3D model. This model will activate if we scan the same environment that we scanned before. Think of this use case as a *marker-based* scenario, but instead of an image or an object, this tracks a bigger environment.

Scanning an environment for VPS

In order to scan an environment and upload to lightship cloud, you need to have a lightship account and the *Niantic Wayfarer* app installed on your device. Currently, a beta version for iOS devices is available and a full Android version available from the Google play store.

Download the *Niantic Wayfarer* app and install it. Login with the same lightship developer account to get access to the application page. You might want to provide camera and precise location permissions since the app scans rely on the camera and the location data.

From the Niantic Wayfarer app, you can scan and upload environments as private or public. If the scans are public, it is processed and evaluated before being available to others. If it is private, and may take up to 4 hours for the scans to be processed and be available for development use. In this section, we will scan an interior room and upload the data to the private scan space.

Open the wayfarer app, make sure your location in the given map is precise and click **Scan**, as shown in *Figure 11.8*. In a single scan, move around your camera while noticing how it generates the mesh of the environment. Scan at least 60 seconds and make sure you obtain as many details as possible into the mesh:

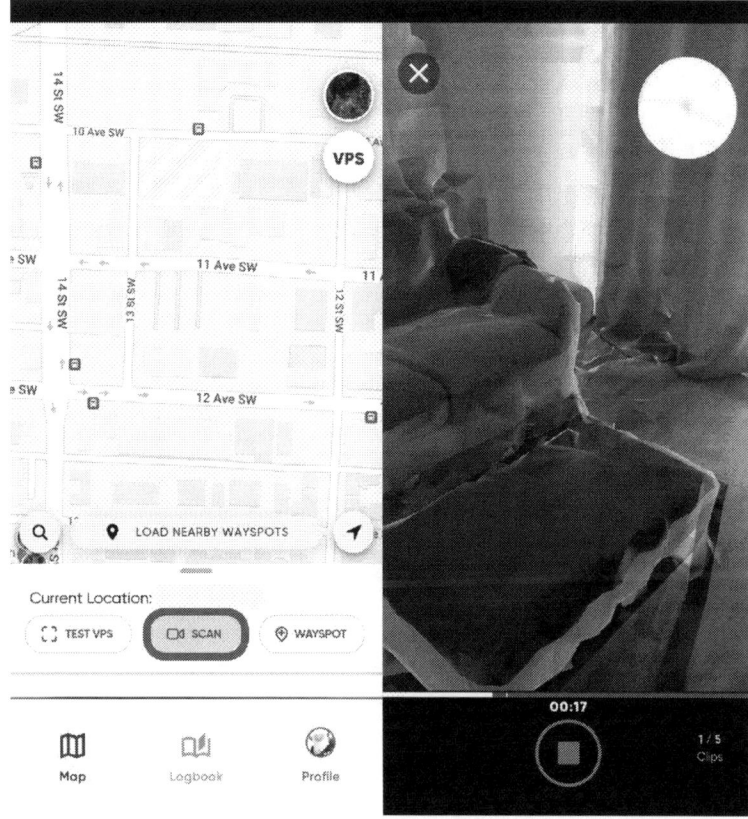

Figure 11.8: Starting an environment scan

Once you are done with the scan, you can continue it to scan nearby places. A single scan allows you to generate meshes for 5 clips, thus allowing you to scan a large environment. In the preceding example, we only needed to scan the room. Therefore, only one clip was created.

Once the scan is completed. Upload your scan as a private scan type. Make sure you immediately upload. If not, you can perform many scans together and upload only the selected scans, as shown in *Figure 11.9*:

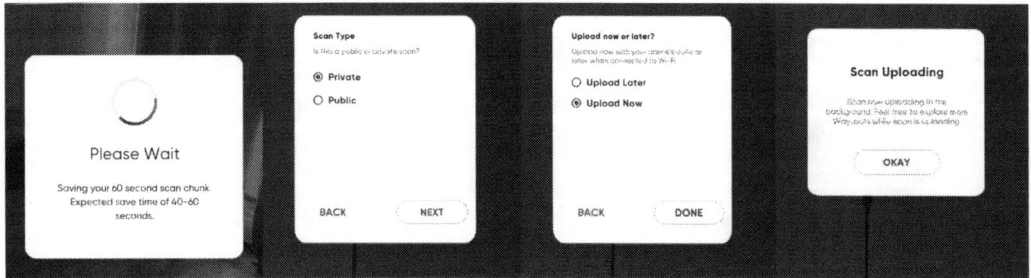

Figure 11.9: Uploading the scanned environment

The size of a single scan may depend on how large your environment is. However, as soon as the upload is started, you can check the status of your upload by visiting the log book, as shown in *Figure 11.10*. If the upload status is **complete**, you will be able to see that the uploaded data is currently in **Processing**, under the **Private meshes** section of your developer dashboard:

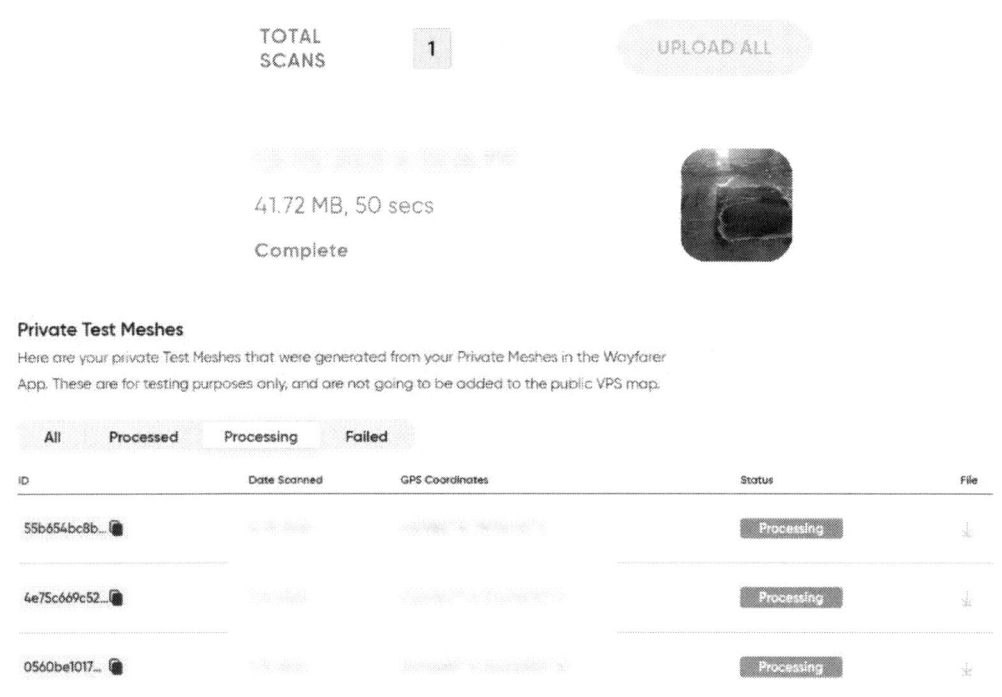

Figure 11.10: Uploaded scan test meshes

After the process is complete (which takes around 10 minutes to 4 hours), you will be able to download the processed scan. Click the **Download** button in the table, in **File** column, once you see the status as **Processed**.

The flow of VPS scan recognition

Before importing our scanned environment and making configurations, we need to understand how Niantic VPS localization works.

There are two main interfaces provided by Niantic to save and load anchors within a scanned location, which are:

- `WayspotAnchorService`: High Level API where the cache is managed by the API.

- **WayspoitAnchorController**: Low Level API where the cache is managed by the developer.

For the simplicity of the implementation, we will be using the `WaypoitAnchorService` to save and load position data.

When we scan an environment, it starts the localization process for a VPS activation location. `WayspotAnchorService` can be used to validate and establish anchors in the environment and generate **payloads** for anchors. There are two ways we can store and retrieve these anchor data, which are:

- **Store and retrieve anchors in run-time:** This allows anyone to scan an environment and store generated payload data within the device (or a remote database) and retrieve them back and show them in the environment. A use case for this would be a collaborative space where people can add spatial post-it notes where others can see them.

- **Use the remote authoring tool to add anchors during development time, and load them in play time:** This allows developers to import a pre-scanned environment and place anchors in the environment to generate payloads, which can then be hardcoded into the application. An example of this would be a game which generates an AR experience around Eifel tower in France or any other landmark.

In this section, let us import the scanned environment to our development project and predefine a location anchor with a prefab that can be loaded when we scan the actual application.

Importing the scanned location

In your project, click **Lightship** menu | **VPS Authoring Assistant** | **Add Location**.

This will open a select dialog to choose the zip file you downloaded from Niantic dashboard. Choosing the file will open another window to generate and save payload data in the editor. Create a new folder inside your assets folder (for example, **Private meshes**) and choose that folder. This will generate a prefab and an asset that you can import into the scene.

Moreover, it will open a new **VPS Authoring** window, along with a new scene that has the scanned environment as a 3D object with a warning not to add or delete any objects to the scene, as shown in *Figure 11.11*:

Figure 11.11: VPS Authoring tool with a private scan

Adding anchors using the VPS authoring tool

Close the VPS Authoring tool by **Lightship** | **ARDK** | **VPS Authoring assistant** | **Close.**

This will remove the additional scene with the environment we added before.

Create a new empty game object with a scale of 1,1,1 and add a sphere as a child object.

Now change the scale of the sphere to (0.3, 0.3, 0.3).

Rename the game object and convert it to a prefab.

Open the VPS authoring tool again. Check the following *Figure 11.12* for step-by-step process:

1. Click the dropdown and select the ID of the private scan you imported.
2. By default, there will be a single anchor attached to the environment. However, we will add one more by clicking **Create New Anchor** button. This will generate a new empty game object in the new scene called **Anchor**.

3. Drag and drop the prefab we created earlier into the **Associated Prefab** placeholder in the VPS authoring tool. You can also rename the Anchor by clicking the pencil icon next to the name of the anchor in *(2)*. In *Figure 11.12*, it is renamed to **Sofa**.

4. Select the anchor object in the editor, and use your transform tools to move, rotate and scale the prefab. You will not be able to edit the prefab this time, but you can copy and transform the data of the anchor to do prefab modifications later. Copy the values individually (in section *(6)* of *Figure 11.12*) and save them for later.

5. Now click **Save All Anchors** button. This will update a manifest in the folder you added your private mesh into. Also, a **Payload** will be generated uniquely for this anchor.

6. Click the **Payload** to copy the payload string. Save this for later.

You can also add multiple anchors to this. If you do, copy the payloads and save them for retrieval process later. Refer to the following *Figure 11.12*:

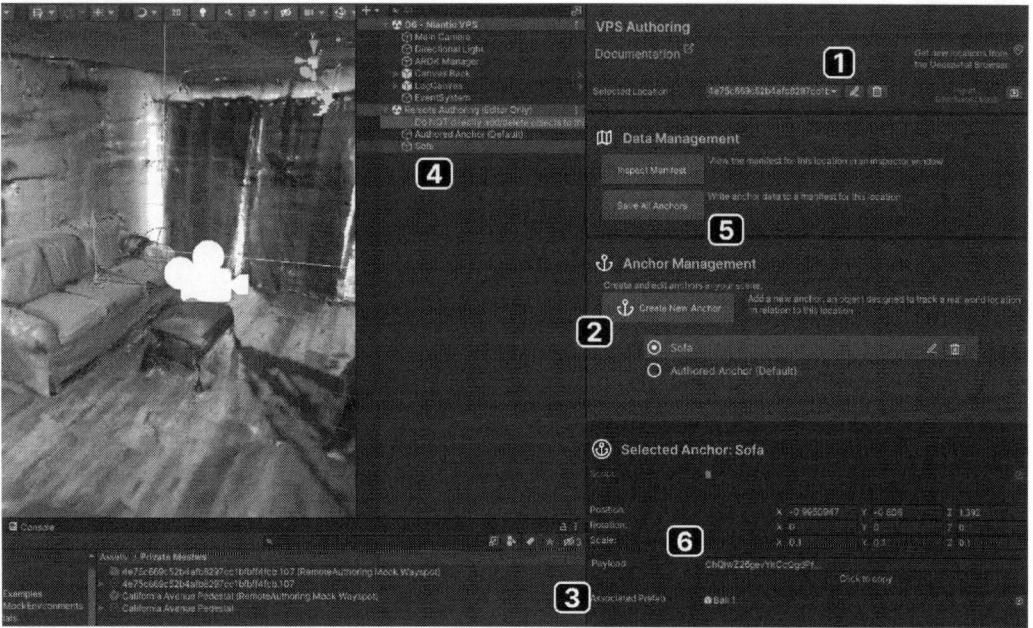

Figure 11.12: Adding and saving an anchor using VPS Authoring tool

Close the VPS Authoring tool to set up the prefab.

Updating the prefab with proper visual elements

Open the folder that the private mesh has been imported to. You will be able to see a prefab and an asset that holds your anchor data. Drag and drop the prefab directly to the hierarchy. Make sure the position and rotation values are zero, and the scale is one. This will add a 3D model of the scan of your environment.

Now, drag and drop the prefab you associated with the anchor to the scene as well.

Select the prefab, paste the position data you copied from step *(4)* earlier to the new prefab. Make sure that the prefab is placed correctly on the anchor you placed before, as shown in *Figure 11.13*:

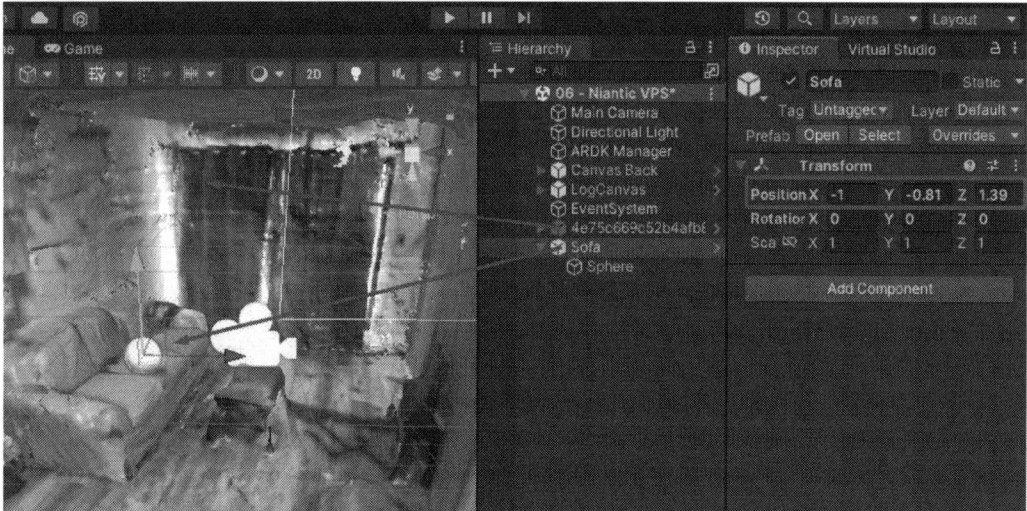

Figure 11.13: Placing an instance of the anchor prefab for modification

Now, you can add any object within the prefab that matches the environment 3D model. In *Figure 11.13*, a sample living room is scanned and an anchor is placed on top of the sofa. We can use this prefab to instantiate once the scan is complete and the anchors are validated.

The following example in *Figure 11.14* shows how text objects and other elements are placed inside the prefab, which will be generated when the app localizes the area. Here, a quad and a text object are added to annotate the sofa, and a flower pot is placed behind the tea table.

Now click the Sofa prefab and apply the changes. Delete both the prefab and the environment mesh from the scene. Refer to the following *Figure 11.14*:

Figure 11.14: Using the scanned model as a reference to modify the anchor-associated prefab

Using Niantic API to restore anchor data

In this section, we will be using the copied payload to load the way spot anchors and position the prefab in the correct location once the environment is localized by the AR session.

Create a new C# script called **VPSLocalizer.cs** and add the following:

1. using System.Collections;
2. using System.Collections.Generic;
3. using UnityEngine;
4. using Niantic.ARDK.AR.WayspotAnchors;
5. using Niantic.ARDK.LocationService;
6. using Niantic.ARDK.AR;
7. using Niantic.ARDK.AR.ARSessionEventArgs;
8. using System;
9.
10. public class VPSLocalizer: MonoBehaviour {
11.   public GameObject anchorPrefab;
12.   [SerializeField] private float desiredAccuracyinMeters,

```
        updateDistanceInMeters;
13.
14.     IARSession session;
15.     IWayspotAnchorsConfiguration wayspotAnchorsConfig;
16.     ILocationService locationService;
17.     IWayspotAnchor[] anchors;
18.
19.     WayspotAnchorService wayspotAnchorService;
20.
21.     Dictionary < System.Guid, GameObject > anchs = new Dictionary < System.Guid, GameObject > ();
22.
23.     void Start() {
24.         ARSessionFactory.SessionInitialized += OnSessionInitialized;
25.     }
26.
27.     private void OnSessionInitialized(AnyARSessionInitializedArgs args) {
28.         ARSessionFactory.SessionInitialized -= OnSessionInitialized;
29.         session = args.Session;
30.
31.         wayspotAnchorsConfig = WayspotAnchorsConfigurationFactory.Create();
32.         locationService = LocationServiceFactory.Create(session.RuntimeEnvironment);
33.
34.         locationService.Start(desiredAccuracyinMeters, updateDistanceInMeters);
35.         wayspotAnchorService = new WayspotAnchorService(session, locationService, wayspotAnchorsConfig);
36.
37.         wayspotAnchorService.LocalizationStateUpdated += HandleLocalizationStateUpdated;
38.     }
```

```
39.
40.    private void HandleLocalizationStateUpdated(LocalizationStateUpdatedArgs args) {
41.        if (args.State == LocalizationState.Localized) {
42.            var payload = WayspotAnchorPayload.Deserialize("PASTE THE PAYLOAD YOU COPIED FROM THE ANCHOR");
43.
44.            anchors = wayspotAnchorService.RestoreWayspotAnchors(payload);
45.
46.            foreach(var item in anchors) {
47.                var go = Instantiate(anchorPrefab);
48.
49.                anchs.Add(item.ID, go);
50.
51.                item.TransformUpdated += OnTransformUpdated;
52.            }
53.        }
54.
55.        if (args.State == LocalizationState.Failed) {
56.            Debug.Log("Localization Failed!");
57.        }
58.    }
59.
60.    private void OnTransformUpdated(WayspotAnchorResolvedArgs args) {
61.        var anchor = anchs[args.ID].transform;
62.        anchor.position = args.Position;
63.        anchor.rotation = args.Rotation;
64.    }
65. }
```

Here, we will be calling the **OnSessionInitialized()** method when the AR session is started to initiate the localization. This is done by starting the location service, and then the way spot anchor service. Once the anchor service is initialized, it keeps tracking its localization status.

We use the AR session, the location service which determines the location accuracy given in meters (as variables) and the way spot anchor configuration object, in line 35.

Once the **WayspotAnchorService** is created, a **HandleLocalizationStateUpdated** method is subscribed along with arguments that explain the status of the localization process. This method will execute every time when there is an update to the localization.

The localization state updated method checks the status of the method. If it is the *Localized* state, then we can restore the anchors from the payload. However, the payload must be first deserialized, as shown in line 42. Here, you need to add the copied anchor that matches the prefab we modified earlier.

Calling the method **RestoreWayspotAnchors()** from the way spot service with the deserialized payload as input, as seen in line 44, will return an array of anchors. (Per payload, this will be one anchor).

Now, we iterate through all the anchors that were restored and instantiate the prefab we associated for the anchor. At the same time, we populate a dictionary using the id of the anchor as the key and the **GameObject** as the value.

When we instantiate a prefab for the first time, it will be placed in the origin position instead of the actual position. Therefore, we need to validate the anchor position with the way spot anchor service, and it will pass the updated position data through an event call. This is implemented by subscribing to the **TransformUpdated** event with **OnTransformUpdated** method, including **WayspotAnchorResolvedArgs** as parameters, as shown in line 51.

OnTransformUpdate method will execute as soon as the anchor transform data are resolved, and the argument will contain position, rotation, and the id of the anchor. We use the dictionary to find the **gameobject** associated with the ID and assign position and the rotation to the prefab. This will be resulted in your prefab populating in the area in origin and setting its position to the correct place after a short period.

Now add this script as a component anywhere in the scene and assign the anchor Prefab. For location accuracy data, add 0.1 for both variables.

Build and run the app. Scan the same environment and see how it populates the 3D prefab exactly on the anchor position you placed inside the editor, as shown in *Figure 11.15*:

Figure 11.15: Localizing and loading anchor data in the private environment

Using Niantic VPS for scalable AR applications

In the preceding example, we added only one anchor to a private mesh scan that is currently in your online database. Localization for private environments only works with your app ID, and the meshes should be yours only. Moreover, deleting the mesh would stop the localization from the app since your app will match the scanned surface only with the meshes you have uploaded.

We hardcoded the payload and assigned only one associated prefab for this example. If you have more than one anchor and different prefabs for each anchor, save the prefab and payload data in a database (it can be internal persistence such as **playerpref** or a file or an external database using HTTP Rest API to retrieve data).

Wayspot anchors are only stored for 6 months. Therefore, we have to check for the time and recreate the anchor in runtime using the wayspot anchor controller.

You can also contribute to the Niantic public scan cloud by scanning and uploading data through the wayfarer app. You can download public meshes from the GeoSpatial Browser page from the lightship dashboard and use them to test public locations using the VPS Authoring tool.

More information on Niantic Lightship ARDK API, including examples, can be checked by logging into Lightship documentation:

https://lightship.dev/docs/ardk/

Conclusion

In this chapter, we learned how to use Niantic Lightship ARDK to develop environment and world scale Augmented reality experiences. Lightship ARDK is powerful to scan and detect the physical boundaries effectively and has very efficient environment detection and localization technology. We can use the occlusion, meshing, and VPS technologies to build AR applications so that we can persist and restore data in AR more efficiently. This can be used to solve localization and tracking issues that many AR applications have. In our next chapter, let us look into enhancing the experience of AR applications we develop using Unity.

Key points

- Niantic ARDK requires a developer account and an app id to enable AR features.
- ARDK natively supports meshing regardless of the hardware capabilities of the device.
- AR occlusion is provided by default, and meshing can be visualized using a simple material attached to the AR Depth Manager.
- Adding a collider to the mesh prefab integrated physical features to scanned boundaries.
- Niantic VPS can be used to scan, create and persist anchor data as payloads and then retrieve data again after localization.
- VPS Authoring tool can be used to create anchors in the development stage for pre-scanned environments.
- The generated payload contains information on the anchors and thus can be used to position the associated prefabs properly.

Question

1. Using Niantic VPS and meshing related components such as depth tracking and occlusion, build an AR exploration application that has a character which takes you around different wayspot anchors of a scanned environment. Utilize unity components such as colliders, raycasts and animations for a better user experiences.

CHAPTER 12
Best Practices in Augmented Reality Application Design

Introduction

So far, we used different tools with Unity to build different kinds of **Augmented Reality** (**AR**) applications. However, we only touched the surface of the capabilities that these SDKs offer. In order to build compelling augmented reality applications, developers must also take design considerations into action. The AR app that you build should not only display 3D content properly, but it should also be user-friendly.

In this chapter, we will be going through some best practices in designing augmented reality applications and also learning how these can be implemented in Unity.

Structure

In this chapter, we will discuss the following topics:

- Safety is key
    - Showing warnings at the beginning
    - Showing warnings while using the app
- Guide the user with interactions
- Be mindful of the scale

- Use audio and visual cues
- Free flow restrictions
- AR interactions
- UI considerations

Objectives

After completing this chapter, you can polish your AR application with proper best design practices. You will make your AR application user-friendly and pleasant for users to interact with. Apart from knowing the best practices, you will also learn how to use Unity's integrated tools, other third-party tools, and C# to implement such best practices into your application, regardless of the type of application.

Safety is key

One of the major considerations in AR app design is how developers implement safety warnings into their applications. Mobile app stores such as the Apple app store and Google Play Store enforce the indication of safety within the application as a part of the compliance process.

People open their cameras on their phones when it comes to AR applications. Instead of focusing on what is in their surroundings, people would look at the world through another lens. This increases immersion of the AR application but, at the same time, creates a risk of facing an accident by being unaware of the surroundings. Therefore, add components to your application that warn the user at the beginning of the experience and, if needed, during the use of the app.

Showing warnings at the beginning

Before opening the camera, we can add another scene in Unity with UI components or a Screen space overlay on the AR experience with a button prompt to provide a list of warnings to make the user aware of the surrounding. The UI scene will be the first to load in build settings. You can also use visual elements to demonstrate the warnings by using the image component in Unity. Refer to *Figure 12.1*:

Figure 12.1: The UI elements show a warning before opening the camera

Some of the warnings that you can provide the user are as follows:

- Please be aware of the surroundings when using this AR application.

- Do not use the app while driving, walking, or operating machinery that requires your attention.

- Do not use the app in public places where you may disturb or endanger others or violate their privacy.

- Do not use the app for prolonged periods; it may cause eye strain, fatigue, or nausea.

- Do not use the app if you have a history of epilepsy or other medical conditions that may be triggered by flashing lights or rapid movements.

An example of warnings views across different AR mobile applications can be seen in *Figure 12.2*:

Figure 12. 2: *Pokémon GO, Mission to Mars AR, and Happy Baby Elephant AR apps show a warning before launching the app*

Showing warnings while using the AR app

The AR feature in Google Maps now allows users to crossroads while looking at the phone. It also warns when the phone is held up for too long to focus on the surroundings. This design feature must be implemented in a way that does not break immersion. Moreover, showing warnings on top of an application causes a negative experience for the user. Therefore, it needs to be done carefully, depending on the AR application type. For example, an action game in AR cannot be interrupted with prompts while a player is playing the game. Therefore, only pre-warnings will be necessary. An app such as Google Maps requires continuous attention to the surrounding and will not hinder the AR experience if the user looks away from the app.

In Unity, you can use the **Input.Gyro** to get access to the gyroscope sensor of the mobile device. The **attitude** variable of the Gyro object is a Vector that matches the device's orientation. This can be used to check if the device is placed perpendicular to the floor surface for a long time, assuming that the device is being used for a longer period. You can use a **coroutine** or a **timer** value to check the time that the device has been in use, and if it reaches an amount you have calibrated, you can show a simple UI prompt at the top of the view without hindering the experience of the user. Refer to *Figure 12.3*:

Figure 12.3: Google Maps AR app showing a warning (photo by frequentmiler)

Guide the user with the interactions

Augmented reality-related interactions within an AR application can be novel to a user. Scanning an environment or a marker, tapping on the floor, or another interactive point are not everyday interactions that a person would do with their mobile phones. As developers, we designed our app to be used by ourselves, assuming that the users would follow our thinking patterns. This is a false assumption, as any app development requires frequent user testing and feedback. Adding novel interaction methods into the mix makes people dislike the experience that the app provides.

Therefore, adding visual guidance for every interaction is a must-have in AR applications. This also validates some of the technical challenges in context recognition. As an example, in a marker-less AR application that uses SLAM to track the planes in a physical environment, the camera should be moved to recognize the movement patterns and predict the planes. For this, a user must rotationally move the device. Many AR applications that use marker-less AR show an animation of a hand moving a phone to indicate how the device should be moved to enable tracking, as shown in *Figure 12.4*:

Figure 12.4: Animation of a hand holding a smartphone

A similar interface can be used in Unity by showing a moving image placed on a canvas. Unity has an integration animation tool that can create a simple animation of the image moving in circles. The animation can be hidden once the app identifies at least one plane in the environment. This is possible in AR Foundation by accessing and subscribing to the **planesChanged** event in **AR Plane Manager**. This action will be invoked whenever a new plane is added, updated, or removed.

For a Marker based AR application, a UI with a translucent image of the marker that needs to be tracked can be placed, as shown in *Figure 12.5*. You can also add an info carousel for users to understand how to interact with the markers that need to be scanned. The user should always be aware of what is to be done next. App stores, such as the Apple app store, does not allow developers to publish marker-based AR apps if the app does not indicate what and how to scan and if the proper interaction instructions are not given within the app. Therefore, it is a must to consider when publishing your apps.

When the scanning has begun, and the objects are placed, the app should instruct what users can and cannot do with *coach marks* and interaction animations. This helps many users get used to new interactions, such as tapping on the floor, pinching, and other interactions.

Refer to *Figure 12.5*:

Figure 12.5: Initializing UI element prototypes for marker-based AR applications

Be mindful of the scale

AR apps can be experienced in different ways. It can be on a table, inside a room, or outside. When placing objects, the developers should scale the experience in a way that matches the surrounding that it is placed. In Unity, scaling objects that are placed is not recommended. Components such as particle systems do not like scaling since it has to scale the particles hierarchically. Moreover, movement and physics may not work as intended if the objects are scaled.

If an AR Foundation is being used for markerless AR, we can scale the camera, which scales the view spectrum of the camera origin. When the camera origin is scaled, the objects that are not scaled will make the illusion that they are being scaled. Therefore, by measuring the distance from the camera to the floor or the tracked plane, you can decide whether it is a small or large space, such as outdoors.

The scale of the objects in the AR experience involves the ability for exploration. One of the main points of AR applications is the flexibility of the movement. Therefore, we can use that to create room for exploration. Games such as Pokémon Go, and Minecraft worlds provide better exploration capabilities by making the objects placed around and scaling them up so users do not have to look for the objects around them.

Refer to *Figure 12.6*:

Figure 12.6: *The scale of the experience depends on the environment (backgrounds by Freepik)*

Use audio and visual cues

AR applications rely on media. It requires people to freely move their devices to engage. However, it is necessary to implement different audio-visual cues to get a better feeling of interactive elements. This allows users to feel the interactions more naturally and helps them find their way around the application. Some audio-visual cues that can be added to your AR app can be as follows.

Indicating objects that are out of camera view

Imagine an AR content that you have placed in a virtual space, but you have moved the camera out of the 3D model view. To find your way back to where the 3D model is, you can show a UI visual marker representing the direction of the object, as shown in *Figure 12.7:*

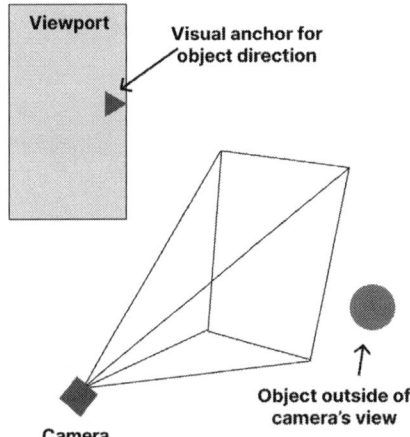

Figure 12.7: *Showing a visual anchor for an AR object outside viewport*

In Unity, this can be done by referencing the target object as **target**, the camera as **cam**, and the anchor on a screen space canvas as **arrow** with the following C# snippet within an update method:

1. `var pos = cam.WorldToViewportPoint(target.position);`
2. `var xx = Mathf.Lerp(0, Screen.width, pos.x) - 1;`
3. `var yy = Mathf.Lerp(0, Screen.height, pos.y) - 1;`
4. `arrow.position = new Vector2(xx,yy);`

Adding visual markers on interactable objects

When you have interactable objects in an AR app, because many are 3D models, it can be hard to distinguish between an interactable object and a non-interactable one. Therefore, the interactable objects must stand out from the other objects. As an example, imagine you are exploring a 3D Art AR installation, and there are some elements that you are supposed to interact with. The object that you will tap can have a simple visual indicator to stand out, such as:

- A simple glowing effect on the 3D model can be done using the particle system of Unity.

- With an outline using custom shaders URP, you can use shader graph to create and apply an outline shader.

- Using text annotations with interactions tooltips. Looking at a text from different angles can break the immersion. Use the *Billboard* concept to rotate a text object towards the camera always. This way, the text will always be facing the camera.

- Simple animations such as growing and shrinking. Animations can be made easily using the animation tool within Unity.

An example of how an object can stand out, demonstrating the preceding examples in *Figure 12.8*:

Figure 12.8: Visual cues to stand out (glowing, outline, tooltip, and animations)

Using 3D audio cues

Adding audio is always an improvement to the feel of the application. Having a simple audio cue for taps and movement of objects that are similar to real sounds can enhance the experience. Apart from normal sound effects, Unity Audio Source supports 3D sound that can be heard based on proximity.

Imagine an AR app that requires you to get closer to an object that emits a sound effect. You can make the sound effect realistic by setting up the audio source to emit sounds based on the proximity, which increases the volume of it when you are closer to the object. This can be done by setting up 3D audio settings in the **Audio Source** component, as shown in *Figure 12.9*:

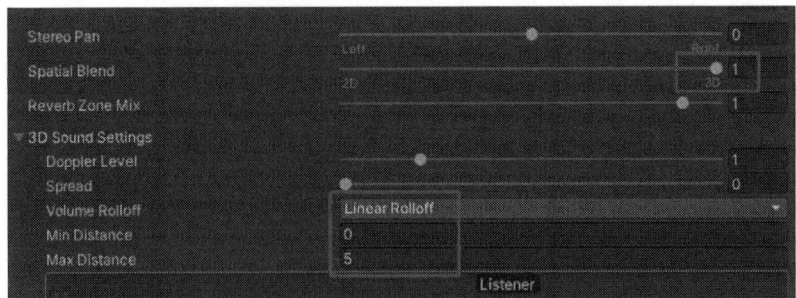

Figure 12.9: Enable 3D spatial audio in Audio Source Component

In any audio source attached to a game object in a scene, set the spatial blend to 3D. Change volume roll-off to linear and set the min and max distances as required to have proper 3D spatial audio in AR.

Showing physical properties in visual cues

In some AR applications, you may have different objects representing different physical properties, such as weight, color, speed, etc. Visual elements can easily represent some properties, while some cannot. For example, weight cannot be presented directly in a visual format. Imagine an interaction allowing users to pick and move physical objects in AR. A simple way to show the weight with a visual cue is to have a simple line that bends depending on the weight/mass of the object. This will provide the illusion that the object has a weight, and tweaking the bending of the curve can make the users feel the difference of each object that is being lifted. *Figure 12.10* shows a simple example of how it can look in 3D:

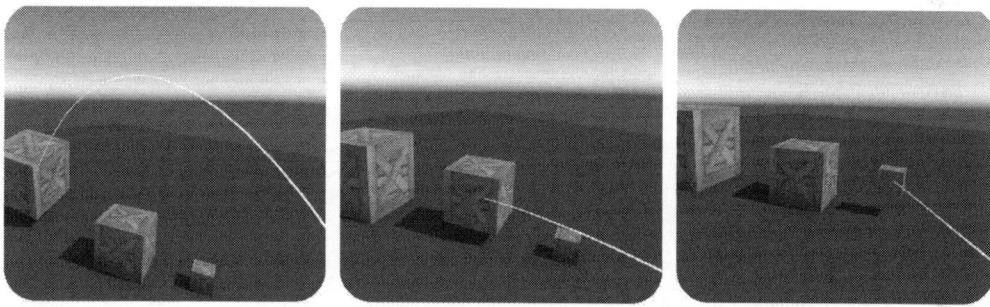

Figure 12.10: Using a curved line to represent weight

The following is a code snippet that can be used to tap (the code uses a mouse click) and move an object by lifting. It uses a spring joint to attach to the object with different masses and curves using linear interpolation:

```
1.  using Unity.VisualScripting;
2.  using UnityEngine;
3.
4.  public class LiftObject: MonoBehaviour {
5.      [SerializeField] private float curveHeight;
6.      [SerializeField] private Material lineMat;
7.      [SerializeField] private Gradient lineColor;
8.      [SerializeField] private int lineFrequency = 20;
9.
10.     private Camera cam;
```

```
11.    private SpringJoint joint;
12.    private LineRenderer line;
13.    private Rigidbody pointRB;
14.    private Rigidbody objectRB;
15.    private RaycastHit hit;
16.    private GameObject pointer;
17.    private Vector3 localHitpoint;
18.    private bool isConnected;
19.
20.    Vector3 pointA, pointB, pointC, pointAB, pointBC;
21.
22.    void Start() {
23.       cam = Camera.main;
24.       isConnected = false;
25.    }
26.
27.    private void Update() {
28.       if (Input.GetMouseButtonDown(0)) {
29.          if (!isConnected && Physics.Raycast(cam.ScreenPointToRay(Input.mousePosition), out hit)) {
30.             if (!hit.transform.CompareTag("liftable"))
31.                return;
32.
33.             isConnected = true;
34.             localHitpoint = hit.transform.InverseTransformPoint(hit.point);
35.
36.             pointer = new GameObject("pointer");
37.             pointer.transform.position = hit.point;
38.             pointer.transform.parent = cam.transform;
39.
40.             pointRB = pointer.AddComponent < Rigidbody > ();
41.             pointRB.isKinematic = true;
```

```
42.        objectRB = hit.transform.GetComponent < Rigidbody > ();
43.
44.        joint = objectRB.AddComponent < SpringJoint > ();
45.        joint.spring = 500;
46.        joint.damper = 1;
47.        joint.tolerance = 0.001 f;
48.        joint.connectedBody = pointRB;
49.
50.        line = gameObject.AddComponent < LineRenderer > ();
51.        line.material = lineMat;
52.        line.startWidth = 0.01 f;
53.        line.endWidth = 0.005 f;
54.        line.colorGradient = lineColor;
55.        line.positionCount = lineFrequency;
56.      } else {
57.        //clear line, rotate and drop object
58.        isConnected = false;
59.        isConnected = false;
60.        Destroy(pointer.gameObject);
61.        Destroy(line);
62.      }
63.
64.    }
65.
66.    if (isConnected && pointer != null) {
67.      if (line != null) {
68.        pointA = cam.ScreenToWorldPoint(new Vector3(Screen.width, 0, 1));
69.        pointC = hit.transform.TransformPoint(localHitpoint);
70.        pointB = pointA + (pointC - pointA) / 2 + Vector3.up * curveHeight * objectRB.mass;
71.
72.        for (int i = 0; i < lineFrequency; i++) {
```

73.   pointAB = Vector3.Lerp(pointA, pointB, i / (float) lineFrequency);

74.   pointBC = Vector3.Lerp(pointB, pointC, i / (float) lineFrequency);

75.

76.   line.SetPosition(i, Vector3.Lerp(pointAB, pointBC, i / (float) lineFrequency));

77.   }

78.   }

79.   }

80.   }

81. }

Free flow restrictions

One of the biggest use cases of AR applications is the ability to freely move the virtual camera, which moves with the physical device to explore. However, 3D applications use different methods to build interactions, which users can easily identify by moving the camera. For example, imagine an AR treasure hunt game that requests players to guess the content inside a 3D box in AR. Having the flexibility to move the camera around, users can take a peek inside the 3D model and see how it has been implemented. Sometimes, accidentally peeking into a 3D model can break the immersion of the experience.

In order to stop users from peeking inside 3D models, they can be configured to send an event to the UI to block the view by adding an overlay. The event can be triggered either using trigger colliders or checking the distance from the camera to the center of the object.

Figure 12.11 is an example overlay that can be used to inform users to move the device away if it collides with a 3D model in the scene.

This can sometimes create unnecessary performance issues due to unnecessary collision requirements. Therefore, it is ideal to choose only the objects that could break immersion or be unfair to the rules of the AR application:

Figure 12.11: UI overlay to inform users not to clip objects

AR interactions

Interacting with elements in AR through a smartphone application can contain different types of touch input. Most of the touch inputs can be converted to realistic interactions in order to manipulate objects. In the previous chapters, we implemented different interactions that allow users to move, scale, rotate objects, tap and place, and sometimes auto-recognizable implementations. When it comes to interacting with 3D elements in an AR world, there can be certain design considerations that we can integrate to make these interactions smooth. Some of them are as follows.

Using a reticle to interact with smaller objects

A **reticle** is a small UI point that can be placed as an overlay on the app screen. Instead of touching a smaller object which can be covered by your finger, you can use a button on the screen to point and select it. This will increase the precision of selecting an object in AR than tapping directly above the object. In Unity, this can be done by casting a ray from the screen midpoint towards the camera's forward direction.

Refer to *Figure 12.12*:

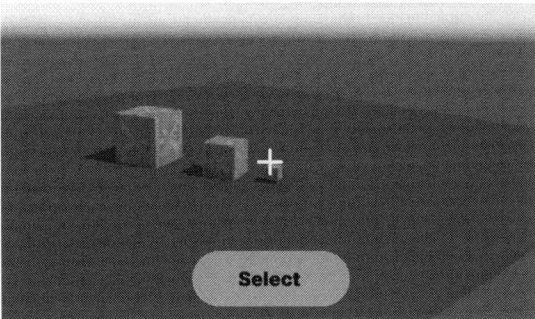

Figure 12.12: Using a reticle with a button instead of a direct tap

Interacting with objects further from camera

AR allows users to move the camera freely. This can cause direct interactable objects to appear smaller when the camera moves further away. Suppose the app depends on touch-based interactions (touch to select an object or press a button in AR, and so on). In that case, the developer must either switch the interaction to a reticle or find another way to interact with the object. Moving back and forth between different interaction methods can confuse the user. Therefore, a simple way to allow interaction with objects that appear smaller is to change the size of the collision boundaries to match the size of a finger regardless of the object it is in. *Figure 12.13* shows an example of how the *sphere collider* of an object changes the size of the collision boundary concerning the distance it has from the camera.

In the example, the distance between the camera with the object has been made indirectly proportional to the scale of the sphere collider, keeping a minimum and a maximum value it can take. On the left side, it shows the distance to the object from the camera when it is closer and away from the object. The right side shows how the object appears from the camera to the user. As it can be inspected, touching on the object in both scenarios can make it selectable due to the scale of the collider.

Refer to *Figure 12.13*:

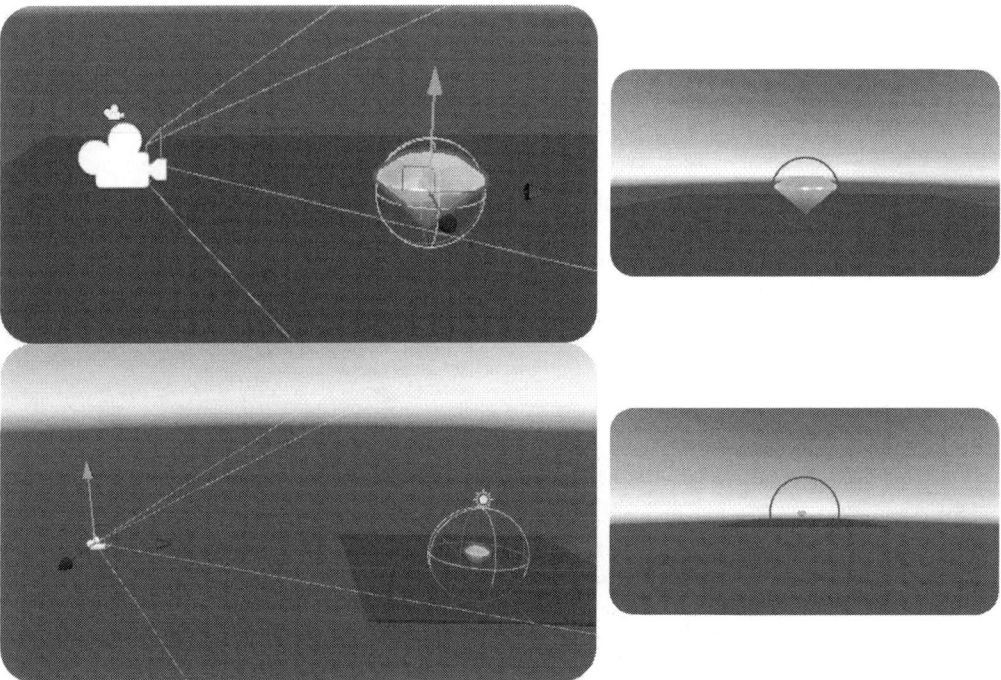

Figure 12.13: *Scaling the touch area for the distance of the object*

UI considerations

Like ordinary smartphone applications, user interface and user experience design for AR applications can be similar to how users interact with non-AR elements such as buttons, pages, and screens. However, user interfaces for AR applications can either enhance or break the immersive experience for the user.

When in AR mode, keep the UI on the screen to a minimum. Users are in the AR mode to move the device and explore the surroundings. Therefore, having different UI components, such as buttons, sliders, toolbars from the side, can be highly distracting. Refer to the following:

- If UI elements require showing information, move them from the overlay canvas to a world space canvas that can be placed as an AR element in 3D space. This allows users to freely move their devices to focus on information that is relevant.

- Having UI popups can be distracting. As an example, winning a reward in an AR game can be presented in a world space UI with additional 3D effects and sounds apart from the UI popup on the screen space of the device. Refer to *Figure 12.14*:

Figure 12.14: *Using world space canvas instead of screen space popups*

- Keep screen space user interface elements to a minimum. Have one or two buttons that open different toolbars or other UI elements but always hide them when the objective of the UI element is complete, as shown in *Figure 12.15:*

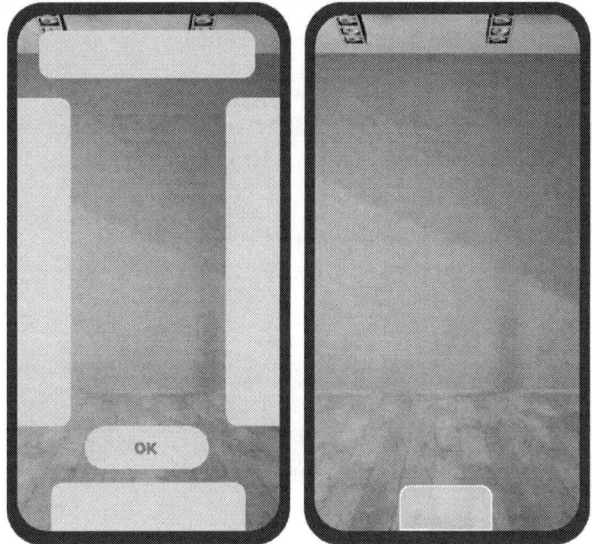

Figure 12.15: Less is better. Keep Screen space UI to a minimum

Conclusion

In this chapter, we learned some best practices for designing a handheld-based AR application. We mainly covered user experience considerations to enhance immersion. These best practices are not mandatory for a working AR app. However, having considered best to worse case scenarios and handling them while polishing the app for users to experience smoothly can make a big difference in the success of your AR app.

In the next chapter, we will cover Unity-based optimization methods to smoothen the 3D apps we develop.

Key points

- Safety is a key factor in building AR applications. Inform users to be safe when using your AR app.
- Never use users guessing. Inform them of all the interactions.
- Use visual and audio cues to convey AR object properties.

- Keep user interfaces for AR simple.
- Use world space user interfaces over screen space to enhance the AR experience.

Question

1. What are some of the best practices that can be used when building an AR based story telling application? Explain with evaluations in terms of input methods, audio and visual user experiences.

Join our book's Discord space

Join the book's Discord Workspace for Latest updates, Offers, Tech happenings around the world, New Release and Sessions with the Authors:

https://discord.bpbonline.com

CHAPTER 13
AR App Performance Optimization

Introduction

Augmented Reality (AR) applications run on mobile devices solve many challenges. It renders 3D models and performs logic based on the codes we have written on top of the algorithms running for context recognition and camera input. Based on the SDK we are using, the algorithm for context recognition can be different. Unlike a non-AR 3D interactive application, the number of resources an AR app requires from a mobile device is significantly larger.

Therefore, when building an AR app, we have resource limitations to adhere to. This involves reducing the rendering, processing, and memory required by an AR app. In this chapter, we will be going through some fundamental elements in Unity that you need to know as an AR application developer to build a smooth AR application.

Structure

In this chapter, we will discuss the following topics:

- Performance metrics
    - Frames per second
    - Tris and verts
    - Draw calls

- Optimization of a 3D app
    - GPU instancing
    - Static and dynamic batching
    - Occlusion culling and frustum culling
    - Textures and UV maps
    - Light baking
    - UI optimizations
- Optimization considerations in coding

Objectives

After completion of this chapter, you will be able to optimize your AR app to reduce the resource requirements needed. You will also learn the key metrics for application performance and use necessary actions to mitigate the performance-related challenges in your app.

Performance metrics

In any application, the performance of the application can be measured by looking at some metrics. The smoothness of the application and the time it takes to load are some of the visual metrics we can inspect in many 3D applications. Just like running a high-end 3D game on a low-end computer makes the game crash and lag, AR apps can cause similar issues when running on devices with less resources, such as mobile devices. In this section, we will learn some of the key performance metrics that can be used to determine the smoothness of the application.

Frames per second

When you run any application, the device it runs allocates its power for calculations and renders everything on the screen. In order to animate objects and move from one screen to another, the processor clears and redraws everything at a high frequency.

If the device takes longer to process calculations, it takes longer pauses in between redraws on the screen. This makes the screen update at a lower frequency. Having low-frequency screen redraws becomes visually significant as it creates a graphical lag on the screen. This frequency of drawing the screen is known as **frames per second (FPS)**.

High frames per second imply that the app takes a little time to process, which validates an optimized application. If the logic of your app is expensive and if it does heavy calculations, the FPS count would drop, and the overall experience is hindered. Therefore, FPS can be considered a performance metric to validate whether your app is optimized enough.

Any app over 30 fps on a normal device can be optimized enough. High-end devices running highly optimized apps can go over 100 fps, or even 400 fps, based on how big the app is. Anything lower than 30 fps is visually significant and can be considered neither optimized nor running on a recommended device.

Figure 13.1 features the varying movement of an object with different FPS:

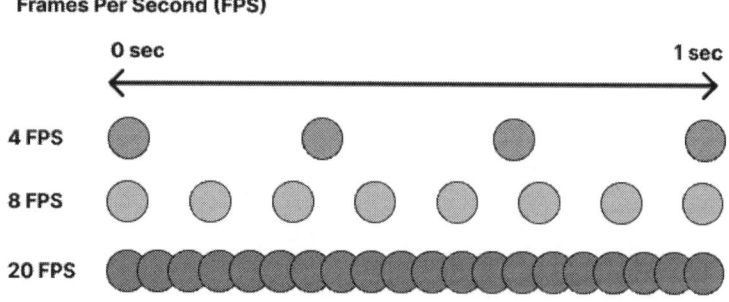

Figure 13.1: How the movement of an object represented with different FPS

Many AR SDKs are optimized enough to render content that clips to higher fps, but with limitations. If the app runs 60 fps, it is 60 times per second that the SDK should calculate the context information, such as the knowledge of planes around the device. If it runs 30 fps, that means that the device can take a rest compared to 60 fps. For Apple iPhone, AR Kit usually runs at 60 fps, while many Android devices that are compatible with AR Core have a maximum of 30 fps even though their logic is highly optimized. Only Google Pixel devices run AR core with 60 fps.

The FPS of a Unity scene at run time can be checked via the **Stats** section in the **Game** window, as shown in *Figure 13.2*:

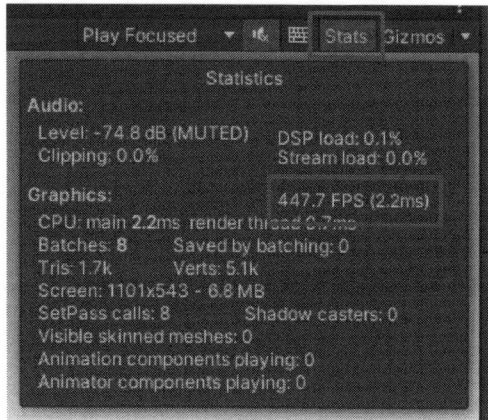

Figure 13.2: FPS counter in Game Window – Stats

There can be multiple factors that can hinder the FPS apart from the expensive calculations the scripts in it do. The number of objects in the scene, lighting, and user interface elements can cause massive drops in fps, if not optimized properly. The second section of this chapter will explain different ways how we can improve fps.

Tris and verts

Every object that is in a 3D scene is rendered in a 3D world. Objects rendered in a 3D world are made out of points (vertices) and lines connecting the points (edges). Combining edges creates triangles (tris). In order to have smooth 3D models, the models should have more vertices and triangles. Every triangle information should be loaded into device memory, and they have to be rendered individually to be visible through the screen. Therefore, it requires higher processing and rendering power to draw an object with a higher number of triangles, compared to a model with lower triangles.

Figure 13.3 features how the triangles of a scene can be viewed through Wireframe view and how they are displayed in the stats:

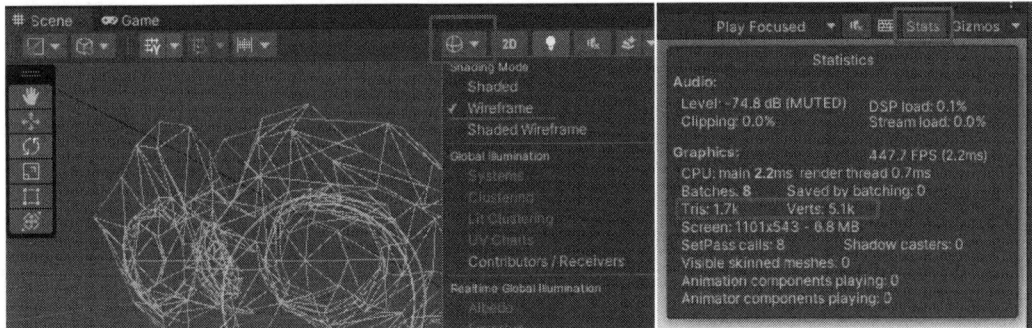

Figure 13.3: *How triangles of a scene can be viewed through Wireframe view and how they are displayed in stats*

Having a higher amount of 3D models or having 3D models with high poly counts (triangles) will cause the app to slow and hinder the user experience. Therefore, we must use 3D models that are low poly with lesser triangle counts. You can use a 3D model viewer or 3D modeling tools such as blender to view the number of triangles and even use them to reduce the triangles as well. However, the lower the poly count means, the lesser the object that appeals to be realistic in AR. Therefore, we need to find a balance and other 3D modeling tips, such as using **normal maps** and **height maps** to make visual illusions to provide details to low poly 3D models.

Draw calls

In 3D applications, it takes numerous iterations to render a scene to be visible to our eyes. For example, a drawing of an object with a light next to it requires the object vertices to be rendered, as well as the color, shadows, and any post-processing effects, which accumulate into multiple draw calls. In Unity, different materials are rendered separately, and different objects are rendered separately. In *Figure 13.4*, you can see how a rendering of a single game object has taken multiple steps to render on the game view. You can also check the number of batches that Unity has taken to render a simple scene:

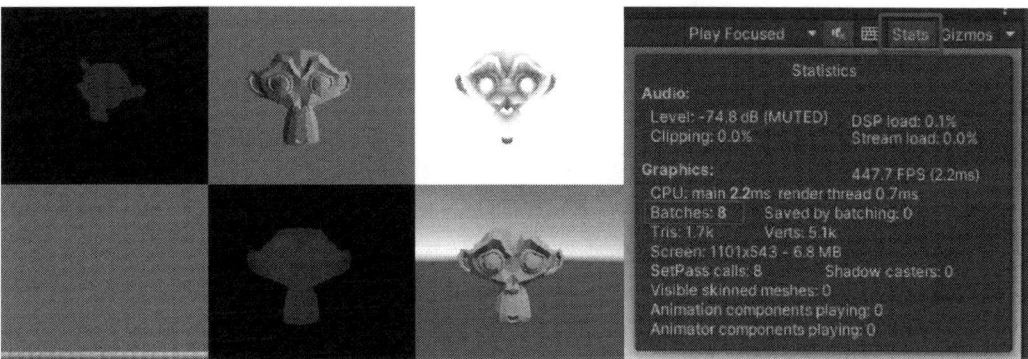

Figure 13.4: *Some steps of rendering a single frame (left) the number of batches it has taken to render the frame*

This implies one conclusion: having a higher number of draw calls and large batch count leads to less performance of the application. Therefore, we must take necessary actions to reduce the number of draw calls and batches to render a frame quickly.

Optimization of a 3D app

In this section, we will go through some methods that we can use to improve the performance of a 3D application both graphically and programmatically. The focus of this section covers some basics to improve the performance metrics discussed in the previous section.

GPU instancing

When Unity renders an object with a material, it takes one draw call per object per material. We can use GPU instancing to draw one material for all the objects in the scene in just one draw call. *Figure 13.5* is an example of a Unity scene with 10000 objects, which uses the same object, and the same material without GPU instancing. This scene with the Unity project is provided along with the book.

Open the scene *02-GPU instancing* to test. The following figure shows that it has taken over 19000 draw calls to render the frame with a fps of 90, without GPU instancing. With GPU Instancing, you get 42 batches with a higher fps of around 150.

> **Note:** If you are using Universal Render Pipeline (URP), there is a *batcher* that comes with it, which supersedes the GPU instancing. You may not get the same result with URP unless the objects are batched (this will be covered in next sub-session).

Refer to the following figure:

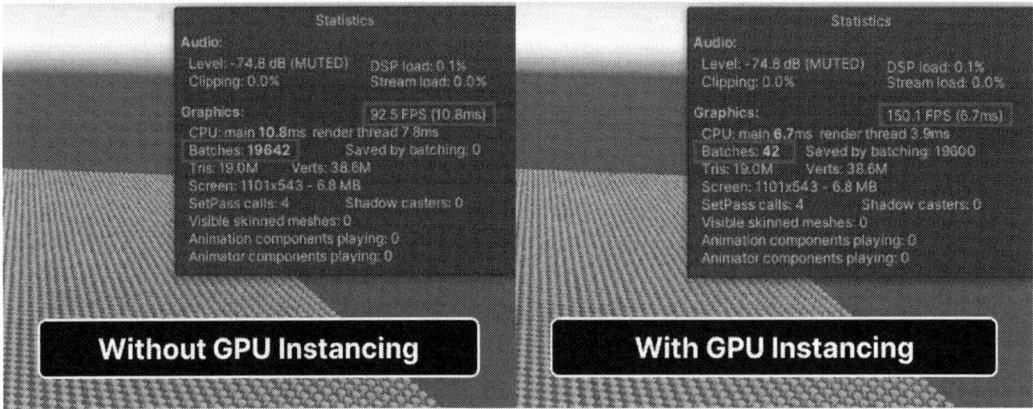

Figure 13.5: Rendering thousands of objects without and with GPU instancing

GPU instancing can be enabled by checking the **GPU Instancing** option in the material. Unity's standard lit and unlit shaders support GPU instancing by default. If you are using a custom shader, that should support GPU instancing to work properly with Unity. *Figure 13.6* shows a material that uses unity Standard shader that allows enabling GPU Instancing:

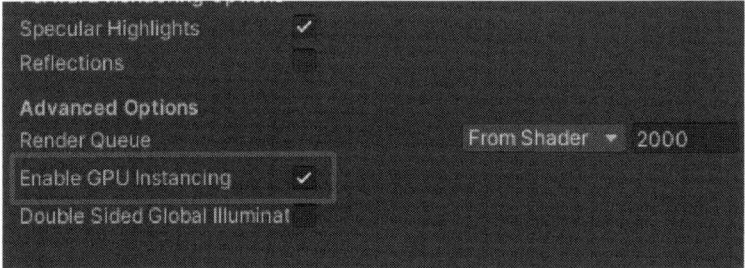

Figure 13.6: Enabling GPU instancing of a material

Static and dynamic batching

Another way to reduce batching and draw calls, is to define the objects that need to be batched together. This allows Unity to get objects with the same mesh and batch them into a single batch, and render is done in just one draw call. This is similar to GPU instancing, and depending on the application, developers must check what is best to use from batching and GPU instancing.

The 3D models in the app are not moving and are static; we can make those objects batched as *static*. This can be done by selecting all the static objects and enabling **Batching Static** from the static dropdown in the inspector window, as shown in *Figure 13.7*. If the objects are moving, the objects can be batched dynamically. Usually, static batching is more performant than dynamic batching since it does not transform object vertices in the CPU. Unity, by default, supports dynamic batching. Using URP, you can enable and disable the dynamic batcher in URP settings.

Figure 13.7 shows the difference between the batches with and without static batching:

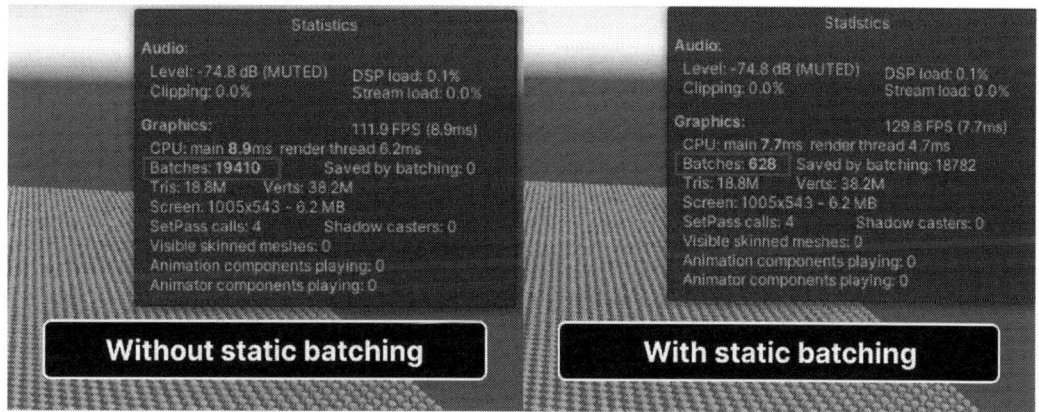

Figure 13.7: Difference of the batch count with static batching

Refer to *Figure 13.8*:

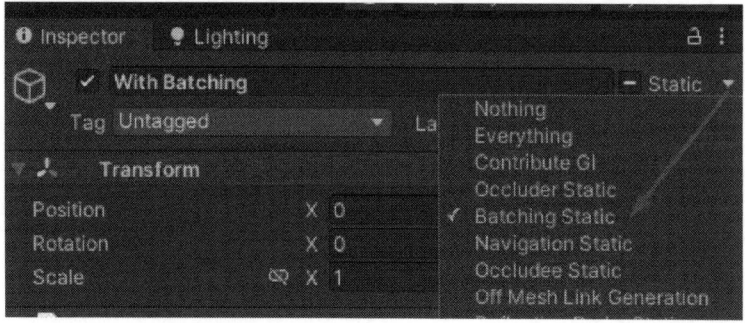

Figure 13.8: Enabling static batching in Unity

Occlusion culling and frustum culling

In 3D applications, there is no need to render any 3D object that is out of the camera's view frustum. This is mainly because the user does not see the objects from the camera. This is known as **frustum culling**. In some scenarios, 3D objects can be occluded (covered) from other 3D objects. In this scenario, the camera does not need to render the covered objects. This is known as **occlusion culling**.

In Unity, both occlusion culling and frustum culling occur by default. This is usually dynamic and checks which are less performant compared to static methods. If any objects are static (not moving, such as buildings, trees, and so on), these objects can also contribute to static occlusion culling. Like batching static, you can choose which object must be statically occluded using the inspector window. *Figure 13.9* shows a simple scene with frustum culling applied to objects only within the camera frustum.

In addition to rendering, you can manually activate different functions of game objects in your code by checking `renderer.isVisible`, a variable of the object. For example, imagine an AR 3D object that calls an API to retrieve data every second. This does not need to happen if the user is not looking at the object. Checking the `render.isVisible` variable, you can pause sending the API request if the value is false and resume it again if it is true.

Refer to the following figure:

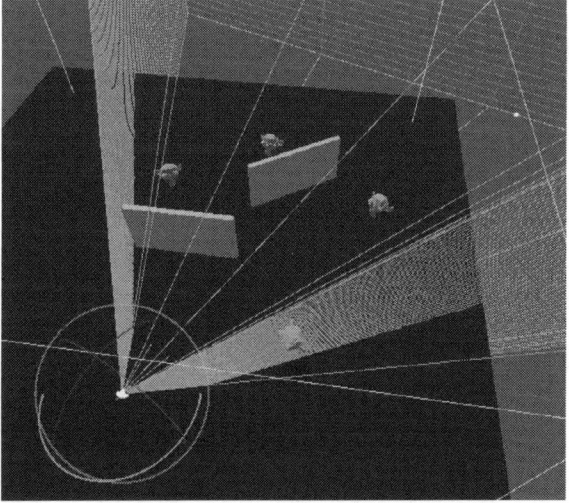

Figure 13.9: Frustrum culling in Unity

Textures and UV maps

In a previous sub-section, we learned that every material on every object contributes to one batch call. If a single object has x number of materials, unity will take x number of iterations to render the complete model. Having a 3D model with multiple meshes (different 3D objects within one object) also increases the number of draw calls required to render the image.

Some 3D models have multiple materials, which defines the colors of different faces of a 3D mesh. *Figure 13.10* is an example of such a 3D model, which has different colors of the 3D model, and they are represented by different materials, via the mesh renderer. Having just one light and rendering a single color in background, the model has taken altogether 22 batches to render the scene:

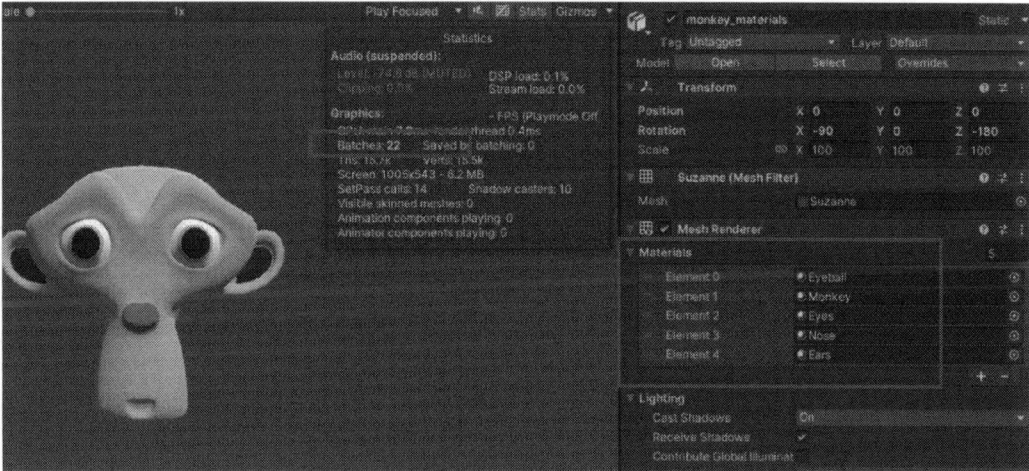

Figure 13.10: 3D model with multiple materials

For an optimized 3D application, this is an overkill. Having multiple materials to render a small portion of a 3D model can drastically increase the number of batch counts.

We can use textures to have multiple colors on a 3D model with just one material. Textures are 2D images that can wrap around a 3D model. There is another concept known as **UV maps**, where different faces of a 3D mesh can be placed on different position values of a texture to map colors. 3D modeling tools like blender can use a single texture to map different faces of the 3D model to it.

316 ■ *Mastering Augmented Reality Development with Unity*

Figure 13.11 is an example of how a color palette texture is mapped (UV Mapped) to different parts of the 3D model (eyes, nose, ears, and so on) in Blender 3D modeling software:

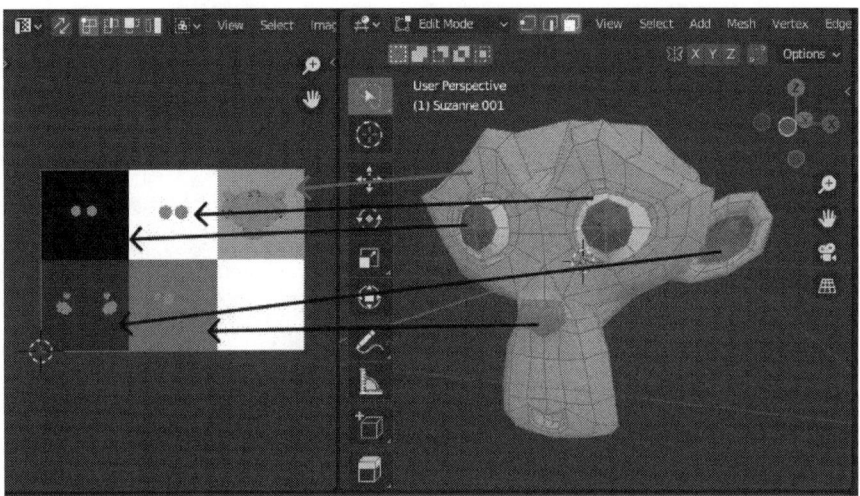

Figure 13.11: Setting up a texture with UV map to create a single material

Once importing this 3D model to Unity, just with a texture on a single material, the batch count of the frame is reduced to 6 from 22, compared to before, as shown in *Figure 13.12*. Visually, both objects look alike:

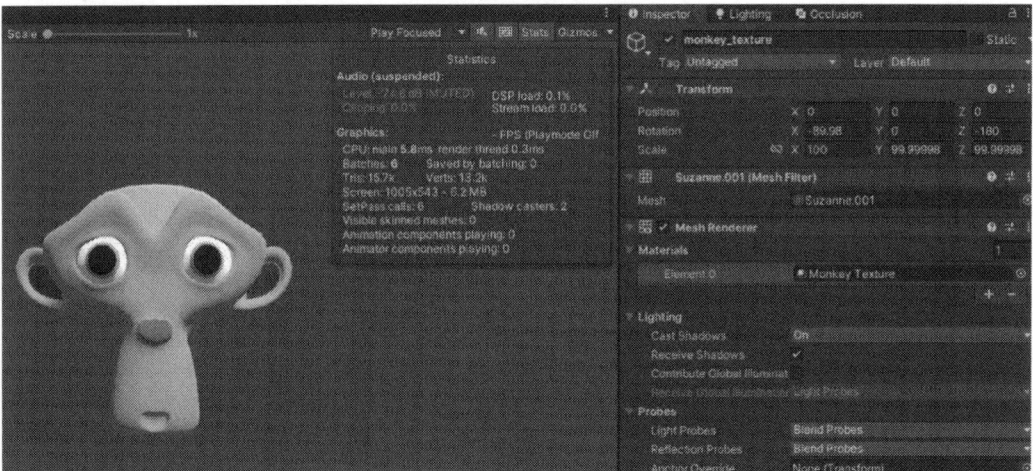

Figure 13.12: Same object with a single material and a texture

Light baking

The amount of lighting is another component that helps increase the number of draw calls of a frame. In Unity, there are different kinds of lights. Directional light, point light, spotlight, and area light are some of those. These lights contribute to additional draw calls since every light, every object needs to be illuminated and rendered apart from its original rendering iterations. Therefore, more lights imply more processing power needed. Hence the reduction of FPS and the increase of draw calls.

Consider a 3D model in AR that does not move over time. The shadows of the object may not move either. In this case, we can mark this 3D object as static. All the static objects can be attributed to a concept known as **light baking**. This means the lights of the scene, its color changes, and shadows can be *painted* onto one giant texture that can be placed over the scene. Light baking might not be useful for AR apps since objects can be dynamic and moved around in an experience. However, it is beneficial to include 3D apps as needed.

In Unity, all the objects that are not moving should be marked as static. Lights that do not contribute to any dynamic objects but make shadows on static objects can be marked as *Baked* as their light mode from the light components. To bake lights, we must use a *light mapper*. Unity already contains a light mapper that can take all the brake lights and static objects to generate a light map texture. This can be viewed from **Window | Rendering | Lighting**. The lighting window has a **Generate Lighting** option under **Scene** tab, which initiates the light mapper that generates the baked content. *Figure 13.13* shows the same scene with dynamic lights alongside baked lights, along with the number of batches it renders:

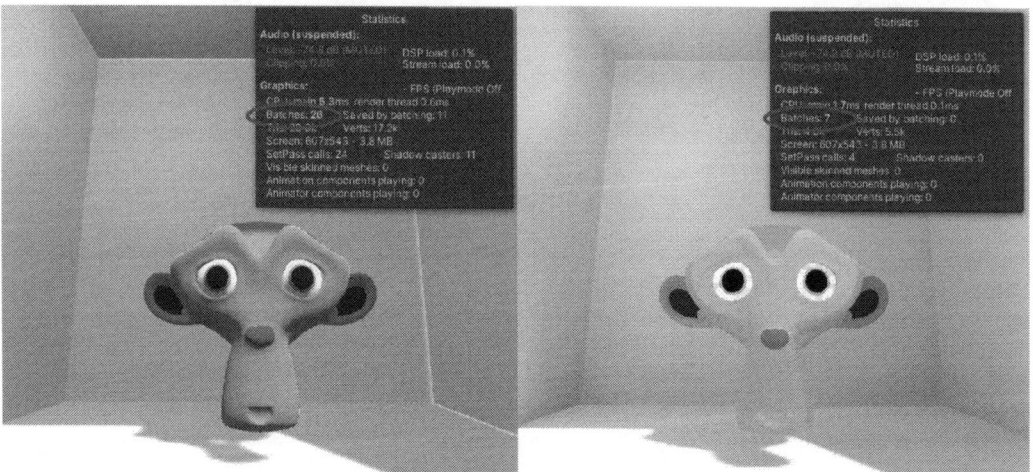

Figure 13.13: *A scene with dynamic light and baked lights*

UI optimizations

In Unity, we use Canvas objects to include user interfaces. Like 3D models, Unity renders any UI content over 2D meshes. Unity's *Canvas*, the object, holds the rendering of all the underlying components of the UI.

Many developers use a single canvas element to hold as many UI components as possible. While this option is not a highly resource incentive for smaller UI elements, large games with highly refreshing UI can have a huge overhead in recalculating the rendering of UI elements. This is due to how the Unity canvas is built. When a single element updates within a canvas game object, the canvas refreshes its children to update the renderer. This is iterative for all the elements within the canvas.

To overcome this, add as many canvases to separate highly changing UI elements and static UI elements. In AR, world space, canvases can contain canvases within canvases to omit updating unnecessary elements. Text that does not update can be added to a texture and be placed in a single material to be added to *quad* 3D planes.

Using a **texture atlas** instead of single images can render many UI elements with 2D sprites in one batch. To achieve this, you need to install *2D sprite* package from Unity's package manager. In *Figure 13.14* it shows an arrangement of 2D assets in a UI which has taken 6 batches to render:

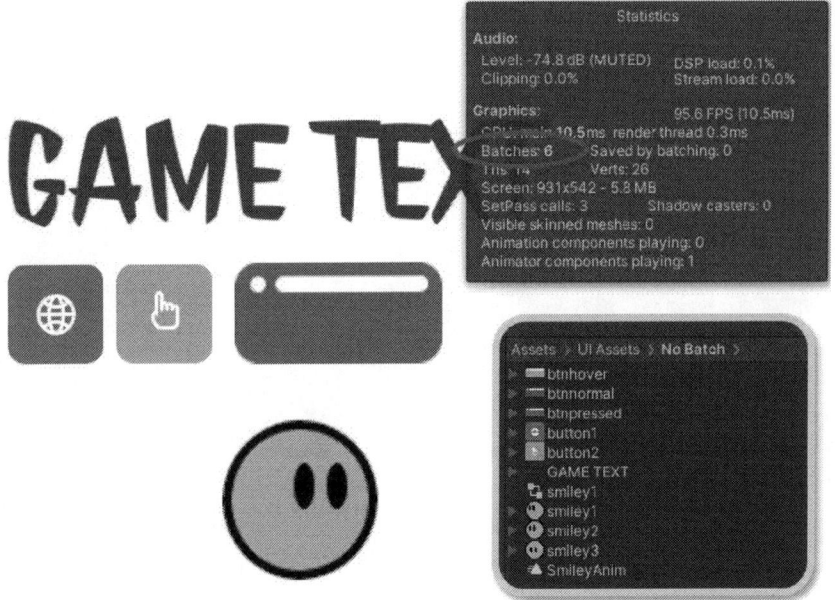

Figure 13.14: Rendering UI elements with different sprites.

You can use all the sprites and group them into a single *atlas* in Unity, which generates a single image of all the sprites combined. This can be created with the 2D sprites pack installed by right-clicking any folder area and click **Create** | **2D** | **Sprite Atlas**.

Select the generated atlas asset and choose the folders containing all your sprites. You must also enable **Sprite packing** from Unity editor by going to **Edit** | **Project Settings** | **Editor**. As shown in *Figure 13.15*, picking the **Pack Preview** button in the sprite atlas generates a single image with all the sprites combined, reducing the batches to 3. For a smaller number of sprites, this is a 50% optimized and it becomes increased with more sprites / 2D images in the scene:

Figure 13.15: Using Same UI elements with sprites packed

Optimization considerations in coding

So far, we have discussed some tips for graphics-related objectives to optimize a 3D app in Unity. Another key objective we need to consider is how optimized your code is. Any code written in any language turns into machine readable code that performs instructions on the CPU. How much work you allocate to the CPU and how much memory you utilize from the **Random Access Memory** (**RAM**) determines how smooth your app could be if all graphical optimizations are achieved.

Following are some objectives that you can fulfill in developing any 3D application:

- **Cache variables**: Creating variables takes up space in memory. If you are reusing variables such as a component reference, which uses `GetComponent` method, calling the reference every frame within the update method can cause a massive performance to hit since the method itself is a search method that must iterate through the components attached to your game object. Therefore, having a variable at the class level and assigning the component only during a single method call, such as the `Awake` or `Start` method, can cache the variable for later use.

- **Reduce using Find methods:** Unity, by default has a series of `Find` methods that allows you to search for different objects and components by either name or type. This is a search method that could iterate over all the objects and all the components in your scene. This is very resource heavy, which can slow your application's performance if it runs at a high frequency. You can use static variables and design patterns such as *singleton*, and dictionary data types to quickly get references to existing objects and components without `Find` methods.

- **Avoid using iterations within iterations:** If there are any iterative code blocks, having more iterative code blocks within iterative code can cause your code to run for longer periods. This is due to the exponential nature of how iterations work in code. For example, having a `for` loop with 10 iterations within another for loop with 10 iterations will have 100 iterations of code execution. If you run this within Unity update method, it will perform 100 iterations per frame. This can sometimes be unnecessary for your code. Therefore, look for ways to reduce the iterations by filtering different code parameters. You can also use recursive functions and other optimized algorithms to replace multiple iterations.

- **Remove Debug code in production:** When you develop any code, using `Debug` methods can be very useful for you to understand your code values, whether the execution reaches your code, and even drawing debug elements in scene view. However, these codes do not reach the final application; rather, they will still be executed within the app. More debug code, such as `Debug.Log` handles strings that can cause additional unnecessary processing power. Therefore, remove all the `debug.log` code from your code before building the app.

- There are many different algorithms that you can use to solve different problems. Even if every algorithm performs the same result, the execution of them can be different. Some algorithms perform well, while others do not. Developing apps continuously trains individuals to use the best and most optimized algorithm that suits their requirements.

Conclusion

In this chapter, we went through some of the basic optimization techniques you can consider to get better outcomes for your 3D application. Developing a 3D application can be overwhelming, with different spectrums that you have to consider. Adding augmented reality on top of that can increase the workload for building a polished Augmented Reality application. However, keeping optimization in mind from the start can be highly beneficial in the long run, as it does not require additional effort at the end to redo your methods.

With this chapter, it ends the complete series of building AR applications. Throughout all the chapters, we identified different methods of AR development using different SDKs. These tools change frequently. They update with optimized algorithms, and the ways of implementing them can change rapidly. However, understanding the principles of how we did during the first chapters of this book remains the same. As developers, we must keep practicing by building different types of projects which force us to read documentation, follow best practices and understand different ways of building AR applications.

Key points

- Frames per second (FPS), Triangle count in 3D models, and draw calls are some of the performance metrics to determine the performance of a 3D app.
- GPU instancing can be used to group the rendering of objects with the same material and reduce draw calls.
- Batching can reduce the batch count when rendering the same object. This can be static or dynamic.
- Frustrum and occlusion culling can reduce the overhead of rendering objects not visible to the camera.
- Reducing the number of materials and different meshes can improve your app's performance massively.
- Combining textures into one atlas reduces the number of draw calls.
- Baking lights of static objects omit additional rendering passes to calculate light estimations. This reduces the draw calls on the screen.
- Processes of the app can be further optimized by following code optimization techniques.

Questions

1. What is the purpose of Level of Detail (LOD) systems in Unity, and how can they improve graphical performance?

2. How can Unity's occlusion culling feature enhance graphical performance in large scenes?

3. Explain the benefits of using a sprite atlas in Unity's 2D rendering and how it optimizes graphical performance.

Answers

1. Level of Detail (LOD) systems in Unity are used to optimize graphical performance by reducing the complexity of 3D models as they move further away from the camera. This means that objects that are distant from the player will have lower-detail versions, reducing the number of polygons and textures being rendered. This optimization technique helps improve frame rates and reduces GPU and CPU workload, resulting in smoother gameplay and better performance.

2. Unity's occlusion culling is a technique that enhances graphical performance by determining which objects are not visible to the camera and therefore do not need to rendered. By identifying and excluding occluded objects from the rendering process, Unity reduces the number of draw calls and minimizes the overall workload on the GPU. This results in improved frame rates and allows developers to create larger and more detailed game environments without sacrificing performance.

3. A sprite atlas in Unity is a texture that contains multiple individual sprites packed into a single image. By using a sprite atlas, Unity reduces the number of texture swaps during rendering, which significantly improves graphical performance. When multiple sprites are combined into one atlas, there are fewer draw calls, and the GPU can efficiently render multiple sprites with a single pass. This optimization technique is particularly useful in 2D games with many different sprites on the screen at once, leading to smoother gameplay and better frame rates.

Join our book's Discord space

Join the book's Discord Workspace for Latest updates, Offers, Tech happenings around the world, New Release and Sessions with the Authors:

https://discord.bpbonline.com

Index

Symbols

3D app optimization 311
  frustum culling 313, 314
  GPU instancing 311, 312
  light baking 317
  occlusion culling 313, 314
  static and dynamic batching 312, 313
  textures 314-316
  UI optimizations 318, 319
  UV maps 314-316
3D audio cues
  using 296
3D Cartesian space 26
3D environment 24-28
3D mobile app development 139
  app debugging 152

app debugging for Android, with ADB console 152, 153
app debugging for iOS, with XCode console 153
Unity build settings 140
3D Universal Render Pipeline (URP) template 68, 69
3D visualization
  mathematic basics 22, 23
8th Wall 54

A

Adobe Illustrator
  URL 195
Alibaba 46
Android build settings 140, 141
Android Open-Source Project (AOSP) 47

Android SDK
　installing 64, 65
Android Studio 51
API endpoint (API path) 193
Apple Reality Composer 53
Apples Vision Pro 49
Application Programming Interface (API) 51, 183
AR applications 8
　education 11, 12
　entertainment 8-10
　health 11
　manufacturing and logistics 10
　marketing and retail 12
　real estate 11
AR app performance optimization 307
　3D app optimization 311
　coding considerations 319, 320
　performance metrics 308
AR best practices 287
　audio and visual cues, using 294
　considerations 288
　free flow restrictions 300
　scaling objects 293, 294
　user interactions 291, 292
　warnings, displaying at beginning 288-290
　warnings, displaying while using AR app 290, 291
ARCore 8, 57
AR development tools
　8th Wall 54
　Apple Reality Composer 53
　Native 51
　Social AR 52
　Unity 3D 54, 55
AR Foundation 57, 58, 256
　Anchors 256
　AR human body manager 256
　Image Tracking 256
　Point Cloud 256
　setting up 230-232
AR interactions 301
　objects, interacting from camera 302
　reticle, for interacting with smaller objects 301
ARKit 8, 57
AR object viewer
　building 235
　object, moving on touch 237, 238
　object, placing on scanned plane 235-237
　object, rotating with single touch and drag 240-243
　object, scaling with two touches 238-240
　plane detection and tracking 235
AR platforms 43
　Android 43
　iOS 43, 44
　Magic Leap 46, 47
　Snapchat spectacles 47
　Social AR 50
　Vuzix Blade device 48, 49
　WebXR AR 50
AR Quick view 53
AR software development kits 55
　ARCore 57
　AR Foundation 57, 58
　ARKit 57

ARToolkit 55, 56
Easy AR 56
Microsoft mixed reality toolkit 55
Niantic Lightship 58, 59
Vuforia 56, 57
Wikitude 56
AR technologies 13
  image recognition and tracking 13-15
  Simultaneous Localization and
      Mapping (SLAM) 15-17
artificial intelligence 17, 18
AR Toolkit 6, 55, 56
  URL 7
AR treasure hunt game
  developing 174-182
assets
  importing, from Unity asset
      store 83, 84
audio
  adding 129-131
  main menu, adding 131-133
  polishing 129-131
  scenes, switching 133, 134
audio-visual cues
  3D audio cues, using 296, 297
  out of camera view objects,
      indicating 294, 295
  physical properties, showing
      in visual cues 297
  using 294
  visual markers, adding on
      interactable objects 295, 296
Augmented Reality (AR) 1
  application 2
  best practices 288

  history 4-7
  implementing 2-4
  over years 8
Autodesk Revit 11

B
Building Information Modelling
      (BIM) 11

C
C# 91
  in Unity 92, 93
Cartesian coordinate system 24
  coordinate system 25
  origin 25
colliders 85, 86
content
  importing, into Unity 82, 83
context recognition 34
  marker-based 34
  marker-less 34, 35
C#, with Unity
  bullet, creating for shooting 109-112
  bullets, shooting 113-115
  enemies, destroying 123-125
  enemies, spawning 123-125
  enemy, setting up 115-121
  player movement 107-109
  player, setting up 121, 122
  scene, setting up 106, 107
cylinder targets
  using 166-170

D
debug class, Unity 95, 96
device tracking 35

device tracking app
  AR shooter, building 249
  enemy, setting up 250, 251
  Game Manager, setting up 251-255
diameter 23
dynamic AR billboard
  AR poster project, setting up 214-216
  asset bundle browser, installing 221, 222
  asset bundles, creating in Unity 221
  asset bundles, uploading in cloud 223
  building 214
  content, displaying in AR 224-227
  content, downloading in AR 224
  meta files, updating for AR experience update 223, 224
  Vuforia Cloud targets, implementing 216-220

E

Easy AR 56
edges 310
environment meshing 269
  ball, throwing at runtime 271, 272
  object, creating to throw 270, 271
  scene, setting up 269, 270
  simple physics simulation, creating 270
Epson Moverio device 49
Euler angles 32
Extensible Markup Language (XML) 186

F

face tracking app
  AR face filter, creating with AR Foundation 243
  custom objects, adding around face 244-246
  default face tracking setup 243, 244
  face interactions, adding 246-248
feature recognition algorithm 13
Fiducial markers 6
float 22
floating-point arithmetic 22
frames per second (FPS) 308-310
free flow restrictions 300
frustum culling 313

G

GameObject structure 84
Game UI 125, 126
  game manager 126-129
Generative Adversarial Networks (GANs) 18
GetComponent 97-99
Gimbal Lock 32
Google 46
Google Pixel device 44
Google Tango 8
Graphical Processing Unit (GPU) 77

H

head-mounted three-dimensional display 5
holograms 1
HoloLens 37, 44

I

image processing algorithms 14
image target
  additional features 165
  best markers/targets, selecting 163-165

multiple image targets, scanning 166
occlusion object, adding 165
similar target image, adding 166
using 159-162
integers 22
Integrated Development Environment (IDE) 65
interactable objects
  visual markers, adding 295, 296
iOS build settings 144
  Configuration | Camera Usage Description 145
  Configuration | Requires AR Kit support 145
  Configuration | Target Device, SDK and minimum iOS version 145
  Identification | Bundle Identifier 144
  Identification | Provisioning profile and Signing team ID 144
irrational number 32

J
JavaScript Object Notation (JSON) 186
Java SDK
  installing 64, 65

K
Kinect 45
kinetic depth effect 4

L
LiDAR sensors 15
light baking 317
light mapper 317
lights
  ambient lights 75
  directional lights 75-77

virtual lights 74
Lightship ARDK 260
Lit 77
local descriptor 14
Localized state 284
local space 33

M
machine inspection tool 184, 185
  simple mock API, creating 192, 193
  Unity deserialization 186-192
  Unity serialization 186-192
  UnityWebRequest, for requesting data based on input 193, 194
machine learning 17
  deep learning 17, 18
MacOS
  Xcode installation 65
Magic Leap 37, 46, 47
marker-based dynamic AR apps
  developing 183
marker-based recognition 34
marker-less recognition 34, 35
marker-less tracking scene
  setting up 232-234
  simulating, in editor 234
materials
  creating 77-79
mesh renderer 85
Microsoft HoloLens 44-46
  reference link 46
MonoBehaviour component
  exploring 93, 94
multi targets
  using 170-173

N

Native AR development 51
Native Development Kit (NDK) 140
Niantic Geospatial library 273
Niantic Lightship 58, 260
Niantic Lightship SDK 260
Niantic lightship VPS 273, 274
  anchors, adding with VPS authoring tool 278, 279
  environment, scanning 274-276
  for scalable AR applications 285
  Niantic API, for restoring anchor data 281-284
  prefab, using with visual elements 280
  scanned location, importing 277, 278
  scan recognition flow 276, 277
Niantic Lightship with Unity
  application, authenticating 261, 262
  camera, setting up 263, 264
  new license, adding 261, 262
  required tools and assets, downloading 261
  setting up 260
  simple plane tracking scene, setting up 262, 263
Niantic Wayfarer 273
normal maps 310
Nreal Air device 48

O

object occlusion
  enabling 268, 269
object replacement 265-268
object space 34
occlusion culling 314

OpenCV
  URL 15
out of camera view objects
  indicating 294, 295

P

paint bucket 77
performance metrics 308
  draw calls 310, 311
  frames per second (FPS) 308-310
  tris and verts 310
physical input
  converting, into virtual interactions 36, 37
Pokémon Go 8
prefabs
  creating 87, 88
primitive objects
  creating, with transformation tools 71
  manipulating, with transformation tools 71-74
project
  creating 68, 69

Q

Quaternions 33

R

Radian 32
Random Access Memory (RAM) 319
Ray casting 36
ReBlink 9
Representational State Transfer (REST API) 192
reticle 301
Rigid body component 86, 87

S

serialized variables 94, 95
shaders 77
simple 3D clock
 building 99-102
Simultaneous Localization and
  Mapping (SLAM) 15
skybox 74
Smartphones 43
Snapchat Lens Studio 52
Snapchat spectacles 47
Social AR 50
Social AR development
 Snapchat Lens Studio 52
 Spark AR 52
 TikTok 52
Software Development Kit (SDK) 140
spaces 33
 local space 33
 object space 34
 world space 33
Spark AR 52
Story of the Forest 9

T

target platform
 setting up 68
The Sword of Damocles 4
three-dimensional cubic space 33
TikTok 52
Time module
 using 96, 97
TouchBegan method 268
transform component 85
trigonometry 31-33

tris 310

U

UI considerations 303, 304
Unity
 C# 92, 93
 content, importing 82, 83
 debug class 95, 96
 deserialization 186-192
 prefabs, creating 87, 88
 script debugging, with
  Visual Studio 150-152
 serialization 186-192
 Time 96, 97
Unity 3D 54, 55
 installing 62-64
Unity apps
 building 145
 building, for Android 145, 146
 building, for Android without
  ADB 146-148
 building, for iOS 148-150
Unity asset store
 assets, importing 83, 84
Unity build settings
 Android build settings 140, 141
 icon 141
 iOS build settings 144
 other settings 142
 presentation 141
 publishing settings 143, 144
 resolution 141
 splash image 142
Unity components 84
 colliders 85, 86
 mesh renderer 85

Rigid body 86, 87
transform 85
Unity Engine
  user interface 69, 70
Unity Hub 62
Unity package manager
  using 81
Unity Web Request 193
Universal Render Pipeline (URP) 77, 261
UV maps 315

V

vector mathematics 28-30
vectors 28, 29
  cross product 31
  direction 30
  dot product 31
  magnitude 30
  negation 31
  unit vector 31
Videoplace 5
virtual camera 79
  manipulating 80, 81
  working 79, 80
virtual objects
  placement on physical worlds 35, 36
Visual Positioning Service (VPS) 58
Visual Studio
  installing 66
Visual Studio Code
  installing 66-68
Vuforia 56, 57, 156
  basic AR scene, setting up 158
  developer account and login, creating 156

SDK, downloading 157
SDK, installing 157, 158
Vuforia VuMark 195
  data, decoding 203-205
  decoded values, using for data retrieval 206-213
  designing, with Adobe Illustrator 195-201
  marker recognition, connecting with networking 202
  targets, downloading 202
VuMarkBehaviour 205
VuMarks 183-185
Vuzix Blade device 48

W

WayspoitAnchorController 277
WayspotAnchorService 276, 277
WebGL 51
WebXR 51
WebXR AR 50
  URL 50
Wikitude 43, 56
world space 33

X

Xcode
  installing, in MacOS 65

Made in United States
Orlando, FL
29 December 2023